Unity 2020 Mobile Game Development
Second Edition

Discover practical techniques and examples to create and deliver engaging games for Android and iOS

John P. Doran

BIRMINGHAM - MUMBAI

Unity 2020 Mobile Game Development
Second Edition

Commissioning Editor: Pavan Ramchandani
Acquisition Editor: Larissa Pinto
Content Development Editor: Divya Vijayan
Senior Editor: Mohammed Yusuf Imaratwale
Technical Editor: Deepesh Patel
Copy Editor: Safis Editing
Project Coordinator: Kinjal Bari
Proofreader: Safis Editing
Indexer: Priyanka Dhadke
Production Designer: Joshua Misquitta

First published: November 2017
Second edition: August 2020

Production reference: 1210820

Published by Packt Publishing Ltd.
Livery Place
35 Livery Street
Birmingham
B3 2PB, UK.

ISBN 978-1-83898-733-6

www.packt.com

To my wife, Hien, for being my loving partner throughout our joint life journey, and to my parents, who took me seriously when I said I wanted to make games for a living.

– John P. Doran

Packt.com

Subscribe to our online digital library for full access to over 7,000 books and videos, as well as industry leading tools to help you plan your personal development and advance your career. For more information, please visit our website.

Why subscribe?

- Spend less time learning and more time coding with practical eBooks and Videos from over 4,000 industry professionals

- Improve your learning with Skill Plans built especially for you

- Get a free eBook or video every month

- Fully searchable for easy access to vital information

- Copy and paste, print, and bookmark content

Did you know that Packt offers eBook versions of every book published, with PDF and ePub files available? You can upgrade to the eBook version at www.packt.com and as a print book customer, you are entitled to a discount on the eBook copy. Get in touch with us at customercare@packtpub.com for more details.

At www.packt.com, you can also read a collection of free technical articles, sign up for a range of free newsletters, and receive exclusive discounts and offers on Packt books and eBooks.

Contributors

About the author

John P. Doran is a passionate and seasoned technical game designer, software engineer, and author based in Peoria, Illinois.

For over a decade, John has gained extensive hands-on expertise in game development, working in a variety of roles, ranging from game designer to lead UI programmer. Additionally, John has worked in game development education teaching in Singapore, South Korea, and the United States. To date, he has authored over 10 books pertaining to game development.

John is currently an instructor in residence at Bradley University. Prior to his present ventures, he was an award-winning videographer.

I want to thank everyone at Packt Publishing for all of their hard work, and thank you to my colleagues in the Interactive Media department at Bradley University, for all of their support over the course of working on this title.

About the reviewer

Sungkuk Park is a game engineer based in Berlin. He has participated in multiple game jams around the world and has created indie games to polish his skills. He is currently interested in the area of technical art, mainly CG, animation, gameplay, and VFX. He spends most of his time learning new skills, including drawing, animation, and VFX, that might come in handy when he pursues his next goal: being a game director for the next gaming generation!

Packt is searching for authors like you

If you're interested in becoming an author for Packt, please visit `authors.packtpub.com` and apply today. We have worked with thousands of developers and tech professionals, just like you, to help them share their insight with the global tech community. You can make a general application, apply for a specific hot topic that we are recruiting an author for, or submit your own idea.

Table of Contents

Preface

As an indie or AAA game developer, you want to have your games where your customers are. More and more people buy mobile devices every year and there's no sign of this stopping any time soon. One of the big advantages of the Unity game engine is that it is cross-platform, making it easy to write your game once and then port it to other consoles with minimal changes. However, there are certain features unique to working with mobile devices, which is what this book is about.

Unity 2020 Mobile Game Development will take you on an exploration of how to use Unity when trying to deploy your content to mobile devices. Over the course of the book, we will see how to create a mobile game and then see how to deploy it to both iOS and Android. We will explore how to add input for mobile devices and have the interface adapt to the many different screen sizes that phones have. We'll then look at some ways to monetize our game by discussing Unity's in-app purchase and advertisement systems. We will also learn how to use notifications to keep users coming back to our game. Then, we will see how we can share our game with the world by enabling us to use Twitter and Facebook's SDK. Afterward, we will see how to work with Unity's analytics system and then polish our title in a number of different ways, before putting it on the Google Play and iOS app stores. Finally, we will also learn how to use Unity's new AR Foundation framework, which allows you to build future-proof AR apps.

Who this book is for

If you are a Unity game developer and want to build mobile games for iOS and Android, then this is the book for you. Previous knowledge of C# is helpful, but not mandatory.

What this book covers

Chapter 1, *Building Your Game*, covers the creation of a simple project in Unity, which we will be modifying over the course of this book to make use of features commonly seen in mobile games. This chapter will also serve as a refresher for some fundamental concepts when working in Unity.

Chapter 2, *Project Setup for Android and iOS Development*, will show you the setup required to deploy a project to both iOS and Android mobile devices, by installing the Java and Android SDKs for Android and configuring Xcode for iOS.

Chapter 3, *Mobile Input/Touch Controls*, shows a number of ways in which input can work on mobile devices. Starting off with mouse events, we will dive into recognizing touch events and gestures, as well as how to use the accelerometer and accessing information using the `Touch` class.

Chapter 4, *Resolution-Independent UI*, discusses how to build the user interface for our game, starting with a title screen, and then build the other menus that we will want to use for our future chapters.

Chapter 5, *Advertising Using Unity Ads*, shows how to integrate Unity's ad framework into our project and then learn how to create both simple and complex versions of advertisements.

Chapter 6, *Implementing In-App Purchases*, talks about how to integrate Unity's **In-App Purchase (IAP)** system into our project and then takes a look at how to create an IAP that is used for consumable content as well as permanent unlocks.

Chapter 7, *Getting Social*, shows how to integrate social media into your projects, starting off with sharing high scores using Twitter and then taking a look at how we can use the Facebook SDK in order to display our player's name and profile picture while inside our game.

Chapter 8, *Keeping Players Involved with Notifications*, shows how to integrate notifications into your projects starting with the setup, before creating basic notifications ahead of time, and then seeing how to customize how the notifications are presented.

Chapter 9, *Using Unity Analytics*, covers some of the different ways that we can integrate Unity's analytics tools into our projects, tracking custom events as well as using remote settings to allow us to tweak the gameplay without having people re-download the game from the store.

Chapter 10, *Making Your Title Juicy*, introduces the concept of making games *juicy* with different ways that we can integrate features of juiciness into our projects, including tweening animations, materials, and postprocessing effects, and adding particle effects.

Chapter 11, *Game Build and Submission*, goes over the process of submitting our game to the Google Play or iOS app stores, with tips and tricks to help the process go smoother.

Chapter 12, *Augmented Reality*, shows the process of adding augmented reality to your games. We start off by setting up the project and going through the installation and setup process for ARCore, ARKit, and AR Foundation. We will then see how to detect surfaces in the real world before seeing how the user can interact with their environment and how to spawn objects within an AR space.

To get the most out of this book

Throughout this book, we will work within the Unity 3D game engine, which you can download from `http://unity3d.com/unity/download/`. The projects were created using Unity 2020.1.0f1, but the project should work with minimal changes in future versions of the engine. If you would like to download the exact version used in this book, and there is a new version out, you can visit Unity's download archive at `https://unity3d.com/get-unity/download/archive`. You can also find the system requirements for Unity at `https://docs.unity3d.com/2020.1/Documentation/Manual/system-requirements.html` in the *Unity Editor system requirements* section. To deploy your project, you will need an Android or iOS device.

For the sake of simplicity, we will assume that you are working on a Windows-powered computer when developing for Android and a Macintosh computer when developing for iOS. For this book, we will be using C# as our scripting language.

If you are using the digital version of this book, we advise you to type the code yourself or access the code via the GitHub repository (link available in the next section). Doing so will help you avoid any potential errors related to the copying and pasting of code.

Download the example code files

You can download the example code files for this book from your account at `www.packt.com`. If you purchased this book elsewhere, you can visit `www.packtpub.com/support` and register to have the files emailed directly to you.

You can download the code files by following these steps:

1. Log in or register at `www.packt.com`.
2. Select the **Support** tab.
3. Click on **Code Downloads**.
4. Enter the name of the book in the **Search** box and follow the onscreen instructions.

Once the file is downloaded, please make sure that you unzip or extract the folder using the latest version of:

- WinRAR/7-Zip for Windows
- Zipeg/iZip/UnRarX for Mac
- 7-Zip/PeaZip for Linux

The code bundle for the book is also hosted on GitHub at
`https://github.com/PacktPublishing/Unity-2020-Mobile-Game-Development-Second-Ed`
`ition`. In case there's an update to the code, it will be updated on the existing GitHub
repository.

We also have other code bundles from our rich catalog of books and videos available
at `https://github.com/PacktPublishing/`. Check them out!

Download the color images

We also provide a PDF file that has color images of the screenshots/diagrams used in this
book. You can download it here: `https://static.packt-cdn.com/downloads/`
`9781838987336_ColorImages.pdf`.

Conventions used

There are a number of text conventions used throughout this book.

`CodeInText`: Indicates code words in text, database table names, folder names, filenames,
file extensions, pathnames, dummy URLs, user input, and Twitter handles. Here is an
example: "Rename the sphere to `Player` and set the **Transform** component's
position to (0, 1, -4)."

A block of code is set as follows:

```
/// <summary>
/// Update is called once per frame
/// </summary>
void Update ()
{
    // Check if target is a valid object
    if (target != null)
    {
        // Set our position to an offset of our target
        transform.position = target.position + offset;

        // Change the rotation to face target
        transform.LookAt(target);
    }
}
```

When we wish to draw your attention to a particular part of a code block, the relevant lines or items are set in bold:

```
[Tooltip("How fast the ball moves forwards automatically")]
[Range(0, 10)]
public float rollSpeed = 5;
```

Bold: Indicates a new term, an important word, or words that you see on screen. For example, words in menus or dialog boxes appear in the text like this. Here is an example: "Select **System info** from the **Administration** panel."

 Warnings or important notes appear like this.

 Tips and tricks appear like this.

Get in touch

Feedback from our readers is always welcome.

General feedback: If you have questions about any aspect of this book, mention the book title in the subject of your message and email us at customercare@packtpub.com.

Errata: Although we have taken every care to ensure the accuracy of our content, mistakes do happen. If you have found a mistake in this book, we would be grateful if you would report this to us. Please visit www.packtpub.com/support/errata, selecting your book, clicking on the Errata Submission Form link, and entering the details.

Piracy: If you come across any illegal copies of our works in any form on the Internet, we would be grateful if you would provide us with the location address or website name. Please contact us at copyright@packt.com with a link to the material.

If you are interested in becoming an author: If there is a topic that you have expertise in, and you are interested in either writing or contributing to a book, please visit authors.packtpub.com.

Reviews

Please leave a review. Once you have read and used this book, why not leave a review on the site that you purchased it from? Potential readers can then see and use your unbiased opinion to make purchase decisions, we at Packt can understand what you think about our products, and our authors can see your feedback on their book. Thank you!

For more information about Packt, please visit `packt.com`.

Building Your Game 1

As we start off on our journey of building mobile games using the Unity game engine, it's important that you are familiar with the engine itself before we dive into the specifics of building things for mobile platforms. Although there is a chance that you've already built a game and want to transition it to mobile, there will also be those of you who haven't touched Unity before or may not have used it in a long time. This chapter will act as an introduction to newcomers and a refresher for those coming back, and it will provide some best practices for those who are already familiar with Unity. While you may skip this chapter if you're already familiar with Unity, I think it's also a good idea to go through the project so that you know the thought processes behind why the project is made in the way that it is, so that you can keep it in mind for your own future titles.

In this chapter, we will build a 3D endless runner game in the same vein as Imangi Studios LLC's *Temple Run* series. In our case, we will have a player who will run continuously in a certain direction and dodge the obstacles that are in their way. We can also add additional features to the game easily, as the game will endlessly have new things added to it.

This chapter will be split into a number of topics. It will contain simple, step-by-step processes for you to follow. Here is an outline of our tasks:

- Setting up the project
- Creating the player
- Moving the player through a C# script
- Improving scripts using attributes
- Having the camera follow the player
- Creating a basic tile
- Making the game endless
- Creating obstacles

Technical requirements

This book utilizes Unity 2020.1.0f1 and Unity Hub 2.3.1, but the steps should work with minimal changes in future versions of the editor. If you would like to download the exact version used in this book, and there is a new version out, you can visit Unity's download archive at `https://unity3d.com/get-unity/download/archive`. You can also find the system requirements for Unity at `https://docs.unity3d.com/2020.1/Documentation/Manual/system-requirements.html` in the **Unity Editor system requirements** section. You can find the code files present in this chapter on GitHub at `https://github.com/PacktPublishing/Unity-2020-Mobile-Game-Development-Second-Edition/tree/master/Chapter%2001`.

Setting up the project

Now that we have our goals in mind, let's start building our project:

1. To get started, open Unity Hub on your computer.
2. From startup, we'll opt to create a new project by clicking on the **New** button.
3. Next, under **Project Name**, put in a name (I have chosen **MobileDev**), and under **Templates**, make sure that **3D** is selected. Afterward, click on **CREATE** and wait for Unity to load up:

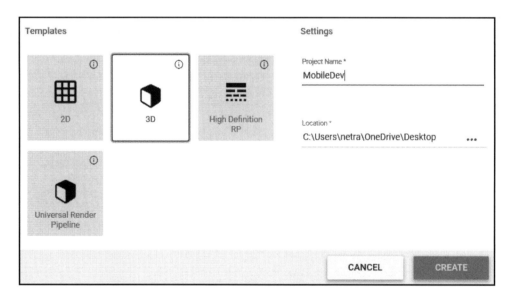

4. After it's finished, you'll see the Unity Editor pop up for the first time:

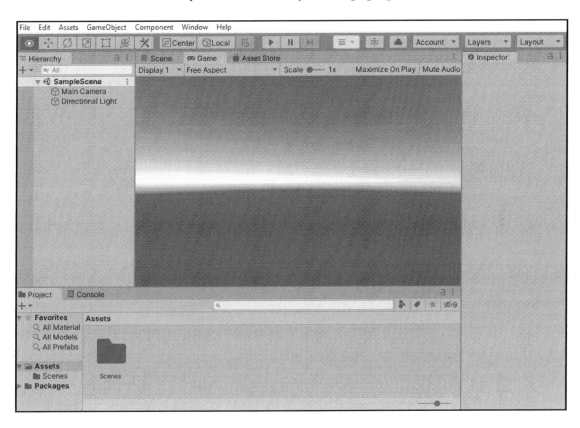

5. If your layout doesn't look the same as in the preceding screenshot, go to the top-right section of the toolbar and select the drop-down menu there that reads **Layout**. From there, select **Default** from the options presented:

In this particular build of Unity, at the time of writing, it appears as if there are some preview packages in use. This likely will not be the case in the future but steps to fix this will be included just in case.

6. If the **Preview Packages in Use** button is visible on the toolbar (the icon looks like a package), select it and click on the S**how Preview Packages...** option:

This will bring up the **Package Manager** window, which will show a list of any packages that are not updated.

7. In the right-hand menu, click on the **Update to 3.0.0** button and wait for it to complete:

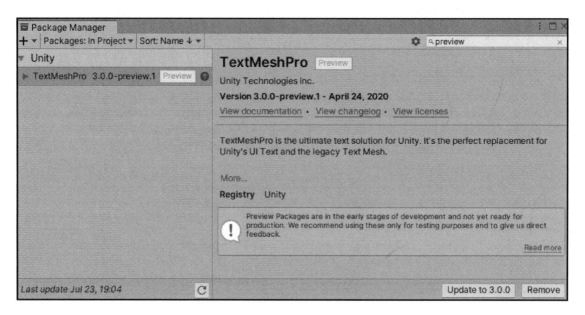

If all went well, the button should go away.

8. Afterward, you can close **Package Manager** if needed, or click on the **Scene** tab to go back to the game editor itself:

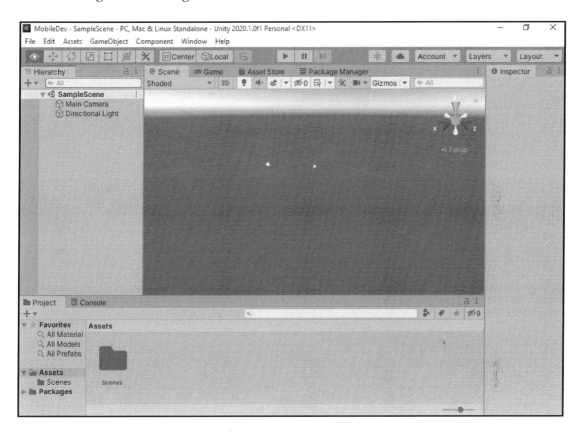

We now have opened up Unity for the first time and have the default layout displayed!

If this is your first time working with Unity, then I highly recommend that you read the *Learning the interface* section of the Unity manual, which you can access at `https://docs.unity3d.com/Manual/Learningthe Interface.html`.

Now that we have Unity open, we can actually start building our project.

Creating the player

To get started, we'll build a player that will always move forward. Let's start with that now:

1. Create some ground for our player to walk on. To do that, go to the top menu and select **GameObject | 3D Object | Cube**.

2. From there, we'll move over to the **Inspector** window and change the name of the object to Floor. Then, for the **Transform** component, set **Position** to (0, 0, 0) if needed, which we can type in, or we can right-click on the **Transform** component and then select the **Reset Position** option.

3. Then, we will set the **Scale** values of the object to (7, 0.1, 10):

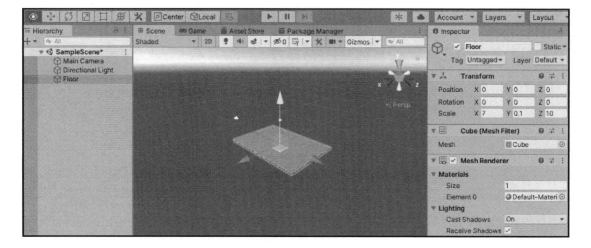

In Unity, by default, 1 unit of space is representative of 1 meter in real life. This will make the floor longer than it is wide (X and Z), and we have some size on the ground (Y), so the player will collide and land on it because we have a **Box Collider** component attached to it.

The **Box Collider** component is added automatically when creating a **Cube** object and is required in order to have objects collide with it. For more information on the **Box Collider** component, check out `https://docs.unity3d.com/Manual/class-BoxCollider.html`

4. Next, we will create our player, which will be a sphere. To do this, we will go to **GameObject | 3D Object | Sphere**.

5. Rename the sphere to `Player` and set the **Transform** component's **Position** values to `(0, 1, -4)`:

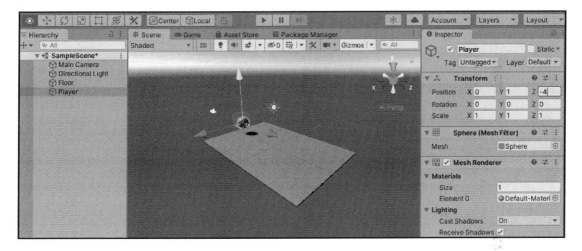

This places the ball slightly above the ground and shifts it back to near the starting point. Note that the camera object (see the camera icon) is pointing toward the ball by default because it is positioned at 0, 1, -10.

6. We want the ball to move, so we will need to tell the physics engine that we want to have this object react to forces, so we will need to add a **Rigidbody** component. To do so, go to the menu and select **Component | Physics | Rigidbody**. To see what happens now, let's click on the **Play** button, which can be seen in the middle of the first toolbar:

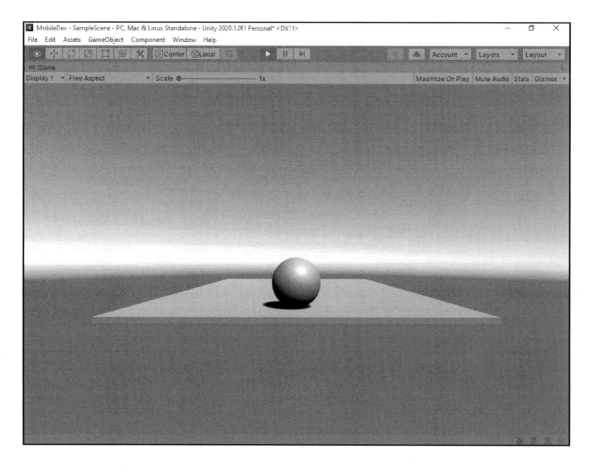

As in the preceding screenshot, you should see the ball fall down onto the ground when we play the game.

You can disable/enable having the **Game** tab take up the entire screen when being played by clicking on the **Maximize On Play** button at the top, or by right-clicking on the **Game** tab and then selecting **Maximize**.

7. Click on the **Play** button again to turn the game off and go back to the **Scene** tab, if it doesn't happen automatically.

We now have the objects for both the floor and player in the game and have told the player to react to physics! Next, we will add interactivity to the player through the use of code.

Moving the player through a C# script

We want the player to move, so in order to do that, we will create our own piece of functionality in a script, effectively creating our own custom component in the process:

1. To create a script, we will go to the **Project** window and select the create button in the top-left corner of the menu by clicking the **+** icon, and then we will select **Folder**:

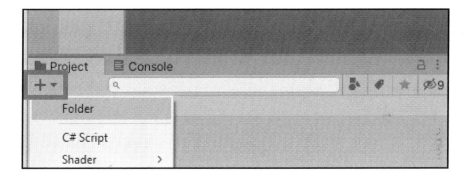

You can also access the **Create** menu by right-clicking on the right-hand side of the **Project** window. With this method, you can right-click and then select **Create** | **Folder**.

2. From there, we'll name this folder Scripts. It's always a good idea to organize our projects, so this will help with that.

If you happen to misspell the name, go ahead and select the object and then single-click on the name, and it'll let you rename it.

3. Double-click on the folder to enter it, and now you can create a script by going to **Create | C# Script** and renaming the newly created item to `PlayerBehaviour` (no spaces).

 The reason I'm using the "behaviour" spelling instead of "behavior" is that all components in Unity are children of another class called `MonoBehaviour`, and I'm following Unity's lead in that regard.

4. Double-click on the script to open up the script editor (IDE) of your choice and add the following code to it:

```csharp
using UnityEngine;

public class PlayerBehaviour : MonoBehaviour
{
    // A reference to the Rigidbody component
    private Rigidbody rb;

    // How fast the ball moves left/right
    public float dodgeSpeed = 5;

    // How fast the ball moves forwards automatically
    public float rollSpeed = 5;

    // Start is called before the first frame update
    void Start()
    {
        // Get access to our Rigidbody component
        rb = GetComponent<Rigidbody>();
    }

    // Update is called once per frame
    void Update()
    {
        // Check if we're moving to the side
        var horizontalSpeed = Input.GetAxis("Horizontal") *
            dodgeSpeed;
        rb.AddForce(horizontalSpeed, 0, rollSpeed);
    }
}
```

In the preceding code, we have a couple of variables that we will be working with. The `rb` variable is a reference to the GameObject's `Rigidbody` component that we added previously. It gives us the ability to make the object move, which we will use in the `Update` function. We also have two variables, `dodgeSpeed` and `rollSpeed`, which dictate how quickly the player will move when moving left/right or when moving forward, respectively.

Since our object has only one `Rigidbody` component, we assign `rb` once in the `Start` function, which is called when the GameObject is loaded into the scene at the beginning of the game.

Then, we use the `Update` function to check whether our player is pressing keys to move left or right as based on Unity's Input Manager system. By default, the `Input.GetAxis` function will return to us a negative value, moving to -1 if we press *A* or the left arrow. If we press the right arrow or *D*, we will get a positive value up to 1 returned to us, and the input will move toward 0 if nothing is pressed. We then multiply this by `dodgeSpeed` in order to increase the speed so that it is easier to be seen.

For more information on the Input Manager, check out `https://docs.unity3d.com/Manual/class-InputManager.html`.

Finally, once we have that value, we will apply a force to our ball's `horizontalSpeed` units on the X-axis and `rollSpeed` in the Z-axis.

5. Save your script, and return to the Unity Editor.

6. We will now need to assign this script to our player by selecting the `Player` object in the **Hierarchy** window, and then in the **Inspector** window, we will drag and drop the `PlayerBehaviour` script from the **Project** window to be on top of the `Player` object. If all goes well, we should see the script appear on our object, as follows:

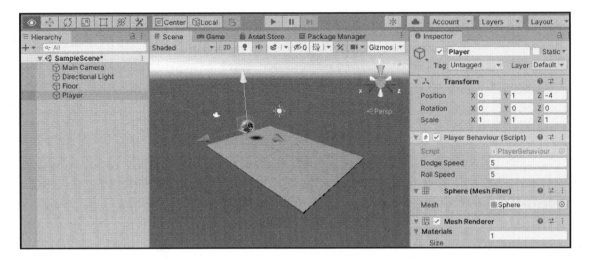

Note that when writing scripts, if we declare a variable as `public`, it will show up in the **Inspector** window for us to be able to set it. We typically set a variable as `public` when we want designers to tweak the values for gameplay purposes, but it also allows other scripts to access the property in code. By default, variables and methods are `private`, which means they can only be used within the class.

For more information on access modifiers and how they work in Unity as well as some additional protections you can put into place, check out `https:/ /www.lumpystudios.com/index.php/the-lumpy-blog/34-access- modifiers-in-unity`.

7. Save your scene by going to **File** | **Save**. Afterward, play the game and use the left and right arrows to see the player moving according to your input, but no matter what, moving forward by default:

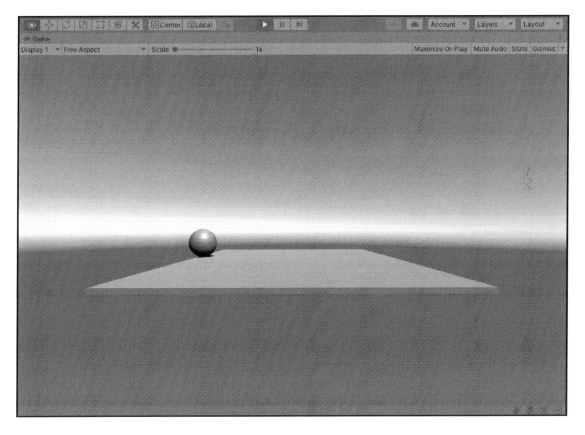

With this, you can see that the ball moves automatically and our input is received correctly!

Improving our scripts with attributes and XML comments

We could stop working with the `PlayerBehaviour` class script here, but I want to touch on a couple of things that we can use in order to improve the quality and style of our code. This becomes especially useful when you start building projects in teams, as you'll be working with other people—some of them will be working on code with you, and then there will be designers and artists who will not be working on code with you, but they will still need to use the things that you've programmed.

When writing scripts, we want them to be as error-proof as possible. Making the `rb` variable `private` starts that process, as now the user will not be able to modify that anywhere outside of this class. We want our teammates to modify `dodgeSpeed` and `rollSpeed`, but we may want to give them some advice as to what it is and/or how it will be used. To do this in the **Inspector** window, we can make use of something called an *attribute*.

Using attributes

Attributes are things we can add to the beginning of a variable, class, or function declaration, which allow us to attach additional functionality to them. There are many of them that exist inside Unity, and you can write your very own attributes as well, but right now, we'll talk about the ones that I use most often.

The Tooltip attribute

If you've used Unity for a period of time, you may have noted that some components in the **Inspector** window, such as the `Rigidbody`, have a nice feature—if you move your mouse over a variable name, you'll see a description of what the variables are and/or how to use them. The first thing you'll learn is how we can get the same effect in our own components by making use of the `Tooltip` attribute. If we do this for the `dodgeSpeed` and `rollSpeed` variables, it will look something like this:

```
[Tooltip("How fast the ball moves left/right")]
public float dodgeSpeed = 5;

[Tooltip("How fast the ball moves forwards automatically")]
public float rollSpeed = 5;
```

Save the preceding script and return to the editor:

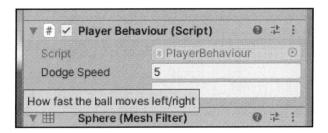

Now, when we highlight the variable using the mouse and leave it there, the text we placed will be displayed. This is a great habit to get into, as your teammates can always tell what it is that your variables are being used for.

 For more information on the Tooltip attribute, check out https://docs. unity3d.com/ScriptReference/TooltipAttribute.html.

The Range attribute

Another thing that we can use to protect our code is the Range attribute. This will allow us to specify a minimum and maximum value for a variable. Since we want the player to always be moving forward, we may want to restrict the player from moving backward. To do that, we can add the following highlighted line of code:

```
[Tooltip("How fast the ball moves forwards automatically")]
[Range(0, 10)]
public float rollSpeed = 5;
```

Save your script, and return to the editor:

We have now added a slider beside our value, and we can drag it to adjust between our minimum and maximum values. Not only does this protect our variable from being changed to an invalid state, but it also makes it so that our designers can tweak things easily by just dragging them around.

The RequireComponent attribute

Currently, we are using the `Rigidbody` component in order to create our script. When working as a team member, others may not be reading your scripts but are still expected to use them when creating gameplay. Unfortunately, this means that they may do things that have unintended results, such as removing the `Rigidbody` component, which will cause errors when our script is run. Thankfully, we also have the `RequireComponent` attribute, which we can use to fix this.

It looks something like this:

```
using UnityEngine;

[RequireComponent(typeof(Rigidbody))]
public class PlayerBehaviour : MonoBehaviour
```

By adding this attribute, we state that when we include this component in a GameObject and it doesn't have a `Rigidbody` component attached to its GameObject, the component will be added automatically. It also makes it so that if we were to try to remove the `Rigidbody` component from this object, the editor will warn us that we can't, unless we remove the `PlayerBehaviour` component first. Note that this works for any class extended from `MonoBehaviour`; just replace `Rigidbody` with whatever it is that you wish to keep.

Now, if we go into the Unity Editor and try to remove the `Rigidbody` component by right-clicking on it in **Inspector** and selecting **Remove Component**, the following message will be seen:

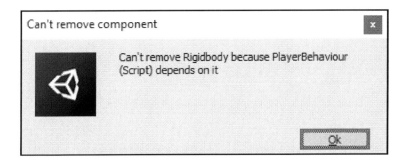

This is exactly what we want, and this ensures that the component will be there, allowing us not to have to include `if` checks every time we want to use a component.

XML comments

Note that previously we did not use a `Tooltip` attribute on the private `rb` variable. Since it's not being displayed in the editor, it's not really needed. However, there is a way that we can enhance that as well, using XML comments. XML comments have a couple of nice things that we get when using them instead of traditional comments, which we were using previously. When using variables/functions instead of code in Visual Studio, we will now see a comment about it. This will help other coders on your team with additional information and details to ensure that they are using your code correctly.

XML comments look something like this:

```
/// <summary>
/// A reference to the Rigidbody component
/// </summary>
private Rigidbody rb;
```

It may appear that a lot more writing is needed to use this format, but I did not actually type the entire thing out. XML comments are a fairly standard C# feature, so if you are using MonoDevelop or Visual Studio and type `///`, it will automatically generate the summary blocks for you (and the `param` tags needed, if there are parameters needed for something such as a function).

Now, why would we want to do this? Well, if you select the variable in IntelliSense, it will display the following information to us:

This is a great help for when other people are trying to use your code and it is how Unity's staff write their code. We can also extend this to functions and classes to ensure that our code is more self-documented.

Unfortunately, XML comments do not show up in the inspector, and the `Tooltip` attribute doesn't show info in the editor. With that in mind, I use `Tooltip` for public instructions and/or things that will show up in the **Inspector** window, and XML comments for everything else.

If you're interested in looking into XML comments more, feel free to check out `https://msdn.microsoft.com/en-us/library/b2s063f7.aspx`.

Update versus FixedUpdate

The next thing to look at is our movement code. You may have noticed that we are currently using the Update function in order to move our player. As the comment above it states, the Update function is called once per frame that the game is running. One thing to consider is that the frequency of Update being called is variable, meaning that it can change over time. This is dependent on a number of factors, including the hardware that is being used. This means that the more times the Update function is called, the better the computer is. We want a consistent experience for all of our players and one of the ways that we can do that is by using the FixedUpdate function.

FixedUpdate is similar to Update with some key differences. The first is that it is called at fixed timesteps, meaning the same time between calls. It's also important to note that after FixedUpdate is called is when physics calculations are done. This means code modifying physics-based objects should be executed within the FixedUpdate function generally, apart from one-off events such as jumping:

```
/// <summary>
/// FixedUpdate is called at a fixed framerate and is a prime place to put
/// Anything based on time.
/// </summary>
private void FixedUpdate()
{
    // Check if we're moving to the side
    var horizontalSpeed = Input.GetAxis("Horizontal") * dodgeSpeed;
    rb.AddForce(horizontalSpeed, 0, rollSpeed);
}
```

By adjusting the code to use FixedUpdate, the ball should be much more consistent in its movement speed.

For more information on FixedUpdate, check out https://docs. unity3d.com/ScriptReference/MonoBehaviour.FixedUpdate.html.

Putting it all together

With all of the stuff we've been talking about, we can now have the final version of the script, which looks like the following:

```csharp
using UnityEngine;

/// <summary>
/// Responsible for moving the player automatically and
/// receiving input.
/// </summary>
[RequireComponent(typeof(Rigidbody))]
public class PlayerBehaviour : MonoBehaviour
{
    /// <summary>
    /// A reference to the Rigidbody component
    /// </summary>
    private Rigidbody rb;

    [Tooltip("How fast the ball moves left/right")]
    public float dodgeSpeed = 5;

    [Tooltip("How fast the ball moves forwards automatically")]
    [Range(0, 10)]
    public float rollSpeed = 5;

    // Start is called before the first frame update
    private void Start()
    {
        // Get access to our Rigidbody component
        rb = GetComponent<Rigidbody>();
    }

    /// <summary>
    /// FixedUpdate is called at a fixed framerate and is a prime place
    ///         /// to put
    /// Anything based on time.
    /// </summary>
    private void FixedUpdate()
    {
        // Check if we're moving to the side
        var horizontalSpeed = Input.GetAxis("Horizontal") * dodgeSpeed;
        rb.AddForce(horizontalSpeed, 0, rollSpeed);
    }
}
```

I hope that you also agree that this makes the code easier to understand and better to work with. Now, we can move on to additional features in the game!

Having the camera following our player

Currently, our camera stays in the same spot while the game is going on. This does not work very well for this game, as the player will be moving while the game is going on. There are two main ways that we can move our camera. We can just move the camera and make it a child of the player, but that will not work due to the fact that the camera would have the same rotation as the ball, which would cause the camera to spin around constantly and likely cause dizziness and disorientation for the players. Due to that, we will likely want to use a script to move it instead. Thankfully, we can modify how our camera looks at things fairly easily, so let's go ahead and fix that next:

1. Go to the **Project** window and create a new C# script called CameraBehaviour. From there, use the following code:

```csharp
using UnityEngine;

/// <summary>
/// Will adjust the camera to follow and face a target
/// </summary>
public class CameraBehaviour : MonoBehaviour
{
    [Tooltip("What object should the camera be looking at")]
    public Transform target;

    [Tooltip("How offset will the camera be to the target")]
    public Vector3 offset = new Vector3(0, 3, -6);

    /// <summary>
    /// Update is called once per frame
    /// </summary>
    private void Update()
    {
        // Check if target is a valid object
        if (target != null)
        {
            // Set our position to an offset of our target
            transform.position = target.position + offset;
```

```
            // Change the rotation to face target
            transform.LookAt(target);
        }
    }
}
```

This script will set the position of the object it is attached to to the position of a target with an offset. Afterward, it will change the rotation of the object to face the target. Both of the parameters are marked as `public`, so they can be tweaked in the **Inspector** window.

2. Save the script and dive back into the Unity Editor. Select the `Main Camera` object in the **Hierarchy** window. Then, go to the **Inspector** window and add the `CameraBehaviour` component to it. You may do this by dragging and dropping the script from the **Project** window onto the GameObject or by clicking on the **Add Component** button at the bottom of the **Inspector** window, typing in the name of our component, and then hitting *Enter* to confirm once it is highlighted.

3. Afterward, drag and drop the `Player` object from the **Hierarchy** window into the **Target** property of the script in the **Inspector** window:

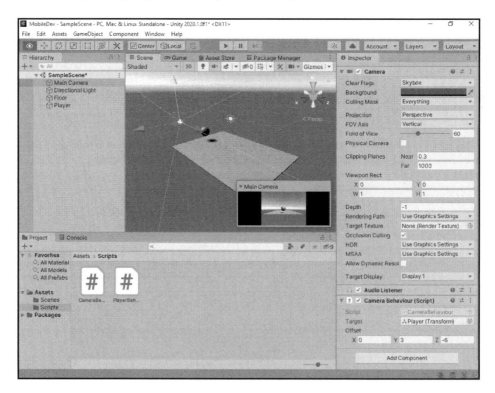

4. Save the scene and play the game:

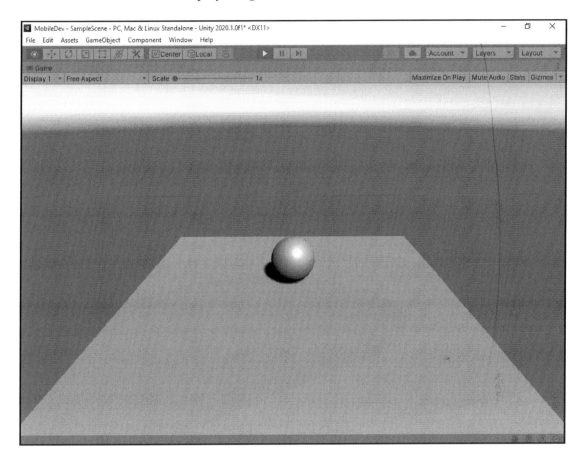

The camera now follows the player as it moves. Feel free to tweak the variables and see how it affects the look of the camera to get the feel you'd like best for the project. After this, we can have a place for the ball to move toward, which we will be covering in the next section.

Creating a basic tile

We want our game to be endless, but in order to achieve that, we will need to have pieces that we can spawn to build our environment; let's do that now:

1. To get started, we will first need to create a single repeatable piece for our runner game. To do that, we'll add some walls to the floor we already have. From the **Hierarchy** window, select the `Floor` object and duplicate it by pressing *Ctrl + D* in Windows or *command + D* on Mac. Rename this new object `Left Wall`.

2. Change the `Left Wall` object's **Transform** component by adjusting the **Scale** values to (1, 2, 10). From there, select the **Move** tool by clicking on the button with arrows on the toolbar or by pressing the *W* key.

 For more information on Unity's built-in hotkeys, check out https://docs.unity3d.com/Manual/UnityHotkeys.html.

3. We want this wall to match up with the floor, so hold down the *V* key to enter **Vertex Snap** mode. In Vertex Snap mode, we can select any of the vertices on a mesh and move them to the same position of another vertex on a different object. This is really useful for making sure that objects don't have holes between them.

4. With Vertex Snap mode on, select the inner edge and drag it until it hits the edge of the floor. Alternatively, you can set the **Position** values to (3, 1.05, 0):

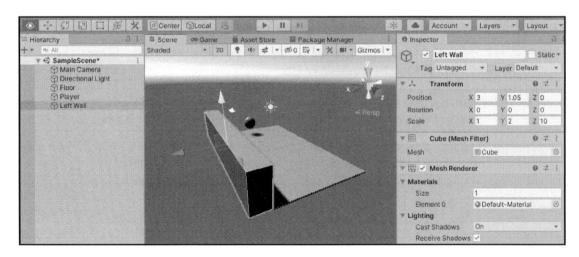

For more information on moving objects through the scene, including more details on Vertex Snap mode, check out `https://docs.unity3d.com/Manual/PositioningGameObjects.html`.

5. Then, duplicate this wall and put the other object on the other side (−3, 1.05, 0), naming it `Right Wall`:

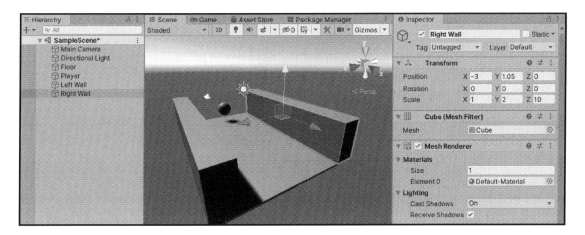

As you can see in the preceding screenshot, we now protect the player from falling off the left and right edges of the play area. Due to how the walls are set up, if we move the floor object, the walls will move as well.

For information on moving Unity's camera or navigating to the scene view, check out `https://docs.unity3d.com/Manual/SceneView Navigation.html`.

The way this game is designed, after the ball rolls past a single tile, we will no longer need it to be there anymore. If we just leave it there, the game will get slower over time due to us having so many things in the game environment using memory, so it's a good idea to remove assets we are no longer using. We also need to have some way to figure out when we should spawn new tiles to continue the path the player can take.

6. Now, we also want to know where this piece ends, so we'll add an object with a trigger collider in it. Select **GameObject** | **Create Empty** and name this object `Tile End`.

7. Then, we will add a **Box Collider** component to our `Tile End` object. Under **Box Collider** in the **Inspector** window, set the **Scale** values to (7, 2, 1) to fit the size of the space the player can walk in. Note that there is a green box around that space showing where collisions can take place. Set the **Position** property to (0, 1, 10) to reach past the end of our tile. Finally, check the **Is Trigger** property so that the collision engine will turn the collider into a **trigger**, which will be able to run code events when it is hit, but will not prevent the player from moving:

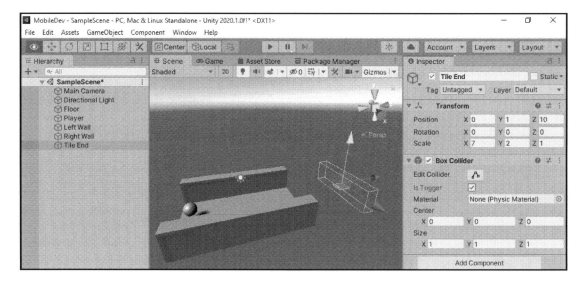

As I mentioned briefly before, this trigger will be used to tell the game that our player has finished walking over this tile. This is positioned past the tile due to the fact that we want to still see tiles until they pass what the camera can see. We'll tell the engine to remove this tile from the game, but we will dive more into that later on in the chapter.

8. Now that we have all of the objects created, we want to group our objects together as one piece that we can create duplicates of. To do this, let's create an **Empty GameObject** instance by going to **GameObject | Create Empty** and naming the newly created object Basic Tile. Set the **Position** values of this new object to (0, 0, 0).

9. Then, go to the **Hierarchy** window and drag and drop the Floor, Tile End, Left Wall, and Right Wall objects on top of it to make them children of the Basic Tile object.

10. Currently, the camera can see the start of the tiles, so to fix that, let's set the Basic Tile **Position** values to (0, 0, -5). As you can see in the following screenshot, now the entire tile will shift back:

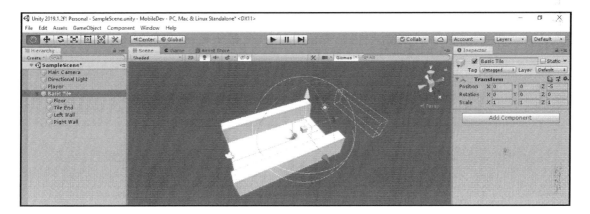

11. Finally, we will need to know at what position we should spawn the next piece, so create another **Empty GameObject** by going to **GameObject | Create Empty** or by pressing *Ctrl + Shift + N*. Make the new object a child of Basic Tile as well, give it the name Next Spawn Point, and set its **Position** values to (0, 0, 5).

 Note that when we modify an object that has a parent, the position is relative to the parent, not its world position.

As you can see, the spawn point position will now be on the edge of our current title:

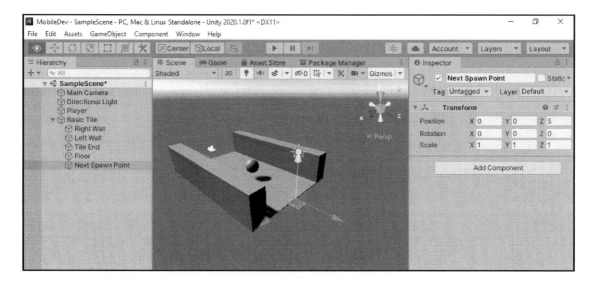

12. Now we have a single tile that is fully completed. Instead of duplicating this a number of times by hand, we will make use of Unity's concept of **Prefabs**. Prefabs, or prefabricated objects, are blueprints of GameObjects and components that we can turn into files, which can be duplicates. There are other interesting features that Prefabs have, but we will discuss them as we make use of them.

From the **Project** window, go to the Assets folder and then create a new folder called Prefabs. Then, drag and drop the Basic Tile object from the **Hierarchy** window to the **Project** window inside the Prefabs folder. If the text for the Basic Tile name in the **Hierarchy** window becomes blue, we will know that it was made correctly:

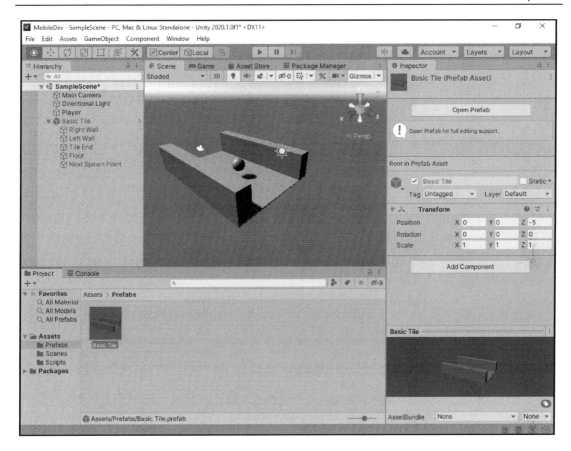

With that, we now have a tile prefab that we can create duplicates of the tile through the code to extend our environment.

Making it endless

Now that we have a foundation, let's make it so that we can continue running instead of stopping after a short time by spawning copies of this basic tile in front of each other:

1. To start off with, we have our prefab, so we can delete the original `Basic Tile` in the **Hierarchy** window by selecting it and then pressing the *Delete* key.
2. We need to have a place to create all of these tiles and potentially manage information for the game, such as the player's score. In Unity, this is typically referred to as a `GameController`. From the **Project** window, go to the `Scripts` folder and create a new C# script called `GameController`.

3. Open the script in your IDE and use the following code:

```
using UnityEngine;

/// <summary>
/// Controls the main gameplay
/// </summary>
public class GameController : MonoBehaviour
{
    [Tooltip("A reference to the tile we want to spawn")]
    public Transform tile;

    [Tooltip("Where the first tile should be placed at")]
    public Vector3 startPoint = new Vector3(0, 0, -5);

    [Tooltip("How many tiles should we create in advance")]
    [Range(1, 15)]
    public int initSpawnNum = 10;

    /// <summary>
    /// Where the next tile should be spawned at.
    /// </summary>
    private Vector3 nextTileLocation;

    /// <summary>
    /// How should the next tile be rotated?
    /// </summary>
    private Quaternion nextTileRotation;

    /// <summary>
    /// Start is called before the first frame update
    /// </summary>
    private void Start()
    {
        // Set our starting point
        nextTileLocation = startPoint;
        nextTileRotation = Quaternion.identity;

        for (int i = 0; i < initSpawnNum; ++i)
        {
            SpawnNextTile();
        }
    }

    /// <summary>
    /// Will spawn a tile at a certain location and setup the next
        /// position
    /// </summary>
```

```
public void SpawnNextTile()
{
    var newTile = Instantiate(tile, nextTileLocation,
                              nextTileRotation);

    // Figure out where and at what rotation we should spawn
    // the next item
    var nextTile = newTile.Find("Next Spawn Point");
    nextTileLocation = nextTile.position;
    nextTileRotation = nextTile.rotation;
}
}
```

This script will spawn a number of tiles, one after another, based on the `tile` and `initSpawnNum` properties.

4. Save your script and dive back in to Unity. From there, create a new **Empty** GameObject and name it `Game Controller`. Drag and drop it to the top of the **Hierarchy** window. For clarity's sake, go ahead and reset the position if you want to. Then, attach the **Game Controller** script to the object and then set the **Tile** property by dragging and dropping the `Basic Tile` prefab from the **Project** window into the **Tile** slot:

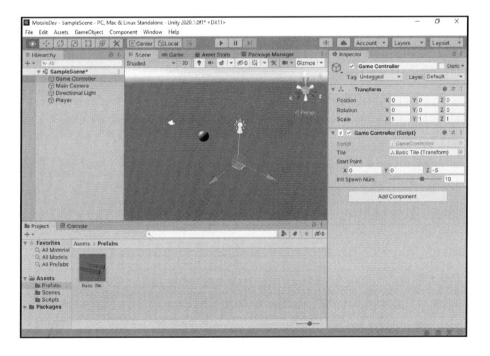

5. Save your scene and run the project:

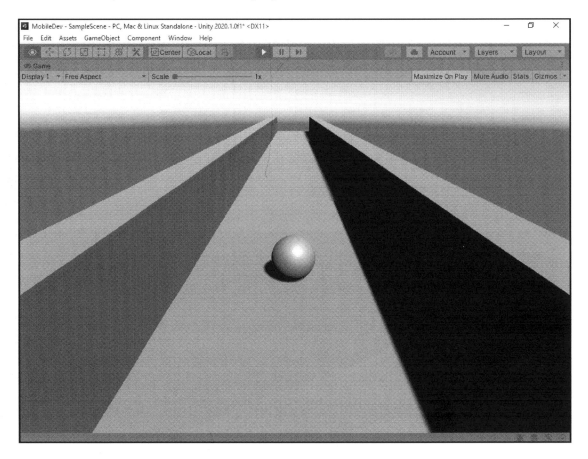

Great, but now we will need to create new objects after these, and we don't want to spawn a crazy number of these at once. It's better that once we reach the end of a tile, we create a new tile and remove it. We'll work on optimizing this more later, but that way we always have about the same number of tiles in the game at any given time.

6. Go into the **Project** window and from the `Scripts` folder create a new script called `TileEndBehaviour,` using the following code:

```
using UnityEngine;

/// <summary>
/// Handles spawning a new tile and destroying this one
/// upon the player reaching the end
/// </summary>
public class TileEndBehaviour : MonoBehaviour
{
    [Tooltip("How much time to wait before destroying " +
             "the tile after reaching the end")]
    public float destroyTime = 1.5f;

    private void OnTriggerEnter(Collider col)
    {
        // First check if we collided with the player
        if (col.gameObject.GetComponent<PlayerBehaviour>())
        {
            // If we did, spawn a new tile
            GameObject.FindObjectOfType<GameController>
                ().SpawnNextTile();

            // And destroy this entire tile after a short delay
            Destroy(transform.parent.gameObject, destroyTime);
        }
    }
}
```

7. Now, to assign it to the prefab, we can go to the **Project** window and then go into the `Prefabs` folder. From there, double-click on the `Basic Tile` object to open up its editor. From the **Hierarchy** tab, select the `Tile End` object and then add a **Tile End Behaviour** component to it:

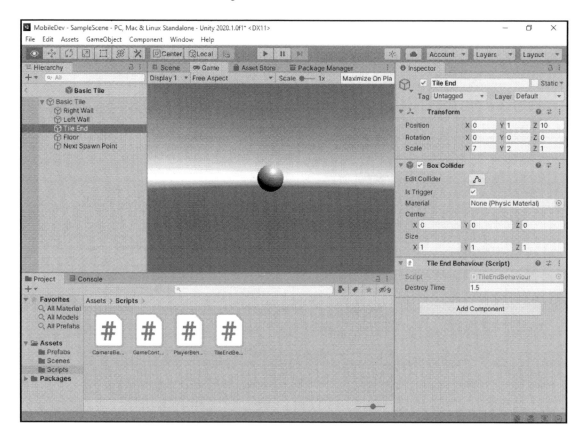

You can also open the prefab editor by selecting the prefab object from the **Project** window, going to the **Inspector** tab, and clicking the **Open Prefab** button.

8. Click on the left arrow next to the prefab name to return to the basic scene:

9. Save your scene and play.

You'll note now that as the player continues to move, new tiles will spawn as you go; if you switch to the **Scene** tab while playing, you'll see that as the ball passes the tiles, they will destroy themselves:

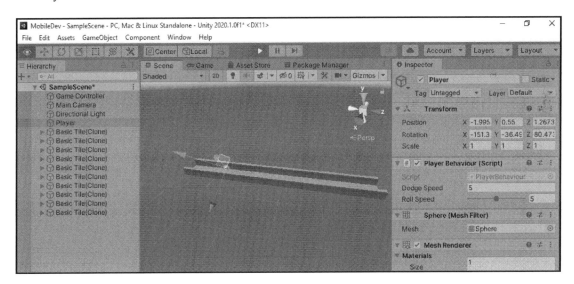

This will ensure that there will be tiles in front of the player to visit! But of course, this is just an endless straight line. In the next section, we will see how to make the game much more interesting.

Creating obstacles

It's great that we have some basic tiles, but it's a good idea to give the player something to do or, in our case, something to avoid. This will provide the player with some kind of challenge and a basic gameplay goal, which is avoiding the obstacles here. In this section, you'll learn how to customize your tiles to add obstacles for your player to avoid. So, let's look at the steps:

1. Just like we created a prefab for our basic tile, we will create a single obstacle through code. I want to make it easy to see what the obstacle will look like in the world and make sure that it's not too large, so I'll drag and drop a `Basic Tile` prefab back into the world.

2. Next, we will create a cube by going to **GameObject** | **3D Object** | **Cube**. We will name this object `Obstacle`. Change the **Y Scale** value to 2 and position it above the platform at (0, 1, 0.25):

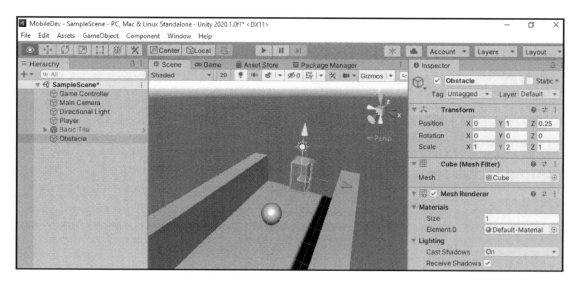

3. We can then play the game to see how that'll work:

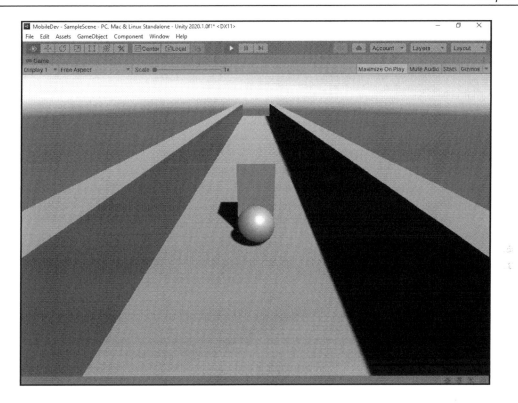

4. As you can see in the preceding screenshot, the player gets stopped, but nothing really happens. In this instance, we want the player to lose when they hit this obstacle and then restart the game; so, to do that, we'll need to write a script. From the **Project** window, go to the Scripts folder and create a new script called ObstacleBehaviour. We'll use the following code:

```
using UnityEngine;
using UnityEngine.SceneManagement; // LoadScene

public class ObstacleBehaviour : MonoBehaviour {

    [Tooltip("How long to wait before restarting the game")]
    public float waitTime = 2.0f;

    private void OnCollisionEnter(Collision collision)
    {
        // First check if we collided with the player
        if (collision.gameObject.GetComponent<PlayerBehaviour>())
        {
            // Destroy the player
            Destroy(collision.gameObject);
```

```
            // Call the function ResetGame after waitTime
              // has passed
            Invoke("ResetGame", waitTime);
        }
    }

    /// <summary>
    /// Will restart the currently loaded level
    /// </summary>
    private void ResetGame()
    {
        // Restarts the current level
        SceneManager.LoadScene(SceneManager.GetActiveScene().name);
    }
}
```

5. Save the script and return to the editor, attaching the script to the **Obstacle** GameObject we just created.

6. Save your scene and try the game:

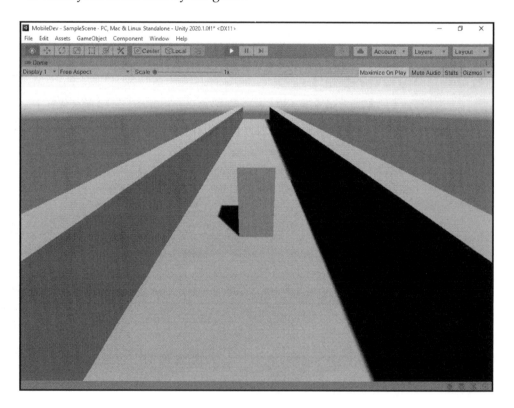

As you can see in the preceding screenshot, once we hit the obstacle, the player gets destroyed, and then after a few seconds, the game starts up again. You'll learn how to use particle systems and other things to polish this up, but at this point, it's functional, which is what we want.

7. Now that we know it works correctly, we can make it a prefab. Just as we did with the original tile, go ahead and drag and drop it from **Hierarchy** into the **Project** tab and into the `Prefabs` folder:

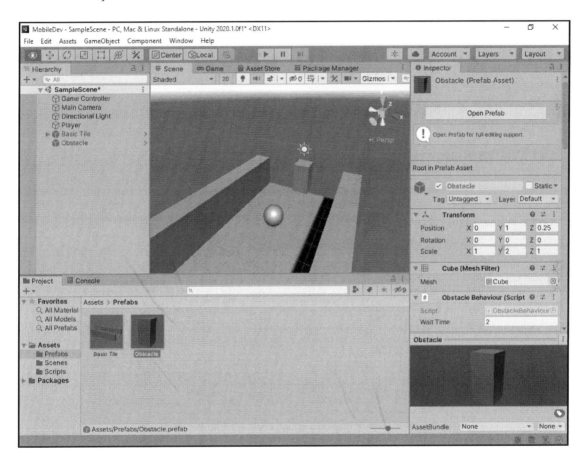

8. Next, we will remove the `Obstacle` object, as we'll spawn it upon creating the tile. To do so, select the `Obstacle` object in the **Hierarchy** window and then press the *Delete* key.

9. We will make markers to indicate where we would possibly like to spawn our obstacles. Expand the `Basic Tile` object to show its children and then duplicate the `Next Spawn Object` object and move the new one's **Position** to (0, 1, 4). We will then rename the object `Center`.

10. Afterward, to help see the objects within the **Scene** window, go to the **Inspector** window and click on the gray cube icon and then at the **Select Icon** menu, select whichever of the color options you'd like (I went with blue). Upon doing this, you'll see that we can see the text inside the editor if we are close to the object (but it won't show up in the **Game** tab by default):

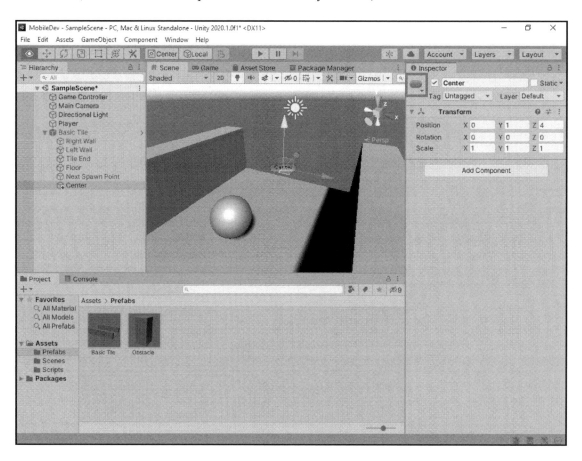

11. We want a way to get all of the potential spawn points we will want in case we decide to extend the project in the future, so we will assign a **tag** as a reference to make those objects easier to find. To do that, at the top of the **Inspector** window, click on the **Tags** dropdown and select **Add Tag...** From the menu that pops up, press the **+** button and then name it `ObstacleSpawn`:

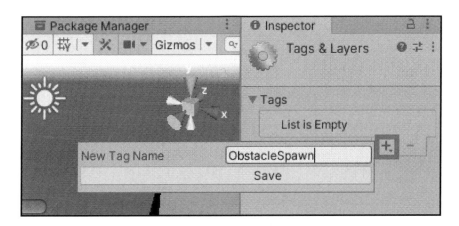

12. Go back and select the `Center` object and assign the **Tag** property to `ObstacleSpawn`:

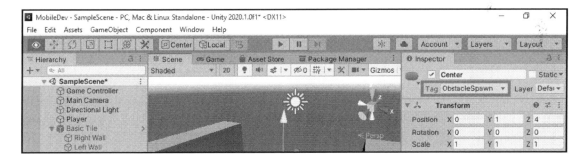

For more information on tags and why we'd want to use them, check out https://docs.unity3d.com/Manual/Tags.html.

13. Go ahead and duplicate this twice and name the others Left and Right, moving them two units to the left and right of the center to become other possible obstacle points:

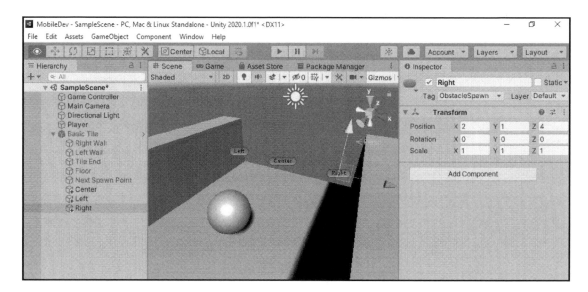

14. Note that these changes don't affect the original prefab, by default; that's why the objects are currently black text. To make this happen, select Basic Tile, and then in the **Inspector** window under the **Prefab** section, click on **Overrides** and select **Apply All**:

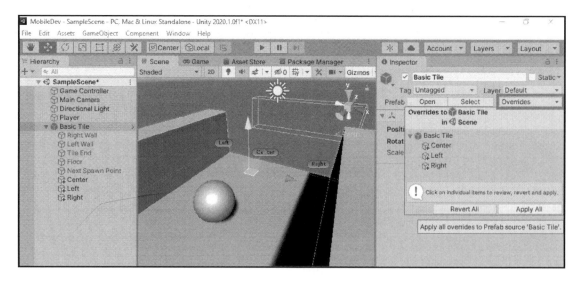

15. Now that the prefab is set up correctly, we can go ahead and remove it by selecting it in the **Hierarchy** window and pressing *Delete*.

16. We then need to go into the GameController script and make some modifications. To start with, we will need to introduce some new variables:

```
/// <summary>
/// Controls the main gameplay
/// </summary>
public class GameController : MonoBehaviour
{
    [Tooltip("A reference to the tile we want to spawn")]
    public Transform tile;

    [Tooltip("A reference to the obstacle we want to spawn")]
    public Transform obstacle;

    [Tooltip("Where the first tile should be placed at")]
    public Vector3 startPoint = new Vector3(0, 0, -5);

    [Tooltip("How many tiles should we create in advance")]
    [Range(1, 15)]
    public int initSpawnNum = 10;

    [Tooltip("How many tiles to spawn initially with
            no obstacles")]
    public int initNoObstacles = 4;
```

The first of these variables is a reference to the obstacle that we will be creating copies of. The second is a parameter of how many tiles should be spawned before spawning obstacles. This is to ensure that the player can see the obstacles before they need to avoid them.

17. Then, we need to modify the SpawnNextTile function in order to spawn obstacles as well:

```
/// <summary>
/// Will spawn a tile at a certain location and setup the next
position
/// </summary>
/// <param name="spawnObstacles">If we should spawn an
///   obstacle</param>

public void SpawnNextTile(bool spawnObstacles = true)
{
    var newTile = Instantiate(tile, nextTileLocation,
                            nextTileRotation);
```

```
// Figure out where and at what rotation we should spawn
// the next item
var nextTile = newTile.Find("Next Spawn Point");
nextTileLocation = nextTile.position;
nextTileRotation = nextTile.rotation;

if (spawnObstacles)
{
    SpawnObstacle(newTile);
}
}
```

Note that we modified the SpawnNextTile function to now have a default parameter set to true, which will tell us whether we want to spawn obstacles or not. At the beginning of the game, we may not want the player to have to start dodging immediately, but we can tweak the value to increase or decrease the number we are using. Because it has a default value of true, the original version of calling this in the Start function will still work without an error, but we will be modifying it later on.

18. Here we ask whether the value is true to call a function called SpawnObstacle, but that isn't written yet. We will add that next, but first we will be making use of the List class and we want to make sure that the compiler knows which List class we are referring to, so we need to add a using statement at the top of the file:

```
using UnityEngine;
using System.Collections.Generic; // List
```

19. Now we can write the SpawnObstacle function. Add the following function to the script:

```
private void SpawnObstacle(Transform newTile)
{
    // Now we need to get all of the possible places to spawn the
    // obstacle
    var obstacleSpawnPoints = new List<GameObject>();

    // Go through each of the child game objects in our tile
    foreach (Transform child in newTile)
    {
        // If it has the ObstacleSpawn tag
        if (child.CompareTag("ObstacleSpawn"))
        {
            // We add it as a possibility
            obstacleSpawnPoints.Add(child.gameObject);
```

```
            }
        }

        // Make sure there is at least one
        if (obstacleSpawnPoints.Count > 0)
        {
            // Get a random object from the ones we have
            var spawnPoint = obstacleSpawnPoints[Random.Range(0,
                            obstacleSpawnPoints.Count)];

            // Store its position for us to use
            var spawnPos = spawnPoint.transform.position;

            // Create our obstacle
            var newObstacle = Instantiate(obstacle, spawnPos,
                                    Quaternion.identity);

            // Have it parented to the tile
            newObstacle.SetParent(spawnPoint.transform);
        }
    }
```

20. Lastly, let's update the `Start` function:

```
/// <summary>
/// Start is called before the first frame update
/// </summary>
    private void Start()
    {
        // Set our starting point
        nextTileLocation = startPoint;
        nextTileRotation = Quaternion.identity;

        for (int i = 0; i < initSpawnNum; ++i)
        {
            SpawnNextTile(i >= initNoObstacles);
        }
    }
```

Now, as long as i is less than the value of initNoObstacles, it will not spawn a variable, effectively giving us a buffer of four tiles that can be adjusted by changing the initNoObstacles variable.

21. Save the script and go back to the Unity Editor. Then, assign the **Obstacle** variable of the **Game Controller (Script)** component in the **Inspector** window with the `Obstacle` prefab we created previously:

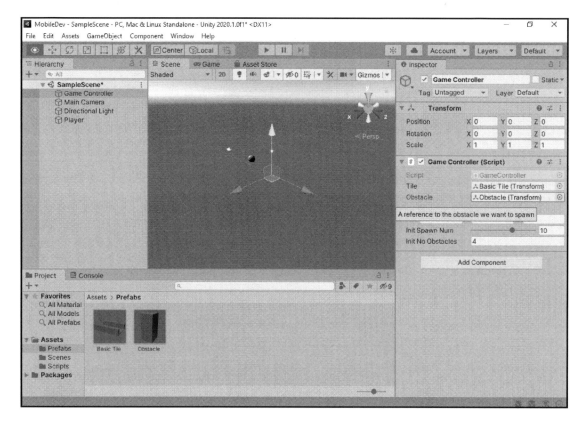

22. It's a bit hard to see things currently due to the default light settings, so let's go to the **Hierarchy** window and select the **Directional Light** object. A directional light acts similarly to how the sun works on Earth, shining everywhere from a certain position.

23. With the default settings, the shadows are too dark by default, so in the **Inspector** window, I changed the **Realtime Shadows | Strength** property to 0.5:

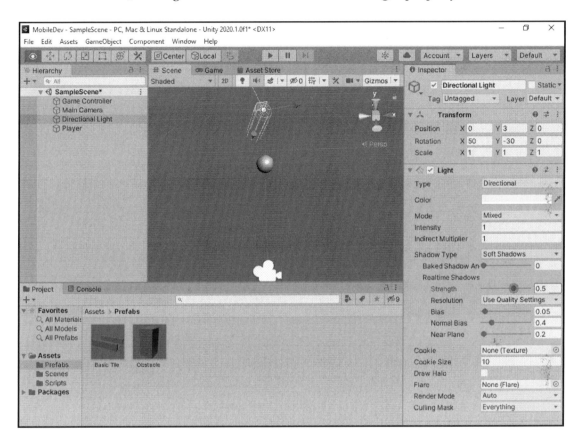

24. Save your scene and play the game:

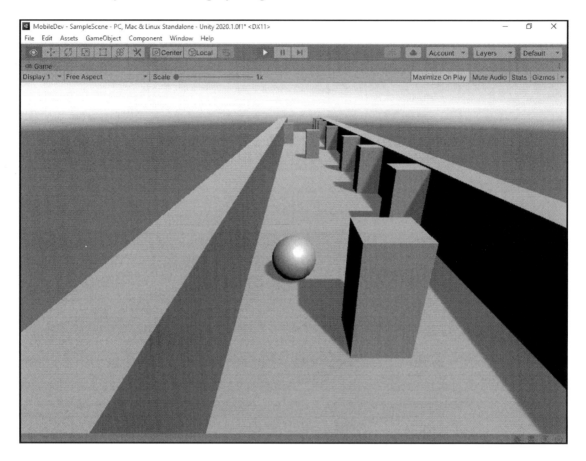

 For more information on directional lights and the other lighting types that Unity has, check out `https://unity3d.com/learn/tutorials/ topics/graphics/light-types?playlist=17102`.

As you can see in the preceding screenshot, we now have a number of obstacles for our player to avoid!

Summary

There you have it! A solid foundation, but just that, a foundation. However, that being said, we covered a lot of content in this chapter. We discussed how to create a new project in Unity, and we built a player that will move continuously, as well as taking inputs to move horizontally. We then discussed how we can use Unity's attributes and XML comments to improve our code quality and help us when working in teams. We also covered how to have a moving camera. We created a tile-based level design system, where we created new tiles as the game continued, randomly spawning obstacles for the player to avoid.

Throughout this book, we will explore more that we can do to improve this project and polish it while changing it to make for the best experience possible on mobile platforms. However, before we get to that, we'll actually need to figure out how to deploy our projects, which is what we will be working on in the next chapter.

Project Setup for Android and iOS Development

We now have a project to start off with, but currently, it's built with playing on a PC in mind. Since this book is about mobile development, it's very important to have the game working on the device itself before we get much further.

In this chapter, we will go through all of the setup that we'll need to perform in order to deploy the project in its current state to our mobile devices. At the time of writing this book, mobile development is typically done either for Android or iOS, so we will cover those two.

This chapter will be split into a number of topics. The chapter itself will be a simple step-by-step process from beginning to end. The following is the outline of our tasks:

- An introduction to build settings
- Building a project for a PC
- Exporting your project for Android
- Putting the project on your Android device
- Unity iOS installation and Xcode setup
- Building a project for iOS

Technical requirements

This book utilizes Unity 2020.1.0f1 and Unity Hub 2.3.1, but the steps should work with minimal changes in future versions of the editor. If you would like to download the exact version used in this book, and there is a new version out, you can visit Unity's download archive at `https://unity3d.com/get-unity/download/archive`. You can also find the system requirements for Unity at `https://docs.unity3d.com/2020.1/Documentation/Manual/system-requirements.html` in the **Unity Editor system requirements** section.

If you wish to deploy to an Android device, you can use Mac, Linux, or Windows, and depending on the features you wish to use, it is possible to export your game in such a way to run apps on Android 4.4 KitKat and above.

 For more information on the different types of Android versions that are supported, check out `https://docs.unity3d.com/ScriptReference/AndroidSdkVersions.html`.

To develop for an iOS device, in addition to the device itself, you'll also need to do some work on a Mac computer that runs OS X 10.11 or a later version. I'll be using 10.14.5 macOS Mojave. If you do not have one, it is possible to develop your game using Windows and, when you want to publish the game, bring your project to a Mac to do the final export.

 There are some other potential ways to build iOS apps using Windows but they are not within the scope of this book. One possible option is to use Unity's Cloud Build service, which will automatically create versions of your game; however, at the time of writing, it is $9.00 a month. For more information, check out `https://unity3d.com/unity/features/cloud-build`.

Another potential option would be to rent a Mac via the cloud to do the building yourself. For more information on that and other potential options, check out `https://mindster.com/how-develop-ios-apps-windows/`.

You can find the code files present in this chapter on GitHub at `https://github.com/PacktPublishing/Unity-2020-Mobile-Game-Development-Second-Edition/tree/master/Chapter%2002/Export`.

An introduction to build settings

There are times during development when you may want to see what your game looks like outside of the editor. It can give you a sense of accomplishment; I know, I felt that way the first time I pushed a build to a console devkit. Whether it's for PC, Mac, Linux, web player, mobile, or console, we have to go through the same menu – the **Build Settings** menu:

1. Start off by opening up the project that we created in `Chapter 1`, *Building Your Game*. In addition, open the Scene we created (`SampleScene.unity`, which is inside the `Scenes` folder):

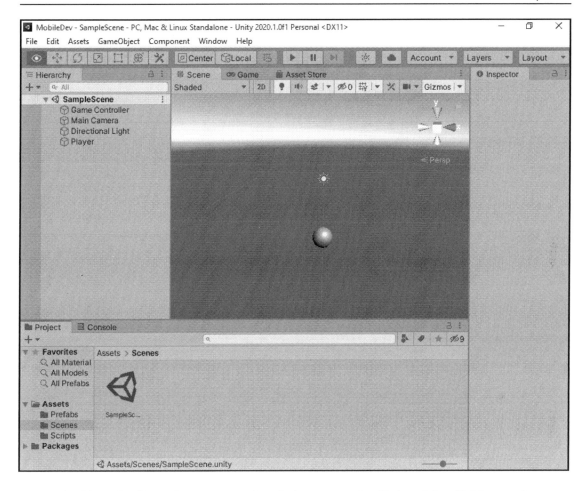

2. Since the Scene is our gameplay, let's rename the file by right-clicking on the object in the **Project** window and selecting **Rename**. Rename the file `Gameplay`. Unity will ask whether you want to reload the Scene. Do so by clicking **Reload**.

3. From here, we will open the **Build Settings** menu by selecting **File** | **Build Settings**:

You may alternatively press *Ctrl + Shift + B* or *command + Shift + B* to bring the menu up as well.

In the preceding screenshot, you will notice that the **Build Settings** menu came up. This menu contains three sections:

- **Scenes in Build**: This window contains the scenes in our project that we want to include when we build our project. This ensures that things such as test levels won't be included unless you specify so.
- **Platform**: This is a list of all of the platforms that you can export your game to. The Unity logo shows up on the current platform you're compiling for. In order to change your platform, you'll need to select it from this list and then click on the **Switch Platform** button, which appears below the list.
- **Options**: To the right of the **Platform** section, you'll see some settings that can be tweaked based on how you want the build to work, with certain options that change based on the platform you will work with.

4. By default, we have no scenes in our build, so let's go ahead and change that. Click on the **Add Open Scenes** button; you should see the Gameplay level appear in the list at index 0, which means that when your game is played, this level will be the first one to load:

 You may also add scenes to the **Scenes in Build** section by dragging and dropping them from the **Project** window. You may also drag the scenes to reorder them however you wish.

Now that we know how the build settings work, let's see how to build the project for PC to understand the general case before continuing to build our mobile game.

Building a project for PC

By default, our platform is set to **PC, Mac & Linux Standalone**. Just to verify that everything is working correctly, let's go ahead and get the game working on our own platform before moving to mobile:

1. To get started, we will select the **Build** option. In my instance, I'll be exporting the project to Windows, but the process is similar for Mac and Linux.

2. Once this is done, a window will pop up asking for a name and a location to put the game in. I'm going create a new `Export` folder located in the same folder that contains `Assets` and `Library`, so it won't show up in the **Project** window, but it will be in the same folder as my project:

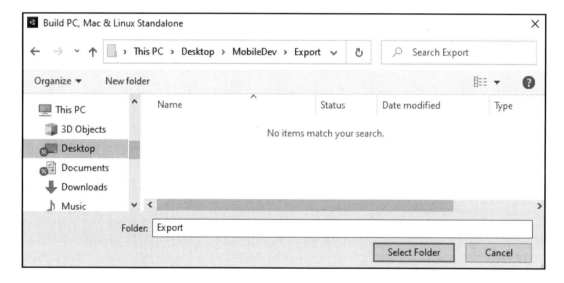

3. Click on **Select Folder** and wait for it to finish. Once it's done, you should have a window appear, as follows:

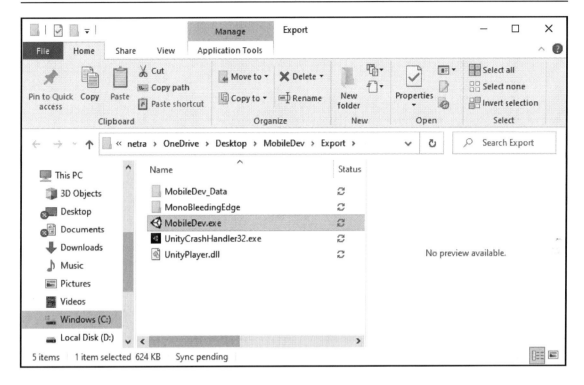

We have the executable, but we also have a data folder that contains all the assets for our application (right now, it's called `MobileDev_Data`). You must include the data folder and the other files created with your game, or it will not run.

If you build for Mac, it will bundle the app and data altogether, so once you export it, all you need to provide is the application.

4. If you double-click on the .exe file to run the game, you'll be taken to the proper game screen, as shown in the following screenshot:

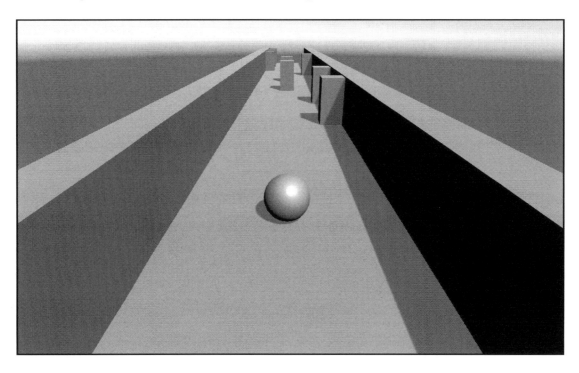

With that, we should be able to control and play the game as we usually would do. This is great!

You'll have to use *Alt + F4* (*command + Q* on Mac) to quit the game, and you can switch to Windowed mode by pressing *Alt + Enter*.

Now that we have talked about the universal ways of building a project, let's dive into the specifics for different platforms. In the next section, we will discuss getting our project onto an Android device.

Exporting a project for Android

Now that we have all of the setup done, we can open Unity with our project and export it for Android devices. In this section, we will first check whether we have Android Build Support installed, and then we will update the build and player settings to export our project. So, let's get started.

Installing Android Build Support for Unity

First of all, if you haven't done so already, you'll need to have selected to add **Android Build Support** as an option when you are installing Unity. If you have installed it, you can skip this section. If you did not install it when doing the initial installation, that is what we will cover in the following steps:

1. Close the Unity Editor and then open up the Unity Hub and select the **Installs** section.

2. From there, click on the three dots to the right of your current version of Unity and select the **Add Modules** option:

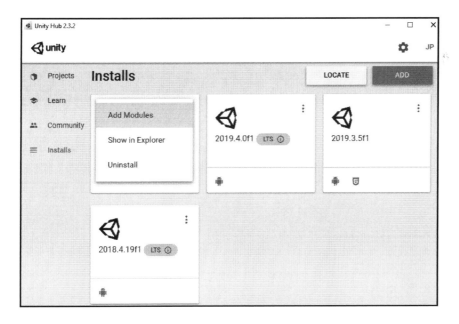

3. Check the **Android Build Support** option, which should also check the **Android SDK and NDK Tools** and **OpenJDK** options. Afterward, click on the **NEXT** button:

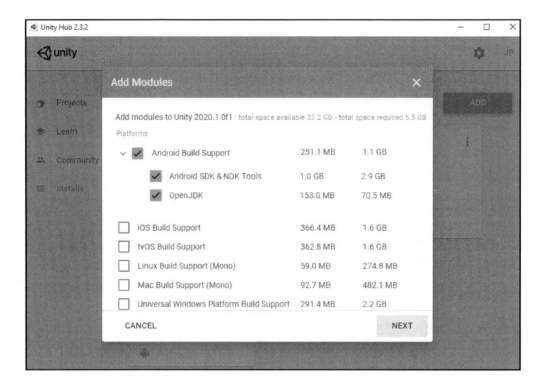

4. You'll be brought to a license terms page. Read it over and if you agree to it, check the agreement box and click on the **DONE** button:

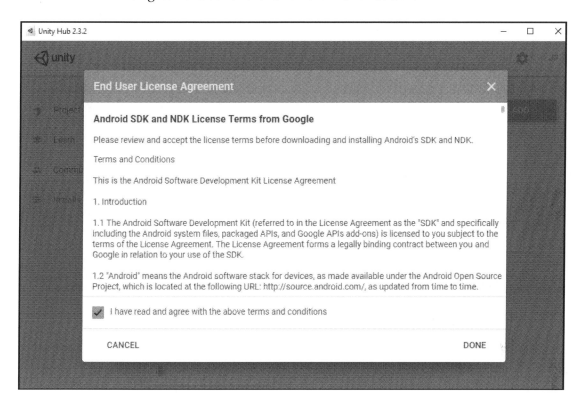

5. Wait for it to finish installing. Once finished, you should see the Android logo at the bottom of your install:

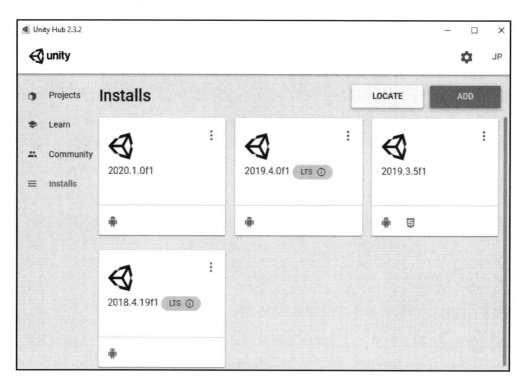

This means that Android Build Support has now been added to our version of Unity and we can build projects there. Next, we will see how to actually build the project for Android and the settings required to do so.

Updating build and player settings for Android projects

Now that we have Android support, let's open up our project again and change the platform we are developing for:

1. At this point, we will dive into Unity and move into our **Build Settings** menu once again by going to **File** | **Build Settings**.

2. Click on the **Android** option from the **Platform** list and then click on the **Switch Platform** button to make the change:

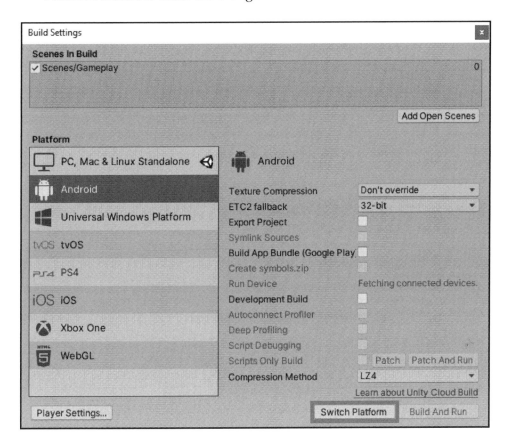

Note that this will make Unity reimport all of the assets in our game, so this may be time-consuming when you start to build larger projects. Once completed, you should notice that the Unity logo is now next to the **Android** option, signifying that's the platform to be built for:

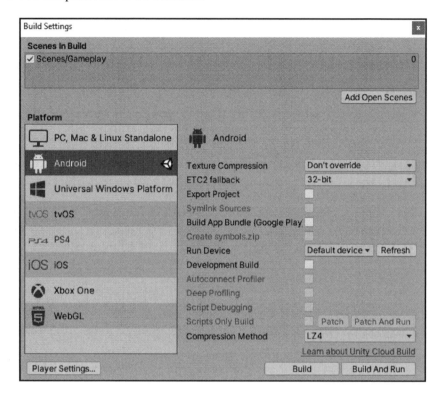

3. Now, in order to be able to build our project, we must set the bundle identifier for our game, which is a string that identifies the app. It's written like a URL in reverse, for example, `com.yourCompanyName.yourGameName`. To modify this, we'll need to open up the **Player Settings** menu, which we can get to by clicking on the **Player Settings...** button in the bottom-left part of the **Build Settings** menu or by going into **Edit** | **Project Settings** | **Player**. You'll note that the menu shows up as a new window:

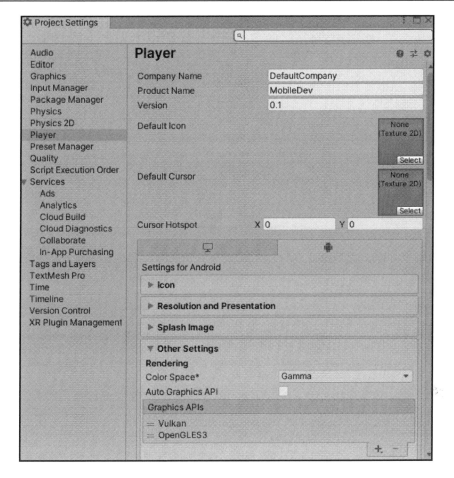

Now that we're in Android mode (note the text on the title bar of the Unity Editor), we can change these properties:

4. We'll discuss more of these in a later chapter, but for now, scroll down until you get to the **Other Settings** option, and from there, you'll see the **Package Name** property. We will change this to something else; for example, I used `com.JohnPDoran.MobileDev`. There's also a **Minimum API Level** option; make sure that your option is set to the same version as your phone or earlier, depending on what you want to support. Note that the earlier you go, the fewer things you'll have access to, but your project will be able to support more phones:

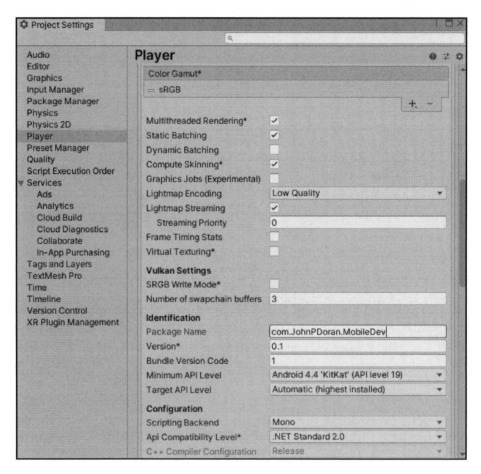

5. Close the **Project Settings** window and open up the **Build Settings** menu again by going to **File | Build Settings**. Now, we can try to build the project by clicking on the **Build** button, saving it in the same `Export` folder we created earlier. It will ask for the name you'd like the file to have. I will use `MobileDev` as we did previously, because instead of a `.exe` file, it will be creating a `.apk` file:

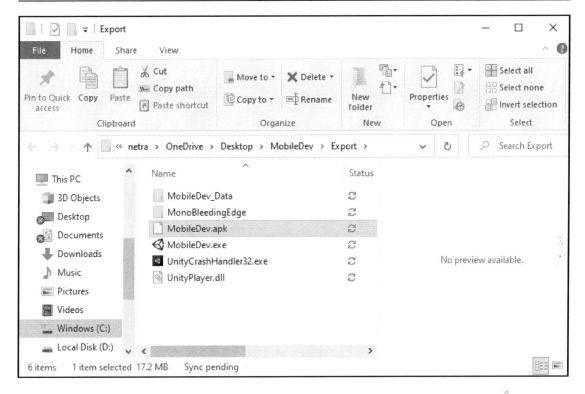

Wait a bit, and once it's finished, you should have a new `.apk` file located in the folder. Of course, just having the APK file doesn't do much if we can't put it on our actual phone; so, in the next section, we will enable our phone to test the game on our device.

Putting the project on your Android device

The following steps may be different for you depending on your Android version. If you are using Android Oreo or higher, start with step 5. If you have version 7 or lower, start at the beginning:

1. On your Android device, you'll need to go to your **Settings** app.
2. From there, scroll down till you get to the **Security** | **Security & location** section or similar, and then tap on it to go into the menu.

3. Inside there, you'll see a section called **Unknown sources**, which you'll want to enable:

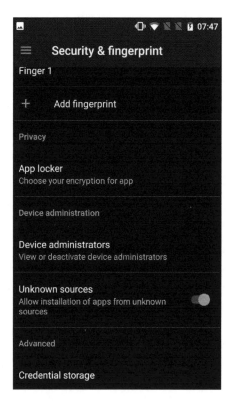

With this enabled, your device can now install the .apk file, but now you will need to move your game over to the device so that you can install it. The easiest way is to transfer it to your device via USB; we'll do that now.

For those of you who'd rather not use USB, I would suggest using a cloud storage app, such as Dropbox, to upload the .apk file and then download it from the app and install that way. There's also another tool called ADB, which can send files to your phone via USB or WiFi. For more information on that and the rest of the Android build process, check out https:// docs.unity3d.com/Manual/android-BuildProcess.html.

4. Connect your phone to your computer via USB. Upon being connected, your phone will show a notification saying that it's connected via USB for charging. Click on that notification and change the option to **File Transfer**:

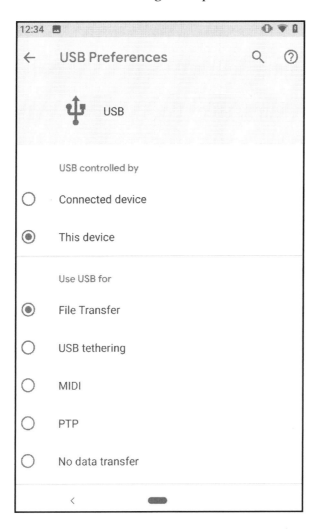

5. After that, go back to your computer and go into **Windows Explorer/Finder**, and then go to the **Devices and Drives** section; you should see your device appear there:

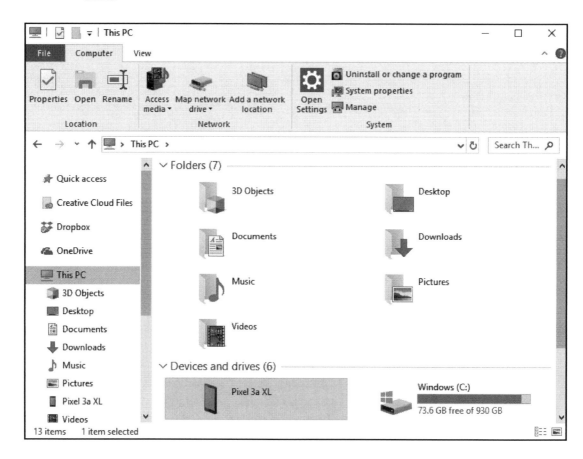

6. Double-click on your device and access the internal shared storage section from there. Then, drag the `.apk` file we made before into this folder:

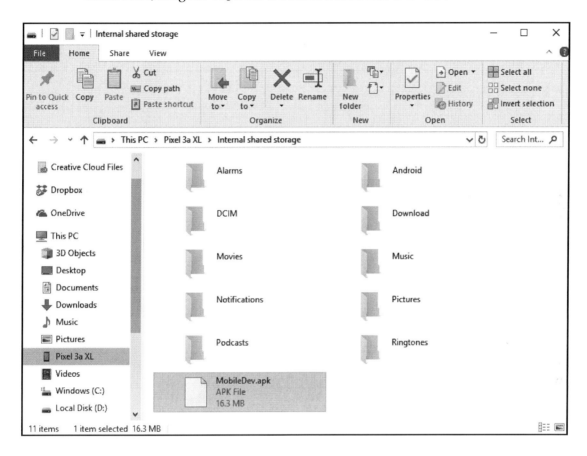

7. Now, back in your phone, open the **Files/File Explorer** app. From there, click on the button on the right-hand side and select **Show internal storage**:

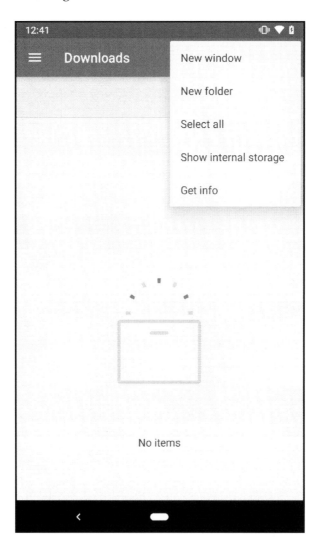

8. Then, click on the button in the top-left corner and select your phone's name (in my case, **Pixel 3a XL**):

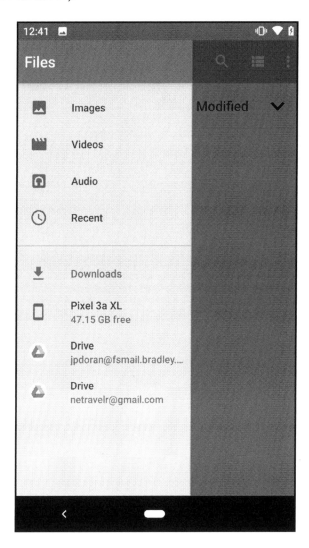

9. From there, select your `.apk` file listed from the files included:

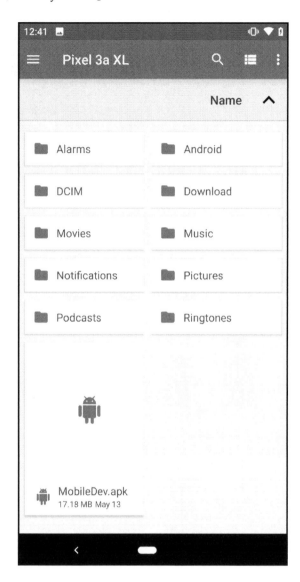

10. You'll be asked to confirm the installation. Hit the **Continue** button:

11. This will open up the installer. Go ahead and click on the **Install** button and wait for it to finish:

12. You may see a window pop up that mentions that Play Protect doesn't recognize the developer. We will see how to solve this issue later on in Chapter 12, *Game Build and Submission,* but for now, click **INSTALL ANYWAY** and wait for the installation to finish:

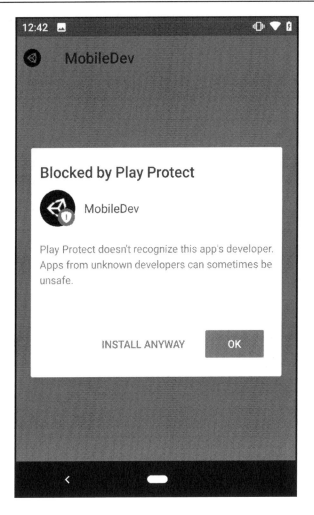

 Of course, I can't note the steps for all devices as some have different drivers that are required or additional steps that need to be performed in order to open files on the device. If these steps do not work and you do not know how to get files onto your device and access them and add new ones to them, go ahead and search for `phone name file transfer`, replacing the phone name with your phone's name.

13. Once it's finished, go ahead and click on the **Open** button to open our game:

As you can see, the game is on there and it's working. Granted, you can't control it yet, and there are a lot of new things that you can't do, but this lets you know that you've set up your Android device properly. Now that you have your game on an Android device, you now need to get it working on iOS, which we will cover in the next section.

Unity for iOS setup and Xcode installation

With Android, there's a lot of setup, but building and getting a game onto your device is less work, whereas, with iOS, there's less work on the setup end and more involvement with getting the game actually onto the device.

Previously, you had to have a paid Apple Developer license in order to get your game onto an iOS device. Although that's still required to get the game on the App Store, you are no longer required to get it for testing. Note that the free option doesn't have everything available to you, most notably **In-App Purchases (IAPs)** and the Game Center; however, for making sure that it works on your device, it'll work just nicely. We will go over how to adjust your project to reflect being in the Apple Developer portal in Chapter 11, *Game Build and Submission*, when we go over putting our project on the App Store.

To develop for an iOS device, in addition to the device itself, you'll also need to go on a Mac computer that runs OS X High Sierra 10.13+ or a later version. I'll be using 10.15.6 macOS Catalina. Just like working with Android, we'll also need to do some setup before we can actually do the exporting. Let's get started on that now:

1. First of all, if you haven't done so already, you'll need to add **iOS Build Support (*)** as an option when you are installing Unity. If you did not install it when doing the initial installation, you may open up the Unity Hub and select the **Installs** section.

2. From there, click on the three dots to the right of your current version of Unity and select the **Add Modules** option:

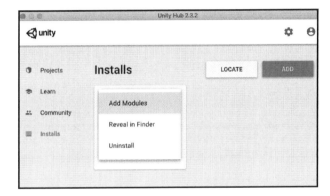

3. From the menu that pops up, check the **iOS Build Support** option:

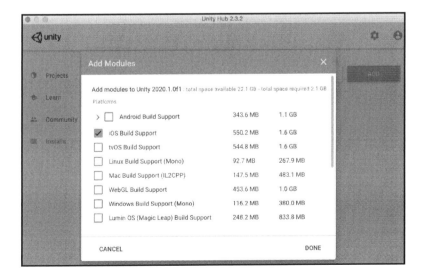

4. Click on the **DONE** button and wait for the installation to finish. Once completed, you should see the icon for iOS support show up:

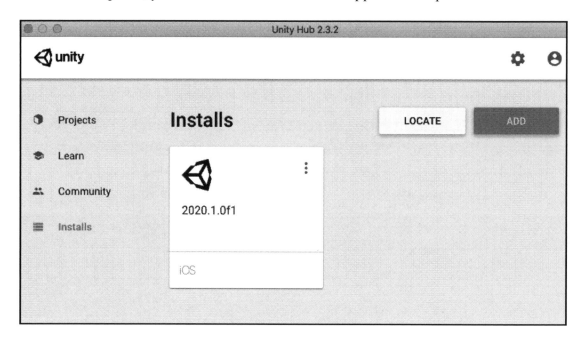

This makes it so you can export your projects for iOS. Since I'll be using my Windows machine mainly, I'm only adding in iOS support, but you can do both iOS and Android from your Mac computer.

5. You'll also need to have **Xcode**, which is the program used to build iOS apps. To download it, you'll need to open up the App Store application on your computer. From the search bar in the top-left corner, type in Xcode and press *Enter*.

6. From there, you'll see the Xcode program at the top left of the page. Click on it and then on the **Install/Update** button:

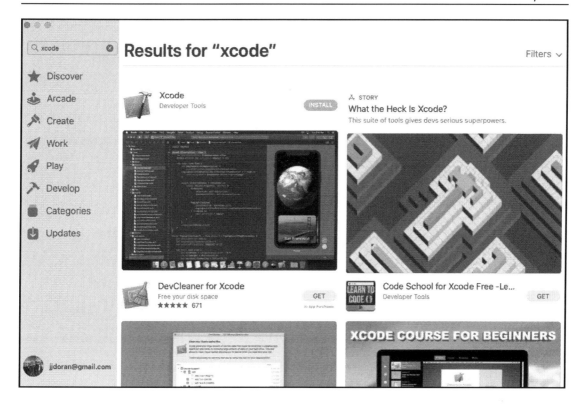

You may need to enter your Apple ID information; go ahead and do so and then wait for it to finish.

 If you do not have an Apple ID, you may get one from `http://appleid.apple.com/`.

7. Once Xcode is installed, open it up. There will be a license agreement for Xcode and the iOS SDK; go ahead and click on **Agree**. It'll then begin installing components that are needed for it to work.

8. You'll then be brought to a welcome screen, but we want to do some setup first. From the top menu bar, go ahead and select **Xcode** | **Preferences** (or press *command* + ,). From there, click on the **Accounts** button. This will display all of the Apple IDs that you want to be able to use in Xcode:

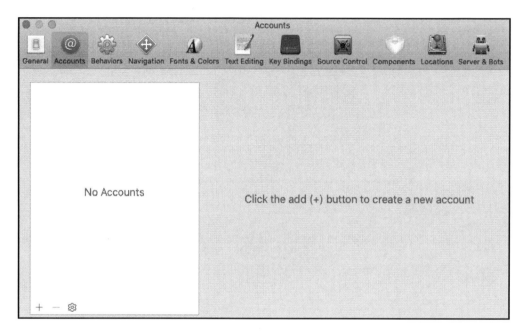

9. Click on the plus icon at the bottom left of the screen and then select **Apple ID** when it asks what kind of account to create:

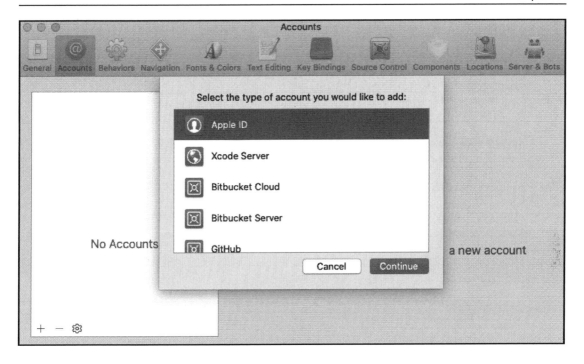

10. From the menu that pops up, go ahead and add in your Apple ID information and you should see it appear on the screen.

If you select the name, you'll see additional information on the right side, such as what teams you are on. If you are not enrolled in the Apple Developer Program, it'll just be a personal team, but if you are paying for it, you should see additional teams there as well.

Now that we have completed the setup and installation of iOS and Xcode, let's continue to building our project.

Building a project for iOS

While there are some similarities to working with Android, there are some differences that are very important to note, so keep that in mind while reading this section. Let's build our project for the iOS device using the following steps:

1. At this point, we will dive into Unity and then move into our **Build Settings** menu once again by going to **File** | **Build Settings**.

2. Click on the **iOS** option from the **Platform** list and then click on the **Switch Platform** button to make the change:

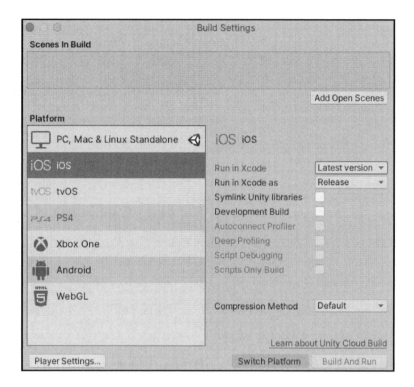

Note that this will make Unity reimport all of the assets in our game, so this may be time-consuming as you build larger and larger projects. This now also means that when we build our project, it will create an Xcode project instead of just an app, which we will need to open and work with once it's built.

3. If we didn't do so earlier when building for iOS, we must set the bundle identifier for our game at this point, which is a string that identifies the app. It's written like a URL in reverse, for example, com.yourCompanyName. yourGameName. To modify this, we'll need to open up the **Player Settings** menu, which we can get to by clicking on the **Player Settings...** button in the **Build Settings** menu or by going to **Edit | Project Settings | Player**.

4. Open up the **Other Settings** section, and then put in a value that you'd like under **Package Name**. (As mentioned in the previous section, I used com.JohnPDoran.MobileDev.)

Note that if you have already changed this property when building for Android, it will already be done; there's no need to do this again.

5. Now, we can try to build the project by clicking on the **Build** button and saving it in the same `Export` folder we created earlier—in this case, I named it `MobileDev_iOS`:

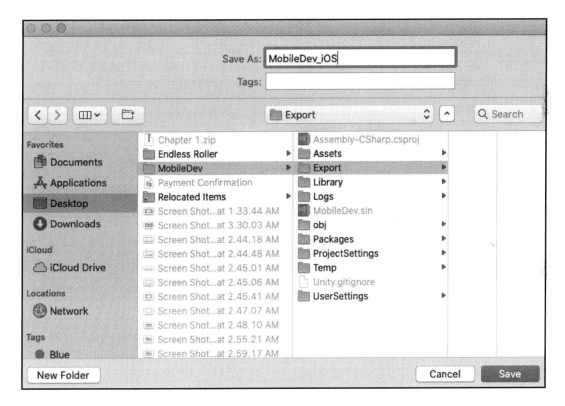

You can press the down arrow button to search for folders in the Finder window that pops up.

6. You may be asked to give permission for the Unity Hub to perform actions to Xcode. Allow it by pressing **OK**:

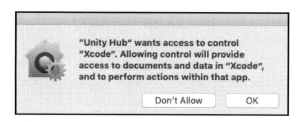

7. Once the project has been built, we will be taken to a Finder window at the location where we created the project. From there, we can double-click on the .xcodeproj file to open the project inside Xcode:

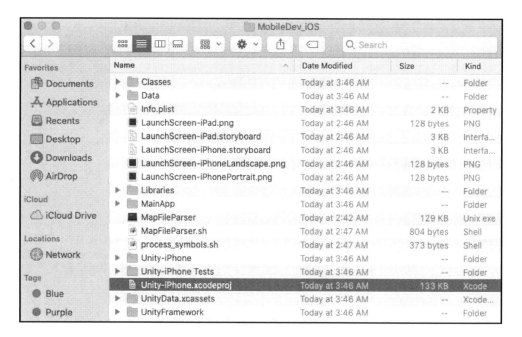

8. In Xcode, after waiting for everything to load in, you'll notice a yellow triangle with a ! in the center of it in the top-center console. If you click on it, you'll see some information appear on the left-hand side.

9. Double-click on the **Update to recommended settings** option on the left-hand side of the screen and then click on the **Perform Changes** button in the window that pops up:

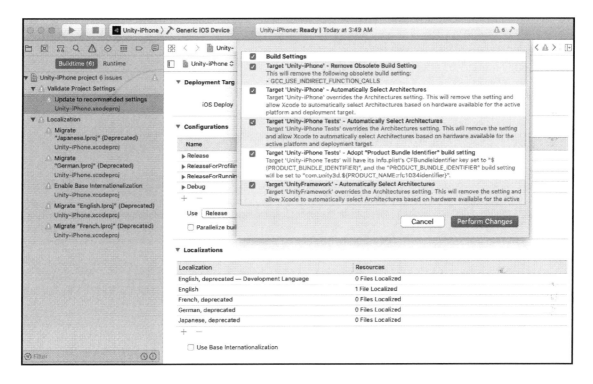

10. Then, go to the drop-down in the middle of the window and select the **Unity-iPhone** option under **Targets**:

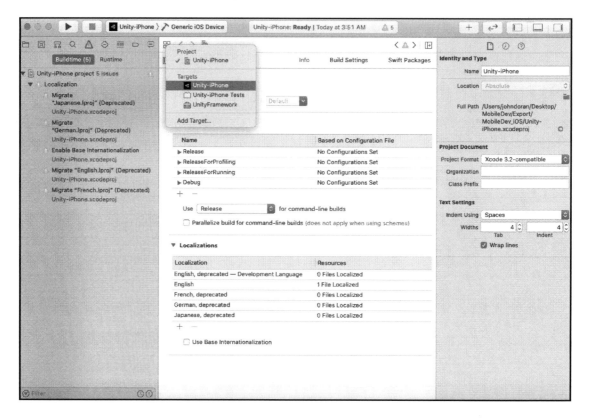

11. Afterward, under the **Signing & Capabilities** section, check the **Automatically manage signing** option, clicking on **Enable Automatic** when the popup comes up. Then, in the window that pops up, assign your team to your profile.

12. If you have an iOS development account or if no errors show up, you can continue to *Step 13*; however, it is also possible that you may see an error stating that you need to set the code signing identity value to **iOS Developer**. If that is the case, from the top-center area go to the **Build Settings** section and under the **Signing** section, change all of the **Code Signing Identity** items to **iOS Developer**:

Afterward, select the **Product | Clean** command from the top toolbar. You should then be able to proceed to *Step 11*.

13. Once all the preceding steps are done, plug in your phone via USB. After loading all of the symbols it needs (wait until the top-middle section says **Ready**); at the top right, instead of **Generic iOS Device**, change it to the device you've connected.

14. When you click on the **Play** button, the computer will ask whether you want to enable developer mode; to do so, go ahead and select **Enable** and enter your password when it asks for it.

15. Your phone may be busy, so you may need to wait a bit before you're able to build to the device. You may get a window asking you to access the key access in your keychain. Go ahead and click **Allow**. You'll also need to unlock your phone at some point as well so that it can make the install.

16. The app will now be on your iOS device, as you can see in the following screenshot:

Right now, it has a generic Unity icon, just like in Android, and we will customize it later on in this book, but for right now, we have an issue: the game won't run.

In order to run the app, you must verify that you want the device to be able to run the app to prevent security issues. To let you know that this is an issue, Xcode will give you a warning that it couldn't launch it, so we'll need to say we want to be able to run it.

17. From your iOS device, open up the **Settings** app. From there, go to **General |
Profiles** or **Profiles & Device Management**. Then, from the menu that pops up,
you'll need to say **Trust [Developer Name]**, with **[Developer Name]** being your
Apple ID account. You'll need to verify again that you wish to trust apps created
by this account, so go ahead and agree, and all of the steps are done.

18. With that, exit out of settings by clicking on the home button and then go over to
the location where the app was installed and tap on it to run:

With that, we have the game running on the iOS side as well.

Note that when building in the following manner, without the paid
license, apps will only work for a limited time, possibly up to a week. If
your game crashes immediately and it worked correctly beforehand, this
is most likely the culprit. Redeploy to the device again to check whether
that is the issue before modifying your actual project.

Summary

We now have our game running on both Android and iOS devices, and we have learned
the steps that we'll need to take each time we want to deploy our games on these devices.

While I will not be writing about exporting to both kinds of devices again until we get to
Chapter 10, *Game Build and Submission*, it's a good idea for you to see how the changes that
we will make will work with both platforms and keep testing on each platform to make
sure that your project works correctly and at a frame rate that you are okay with.

This is especially important to note as running the project on your PC via the editor or an emulator will not always accurately represent how the game will run on a different device. You may find that certain things will slow down your device and make your game choppy. You may also find that certain aspects of your game that run fine on your mobile device will cause your computer to be choppy instead. The thing is, you won't know unless you are always checking the games on devices, so I highly advise that you do so.

We have our game working on mobile devices now, but it currently will not react to anything we do due to how we wrote our input code. In the next chapter, we will explore how we can add input to our project as well as the design considerations we need to make in regards to how the different forms of input will change our game.

Mobile Input/Touch Controls 3

How players interact with your project is probably one of the most important things that can be established as a part of your project. While player input is added for all projects, no matter what platform you are using, this is also one area that can make or break your mobile game.

If the controls that are implemented don't fit the game that you're making, or if the controls feel clunky, players will not play your game for long stretches of time. While many people consider Rockstar's *Grand Theft Auto* series of games to be great on console and PC, playing the game on a mobile device provides a larger barrier of entry, due to all of the buttons on the screen and replacing joysticks with virtual versions that don't have haptic feedback in the same manner as on other platforms.

Mobile and tablet games that tend to do well typically have controls that are simple, finding as many ways to streamline the gameplay as possible. Many popular games require a single input, such as Dong Nguyen's *Flappy Bird* and Ketchapp's *Ballz*.

There are many different ways for games to interact with a mobile device that are different than for traditional games, and we will explore a number of those in this chapter.

In this chapter, we will cover the different ways that inputs will work on mobile devices. We will start off with the input that is already built into our project using the mouse, and then move on to touch events, gestures, using the accelerometer, and accessing information via the Touch class.

This chapter will be split into a number of topics. It will contain a simple, step-by-step process from beginning to end. Here is the outline of our tasks:

- Using mouse input for mobile input
- Movement via touch
- Implementing a gesture

- Scaling the player using pinches
- Using the accelerometer
- Reacting to touch

Technical requirements

This book utilizes Unity 2020.1.0f1 and Unity Hub 2.3.1 but the steps should work with minimal changes in future versions of the editor. If you would like to download the exact version used in this book, and there is a new version out, you can visit Unity's download archive at `https://unity3d.com/get-unity/download/archive`. You can also find the system requirements for Unity at `https://docs.unity3d.com/2020.1/Documentation/Manual/system-requirements.html` in the **Unity Editor system requirements** section. You can find the code files present in this chapter on GitHub at `https://github.com/PacktPublishing/Unity-2020-Mobile-Game-Development-Second-Edition/tree/master/Chapter%2003`.

Using mouse input

Before we dive into mobile-only solutions, I do want to point out that it is possible to write inputs that work on both mobile and PC, namely using mouse controls. Mobile devices support using mouse clicks as taps on the screen, with the position of the tap/click being the location where the finger has been pressed. This form of input provides just the position where the touch happened and that it happened; it doesn't give you all of the features that the mobile-only options do. We will be discussing all of the features you get using mobile-specific input later on in this chapter, but I think it's important to note how to have click events on the desktop as well. I personally use the desktop often for ease of testing on both the PC and on my device, so I don't have to deploy to a mobile device to test every single change made in the project.

The following steps show how to use the desktop-based mouse click events for movement of the player:

1. Inside Unity, open up your `PlayerBehaviour` script and add the following highlighted code to the `Update` function:

```
/// <summary>
/// FixedUpdate is called at a fixed framerate and is a prime place
to put
/// Anything based on time.
/// </summary>
```

```
private void FixedUpdate()
{
    // Check if we're moving to the side
    var horizontalSpeed = Input.GetAxis("Horizontal") * dodgeSpeed;

    // If the mouse is held down (or the screen is pressed
    // on Mobile)
    if (Input.GetMouseButton(0))
    {
        // Converts to a 0 to 1 scale
        var worldPos =
        Camera.main.ScreenToViewportPoint(Input.mousePosition);
        float xMove = 0;

        // If we press the right side of the screen
        if (worldPos.x < 0.5f)
        {
            xMove = -1;
        }
        else
        {
            // Otherwise we're on the left
            xMove = 1;
        }

        // replace horizontalSpeed with our own value
        horizontalSpeed = xMove * dodgeSpeed;
    }

    rb.AddForce(horizontalSpeed, 0, rollSpeed);
}
```

We have added a number of things to the preceding script. First, we check whether the mouse button had been held down or not through the use of the Input.GetMouseButton function. The function will return true if the mouse is held down, and false if it is not. The function takes in a parameter, which is for what mouse button we'd like to check, providing 0 for the left button, 1 for the right, and 2 for the middle button. For mobile, however, only 0 will be picked up as a click.

For more info on the Input.GetMouseButton function, check out https://docs.unity3d.com/ScriptReference/Input. GetMouseButton.html.

To start off, we can get the position that the mouse is at using the `Input.mousePosition` property. However, this value is given to us in screen space. What is screen space? Well, let's first talk about how we traditionally deal with positions in Unity making use of world space.

When dealing with positions in Unity through the **Inspector** window, we have the point **(0,0,0)** in the middle of our world, which we call the origin, and then we refer to everything else based on an offset from there. We typically refer to this method of positioning as **World Space**. Assuming that we have our camera pointing toward the origin, **World Space** looks like this:

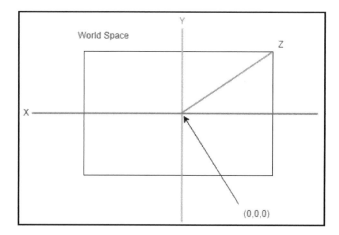

The lines are the *x*, *y*, and *z* axes of our world. If I were to move an object to the right or left, it would move along the *x* axis positively or negatively, respectively. When in school, you may have learned about using graphs and points, and world space works very much like that.

It's not important for the current conversation, but you should note that children of parented objects use a different system in the **Inspector**, which is that they are given positions relative to their parents instead. This system is called **local space**.

When using mouse input, Unity gives us this information in another space, **Screen Space**. In this space, the position is based on where the camera is and isn't involved with the actual game world. This space is also just in 2D, so there's only an *x* and *y* position with *z* always being stuck at 0:

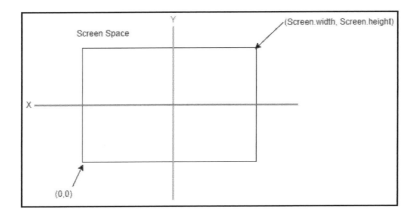

In this case, the bottom left of the screen would be **(0,0)** and the top right would be **(Screen.width, Screen.height)**. **Screen.width** and **Screen.height** are values in Unity that will give us the screen size of the screen window in pixels.

We could use these values as provided and then compare what side of the screen the player pressed, but, in my case, I think it'd be better to convert the position into an easier space to work with. One such space is the **Viewport space**, which goes from **(0,0)** to **(1,1)**:

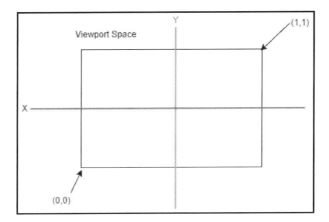

Note that some of Unity's functions will use `Vector3` instead of `Vector2` in order to work with 3D spaces as well.

Instead of searching whether our x position is less than half of the screen width, I can instead just check whether it's less than 0.5, which is what we are doing here. If the value is less than 0.5, it's on the left side of the screen so we return -1; otherwise, it's on the right side, so we give 1.

Once we know that, we can then set the horizontal speed variable to move to the left or right based on our movement.

2. Save the script and dive back into Unity and you will see the following:

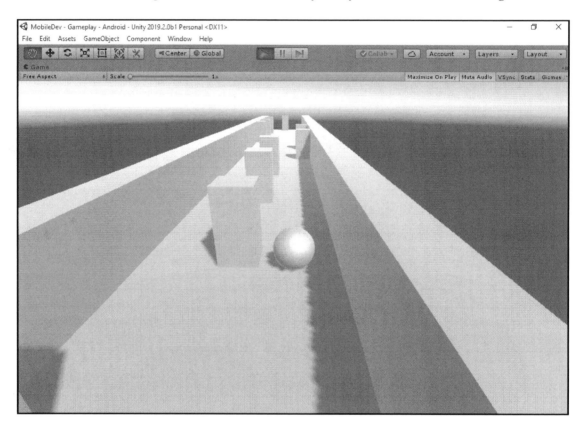

As you can see in the preceding screenshot, we can now use either the mouse (`Input.mousePosition`) or our keyboard (`Input.GetAxis`) to move our player.

This form of input works well enough for what we're doing right now, but I'm assuming that you'll want to know how to use the mobile device's own way of moving, so we will go ahead and learn how to replicate the same functionality using touch instead.

Moving using touch controls

Unity's Input engine has a property called `Input.touches`, which is an array of `Touch` objects. The `Touch` struct contains information on the touch that occurred, having information such as the amount of pressure on the touch and how many times you tapped the screen. It also contains the position property, such as `Input.mousePosition`, that will tell you what position the tap occurred at, in pixels.

For more info on the `Touch` struct, check out https://docs.unity3d.com/ScriptReference/Touch.html.

Let's look at the steps to use touch instead of mouse inputs:

1. Adjust our preceding code to look something like the following:

```
//Check if Input has registered more than zero touches
if (Input.touchCount > 0)
{
    //Store the first touch detected.
    Touch touch = Input.touches[0];

    // Converts to a 0 to 1 scale
    var worldPos = Camera.main.ScreenToViewportPoint
                                        (touch.position);

    float xMove = 0;

    // If we press the right side of the screen
    if (worldPos.x < 0.5f)
    {
        xMove = -1;
    }
    else
    {
        // Otherwise we're on the left
        xMove = 1;
    }

    // replace horizontalSpeed with our own value
    horiztonalSpeed = xMove * dodgeSpeed;
}
```

Now, you may note that this code looks very similar to what we've written in the preceding section. With that in mind, instead of copying and pasting the appropriate code twice and making changes like a number of starting programmers would do, we can instead take the similarities and make a function. For the differences, we can use parameters to change the value instead.

2. Keeping that in mind, let's add the following function to the `PlayerBehaviour` class:

```
/// <summary>
/// Will figure out where to move the player horizontally
/// </summary>
/// <param name="pixelPos">The position the player has
/// touched/clicked on</param>
/// <returns>The direction to move in the x axis</returns>
private float CalculateMovement(Vector3 pixelPos)
{
    // Converts to a 0 to 1 scale
    var worldPos = Camera.main.ScreenToViewportPoint(pixelPos);

    float xMove = 0;

    // If we press the right side of the screen
    if (worldPos.x < 0.5f)
    {
        xMove = -1;
    }
    else
    {
        // Otherwise we're on the left
        xMove = 1;
    }

    // replace horizontalSpeed with our own value
    return xMove * dodgeSpeed;
}
```

Now, instead of using `Input.mousePosition` or the touch position, we use a parameter for the function. Also, unlike previous functions we've written, this one will actually use a return value; in this case, it will give us a floating-point value. We will use this value in the `Update` to set `horiztonalSpeed` to a new value when this function is called. Now, we can call it appropriately.

3. Now, update the `Update` function, as follows:

```
/// <summary>
/// FixedUpdate is called at a fixed framerate and is a prime place
  /// to put
/// Anything based on time.
/// </summary>
private void FixedUpdate()
{
    // Check if we're moving to the side
    var horizontalSpeed = Input.GetAxis("Horizontal") * dodgeSpeed;

    // Check if we are running either in the Unity editor or in a
    // standalone build.
    #if UNITY_STANDALONE || UNITY_WEBPLAYER || UNITY_EDITOR
        // Check if we're moving to the side
        horizontalSpeed = Input.GetAxis("Horizontal") * dodgeSpeed;

        // If the mouse is held down (or the screen is tapped
        // on Mobile)
        if (Input.GetMouseButton(0))
        {
            horizontalSpeed =
                CalculateMovement(Input.mousePosition);
        }

    // Check if we are running on a mobile device
    #elif UNITY_IOS || UNITY_ANDROID
        // Check if Input has registered more than zero touches
        if (Input.touchCount > 0)
        {
            // Store the first touch detected.
            Touch touch = Input.touches[0];
            horizontalSpeed = CalculateMovement(touch.position);
        }
    #endif

    rb.AddForce(horizontalSpeed, 0, rollSpeed);
}
```

In the preceding example, I am using a `#if` directive based on the platform selected. Unity will automatically create a `#define` depending on what has been selected as the platform we are deploying for. What this `#if` does, along with `#elif` and `#endif`, is allow us to include or exclude code from our project based on these symbols.

In Visual Studio, you may note that if you're building for iOS or Android, the code within the UNITY_IOS || UNITY_ANDROID section is grayed out, meaning that it won't be called currently because we are running the game in the Unity Editor. However, when we export the code to our platform, the appropriate code will be used.

To take a look at all of the other platform-dependent #defines, check out https://docs.unity3d.com/Manual/ PlatformDependentCompilation.html.

This will allow us to specify the code for different versions of our project, which is vital when dealing with multi-platform development.

In addition to Unity's built-in #defines, you can create your own by going to **Edit | Project Settings | Player**, scrolling down to **Other Settings** in the **Inspector** window, and changing the **Scripting Define Symbols**. This can be great for targeting specific devices or for showing certain pieces of debug information, in addition to a number of other things.

4. Save the script and dive back into Unity.

Upon exporting your game to your Android device, you should note that the controls now work correctly using our newly created touch code. This allows us to have something that works on mobile as well as PC. Now, let's take a look at some of the mobile-specific ways that we can interpret input.

Implementing a gesture

Another type of input that you'll find in mobile games is that of a swipe, such as in Kiloo's *Subway Surfers*. This will allow us to use the general movement of the touch to dictate a direction for us to move in. This is usually used to have our players *jump* from one position to another or move quickly in a certain direction. So we'll go ahead and implement that using the following steps, instead of our previous movement system:

1. In the PlayerBehaviour script, go ahead and add some new variables for us to work with:

```
[Header("Swipe Properties")]
[Tooltip("How far will the player move upon swiping")]
public float swipeMove = 2f;
```

```
[Tooltip("How far must the player swipe before we will execute the
action (in inches)")]
public float minSwipeDistance = 0.25f;

/// <summary>
/// Used to hold the value that converts minSwipeDistance to pixels
/// </summary>
private float minSwipeDistancePixels;

/// <summary>
/// Stores the starting position of mobile touch events
/// </summary>
private Vector2 touchStart;
```

In order to determine whether we are swiping, we will need to first check the start and the end of our movement. We will store the starting position in the `touchStart` property. We will also have the `swipeMove` property to set how far we will *jump* when the swipe happens. Lastly, we have the `minSwipeDistance` variable, which will make sure that the player has moved on the *x* axis a little before actually making the jump – in this case, we want the user to move at least a quarter of an inch in order for the input to be counted as a swipe.

You'll also note that the `Header` attribute has been added to the top of the first variable. This will add a header to the **Inspector** tab, making it easier to break apart different sections of your script. If you were to save the script and dive into Unity, you should note that it has been added when you select the player:

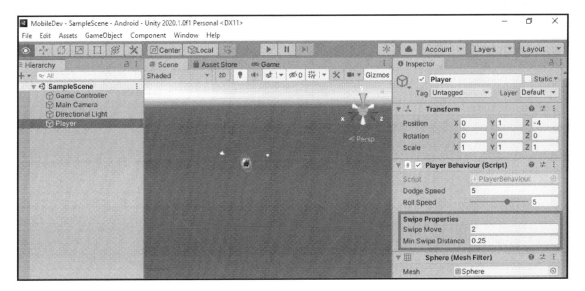

Our next step will be to convert the `MinSwipeDistance` value from inches into the pixel equivalent, which can be used to see how far the user's swiping motion moves the player's character.

2. Go back in the `PlayerBehaviour` script and update the `Start` function to add the following highlighted code:

```
// Start is called before the first frame update
private void Start()
{
    // Get access to our Rigidbody component
    rb = GetComponent<Rigidbody>();

    minSwipeDistancePixels = minSwipeDistance * Screen.dpi;
}
```

The `Screen.dpi` value stands for dots per inch and generally can be thought of as how many pixels are there per inch on the screen. By multiplying the value of `minSwipeDistance` with `Screen.dpi`, we know how long the movement in pixels needs to be to count as a swipe.

 For more information on the `Screen.dpi` variable, check out `https://docs.unity3d.com/ScriptReference/Screen-dpi.html`.

Now that we know the length of a swipe, we need to add the ability to trigger one. As we mentioned before, we have been using the `FixedUpdate` function for our player's movement. This is because Unity's physics engine is only updated once between each `FixedUpdate`, which is generally called less often than the `Update` function. We use the `Input.GetAxis` and `Input.GetMouseButton` functions, which return true every single frame that the button is held down and will continue to respond during `FixedUpdate` loops as well. This works great for events that happen over time, but `FixedUpdate` can miss the start and ending frames where input events happen, which is required for swipe events and certain actions like jumping in games. If you want something to happen the moment an input starts or finishes, you will likely want to utilize the `Update` function instead, and that is what we will be doing with our gesture.

3. Now, back in the `PlayerBehaviour` script, add the following function to the project:

```
/// <summary>
/// Update is called once per frame
```

```
/// </summary>
private void Update()
{
    // Check if we are running on a mobile device
    #if UNITY_IOS || UNITY_ANDROID
        //Check if Input has registered more than zero touches
        if (Input.touchCount > 0)
        {
            //Store the first touch detected.
            Touch touch = Input.touches[0];

            SwipeTeleport(touch);
        }
    #endif
}
```

In the preceding code, we added a new behavior called `SwipeTeleport` that will only be called if the game is running on a mobile device. It hasn't been created yet, but this will take in the `Touch` event and use its properties to move the player if a swipe happens.

4. We will then create a function to handle this new swiping behavior, as follows:

```
/// <summary>
/// Will teleport the player if swiped to the left or right
/// </summary>
/// <param name="touch">Current touch event</param>
private void SwipeTeleport(Touch touch)
{
    // Check if the touch just started
    if (touch.phase == TouchPhase.Began)
    {
        // If so, set touchStart
        touchStart = touch.position;
    }

    // If the touch has ended
    else if (touch.phase == TouchPhase.Ended)
    {
        // Get the position the touch ended at
        Vector2 touchEnd = touch.position;

        // Calculate the difference between the beginning and
        // end of the touch on the x axis.
        float x = touchEnd.x - touchStart.x;

        // If we are not moving far enough, don't do the teleport
        if (Mathf.Abs(x) < minSwipeDistancePixels)
```

```
{
    return;
}

Vector3 moveDirection;

// If moved negatively in the x axis, move left
if (x < 0)
{
    moveDirection = Vector3.left;
}
else
{
    // Otherwise we're on the right
    moveDirection = Vector3.right;
}

RaycastHit hit;

// Only move if we wouldn't hit something
if (!rb.SweepTest(moveDirection, out hit, swipeMove))
{
    // Move the player
    rb.MovePosition(rb.position + (moveDirection *
                    swipeMove));
}
    }
}
```

In this function, instead of just using the current touch position, we instead store the starting position when the touch begins. When the player lifts their finger, we get the position as well. We then get the direction of that movement and then apply that movement to the ball, checking whether we'll collide with something before actually causing the movement.

5. Save your script and dive back into Unity, exporting your project onto your mobile device.

Now, whenever we swipe to the left or right, the player will move accordingly. Let's learn about another action that we can use while playing the game in the next section.

Scaling the player using pinches

The concept of using touch events to modify things in the game can also be applied to other methods of touch interaction such as using finger pinches to zoom in and out. To see how to do this, let's make it so we can change the player's scale using two fingers to pinch or stretch out the view:

1. Open up the `PlayerBehaviour` script and add the following properties:

   ```
   [Header("Scaling Properties")]

   [Tooltip("The minimum size (in Unity units) that the player should
   be")]
   public float minScale = 0.5f;

   [Tooltip("The maximum size (in Unity units) that the player should
   be")]
   public float maxScale = 3.0f;

   /// <summary>
   /// The current scale of the player
   /// </summary>
   private float currentScale = 1;
   ```

2. Next, add the following function:

   ```
   /// <summary>
   /// Will change the player's scale via pinching and stretching two
   /// touch events
   /// </summary>
   private void ScalePlayer()
   {
       // We must have two touches to check if we are scaling the
           object
       if (Input.touchCount != 2)
       {
           return;
       }
       else
       {
           //Store the touchs detected.
           Touch touch0 = Input.touches[0];
           Touch touch1 = Input.touches[1];

           // Find the position in the previous frame of each touch.
           Vector2 touch0Prev = touch0.position -
                               touch0.deltaPosition;
   ```

```
        Vector2 touch1Prev = touch1.position -
                             touch1.deltaPosition;

        // Find the the distance (or magnitude) between the touches
        // in each frame.
        float prevTouchDeltaMag = (touch0Prev -
                                  touch1Prev).magnitude;

        float touchDeltaMag = (touch0.position -
                              touch1.position).magnitude;

        // Find the difference in the distances between each frame.
        float deltaMagnitudeDiff = prevTouchDeltaMag -
                                  touchDeltaMag;

        // Keep the change consistent no matter what the framerate
           //is
        float newScale = currentScale - (deltaMagnitudeDiff
                                        * Time.deltaTime);
        // Ensure that it is valid
        newScale = Mathf.Clamp(newScale, minScale, maxScale);

        // Update the player's scale
        transform.localScale = Vector3.one * newScale;

        // Set our current scale for the next frame
        currentScale = newScale;

    }
}
```

Instead of using a single touch event, in this example, we are using two. Using both touches, we can see how they changed over the course of the previous frame (the delta). We then use that difference to modify the scale of the player. To ensure the ball will always have a valid value we use the `Mathf.Clamp` function to keep the values between what is set in `minScale` and `maxScale`.

3. Next, we need to call the function by updating the `Update` function:

```
/// <summary>
/// Update is called once per frame
/// </summary>
private void Update()
{
    // Check if we are running on a mobile device
    #if UNITY_IOS || UNITY_ANDROID
        //Check if Input has registered more than zero touches
```

```
if (Input.touchCount > 0)
{
    //Store the first touch detected.
    Touch touch = Input.touches[0];

    SwipeTeleport(touch);

    ScalePlayer();
}
#endif
}
```

4. Save your script and return to the Unity editor. Export your game and you should be able to see the player scaling in action – by pulling two fingers apart, you'll see the ball expand, and vice versa:

Hopefully, this demonstrates the power given by having the ability to use multi-touch and some of the advantages of utilizing touch events instead of just a single mouse click. Next, we will explore another type of input method that PCs don't have.

Using the accelerometer

Another type of input that mobile has, that PC doesn't, is the accelerometer. This allows you to move in game by tilting the physical position of the phone. The most popular example of this is likely the movement of the player in games such as Lima Sky's *Doodle Jump* and Gameloft's *Asphalt* series. To do something similar, we can retrieve the acceleration of our device using the `Input.acceleration` property and use it to move the player. Let's look at the steps to do just that:

1. We may want to allow our designers to set whether they want to use this mode, or the `ScreenTouch` we used previously. With that in mind, let's create a new enum with the possible values to place in the `PlayerBehaviour` script above the **Swipe Properties** header:

   ```
   [Tooltip("How fast the ball moves forwards automatically")]
   [Range(0, 10)]
   public float rollSpeed = 5;

   public enum MobileHorizMovement
   {
       Accelerometer,
       ScreenTouch
   }

   public MobileHorizMovement horizMovement =
       MobileHorizMovement.Accelerometer;

   [Header("Swipe Properties")]
   [Tooltip("How far will the player move upon swiping")]
   public float swipeMove = 2f;
   ```

   The preceding script utilizes an enum to define a custom type called `MobileHorizMovement`, which can be one of two values, `Accelerometer` and `ScreenTouch`. We then create a variable of this new type called `horizMovement`.

2. Now, if you were to save the `PlayerBehaviour` script and dive back into the **Inspector** tab, you can see we can select one of these two options (**Accelerometer** or **Screen Touch**). By using this drop-down menu, the game designer of the project can easily select which of the two options we'd like to use, and then we can expand to even more if we'd like to in the future:

3. Next, let's update the Update function with the following highlighted code:

```
// Check if we are running on a mobile device
#elif UNITY_IOS || UNITY_ANDROID

    if(horizMovement == MobileHorizMovement.Accelerometer)
    {
        // Move player based on direction of the accelerometer
        horizontalSpeed = Input.acceleration.x * dodgeSpeed;
    }

    //Check if Input has registered more than zero touches
    if (Input.touchCount > 0)
    {
        if (horizMovement == MobileHorizMovement.ScreenTouch)
        {
            //Store the first touch detected.
            Touch touch = Input.touches[0];
            horizontalSpeed = CalculateMovement(touch.position);
        }
    }
#endif
```

This will make use of the acceleration of our device, instead of the position of a touch on screen.

4. Save your script and export the project.

With that, you'll note that we can now tilt our screen to the right or left and the player will move in the appropriate direction.

In Unity, acceleration is measured in g-force values, with 1 being 1g of force. If you hold the device upright (with the home button at the bottom) in front of you, the *x* axis is positive along the right, the *y* axis is positive upward, and the *z* axis is positive when pointing toward you.

 For more information on the accelerometer, check out `https://docs.` `unity3d.com/Manual/MobileInput.html`.

It's great to know that our regular input is working, but you may want to check whether a game object in our scene has been touched so that the game can react to it. Let's do that next.

Detecting touch on game objects

To add something else for our player to do, as well as to demonstrate some additional input functionality, we'll make it so that if the player taps an obstacle, it will be destroyed. We will use the following steps to modify our existing code to add this new functionality and utilize the concept of raycasts:

1. In the `PlayerBehaviour` script, add the following new function:

```
/// <summary>
/// Will determine if we are touching a game object and if so
/// call events for it
/// </summary>
/// <param name="touch">Our touch event</param>
private static void TouchObjects(Touch touch)
{
 // Convert the position into a ray
 Ray touchRay = Camera.main.ScreenPointToRay(touch.position);

 RaycastHit hit;

 // Create a LayerMask that will collide with all possible
    // channels
 int layerMask = ~0;

 // Are we touching an object with a collider?
 if (Physics.Raycast(touchRay, out hit, Mathf.Infinity,
        layerMask, QueryTriggerInteraction.Ignore))
  {
     // Call the PlayerTouch function if it exists on a
```

```
        // component attached to this object
        hit.transform.SendMessage("PlayerTouch",
                SendMessageOptions.DontRequireReceiver);
    }
}
```

Here, we use a different version to determine collisions: a raycast. The **raycast** is basically an invisible vector leading in a given direction, and we will use it to check whether it collides with any objects inside of our scenes. This is often used in games, such as first-person shooters, to determine whether the player has hit an enemy or not without spawning a projectile and moving it there.

The version of `Physics.Raycast` that we use here takes in five parameters:

- The first specifies what ray to use.
- The second is `hit`, which holds information about the collision that occurred if it happened.
- The third parameter specifies how far to check for a collision.
- The fourth is a layer mask, which is a way to only collide with certain objects. In our case, we want to collide with all colliders, so we use the bit-wise complement operator (~) to change a 0 into the number possible by flipping all the bits used to create the number.
- Lastly, we have an enumeration called `QueryTriggerInteraction`, which we say to `Ignore`. This means that the **Tile End** objects with the triggers we created in Chapter 1, *Building Your Game*, will not block our touch events, which would happen by default even if we couldn't see them.

For more information on the bitwise complement operator (~) check out `https://docs.microsoft.com/en-us/dotnet/csharp/language-reference/operators/bitwise-and-shift-operators#bitwise-complement-operator-`.

For more information on raycasting, check out `https://docs.unity3d.com/ScriptReference/Physics.Raycast.html`.

If we do hit something, we call a function named SendMessage on the object that we collided with. This function will attempt to call a function with the same name as the first parameter if it exists on any component on the game object. The second parameter lets us know whether we should display an error if it doesn't exist.

For more info on the SendMessage function, check out https://docs. unity3d.com/ScriptReference/GameObject.SendMessage.html.

2. Now, in the Update function, let's actually call the aforementioned Touch Objects function:

```
/// <summary>
/// Update is called once per frame
/// </summary>
private void Update()
{
  // Check if we are running on a mobile device
  #if UNITY_IOS || UNITY_ANDROID
  //Check if Input has registered more than zero touches
  if (Input.touchCount > 0)
  {
    //Store the first touch detected.
    Touch touch = Input.touches[0];

    SwipeTeleport(touch);

    TouchObjects(touch);
    ScalePlayer();
  }
  #endif
}
```

3. Save the PlayerBehaviour script at this point.

4. Finally, we call a `PlayerTouch` function if it exists. So, let's open up the `ObstacleBehaviour` script and add the following code:

```
public GameObject explosion;

/// <summary>
/// If the object is tapped, we spawn an explosion and
/// destroy this object
/// </summary>
private void PlayerTouch()
{
 if (explosion != null)
 {
    var particles = Instantiate(explosion, transform.position,
       Quaternion.identity);
    Destroy(particles, 1.0f);
 }

  Destroy(this.gameObject);
}
```

This function will basically destroy the game object it is attached to, and create an explosion that will also destroy itself after 1 second.

It is possible to get similar results to what we are writing by making use of Unity's `OnMouseDown` function. As we have already discussed, it is possible to use mouse events when developing for mobile. Keep in mind, though, that the use of that function is computationally more expensive than the method I'm suggesting here.

This is because when you tap the screen, every object that has an `OnMouseDown` method will do a raycast to check whether it was touched. When you have many objects on the screen, you'll note massive performance differences between one raycast and one hundred, and it's important to keep performance in mind when dealing with mobile development. For more information on this, check out `http://answers.unity3d.com/questions/1064394/onmousedown-and-mobile.html`.

5. Save the scripts and dive back into Unity.

We haven't created an explosion particle effect yet. To create this effect, we will make use of a **particle system**. We'll be diving into particle systems at a much deeper level in Chapter 10, *Making Our Game Juicy*, but, for now, we can consider a particle system as a game object that is made as simply as possible so that we can spawn many of them on the screen at once without causing the game to slow down too much. This is mostly used for things such as smoke or fire, but, in this case, we will have our obstacle explode. Use the following steps to create an explosion particle effect:

1. Create a particle system by going to **GameObject** | **Effects** | **Particle System**.

2. Select the game object in the **Hierarchy** window and then open the **Particle System** component in the **Inspector** tab. In there, click on the **Renderer** section to expand it and change **RenderMode** to **Mesh** and **Material** to **Default-Material** by clicking on the circle next to the name and selecting it from the menu that pops up:

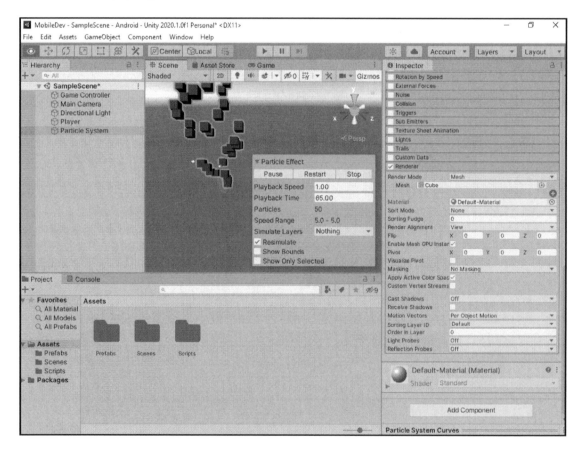

This will make the particles look like the obstacles that we've already created as a box with the default material.

3. Next, under the top **Particle System** section, change the **Gravity Modifier** property to 1. This makes it so the objects will fall over time, much like normal objects with rigid bodies do, but with less computation.

4. Then, under **Start Speed**, move to the right side and click on the downward-facing arrow, and from that menu, select **Random Between Two Constants**:

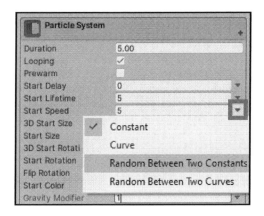

5. This will change the single window to two, signifying the minimum and maximum values that can be used for this property. From there, set the two values to 0 and 8. This makes the objects spawned have starting speeds between 0 and 8.

6. Then, change the **Start Size** to something between 0 and 0.25. This will ensure that we are creating a bunch of cubes that are smaller than the one we are planning to replace.

7. Change **Duration** to 1 and uncheck the **Looping** option. This makes it so that the particle system will last only for 1 second, and unchecking looping means that the particle system will happen only once.

You can still see the effect of each of the changes made by clicking on the **Play** button on the bottom-right menu of the **Scene** window with the **Particle System** object selected.

8. Finally, change the **Start Lifetime** property to 1 so that we can ensure that all of the particles will be dead before the game object is destroyed.

9. Under the **Emission** section, change **Rate over Time** to 0. Then, under **Bursts**, click on the **+** button and then set **Count** to 50:

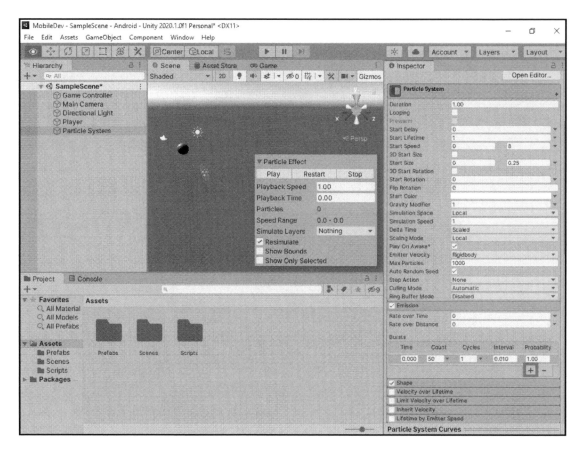

This makes it so that 50 particles will be spawned right at the beginning of the particle system being created, much like an explosion.

10. Then, check **Size over Lifetime** and click on the text next to the checkmark to show more details. From there, change the **Size** property by selecting a curve that decreases over time so that at the end they'll all be 0. This can be done by first selecting the curve itself and then going to the **Particle System Curves** section at the bottom of the **Inspector** window (If you do not see the contents shown in the following screenshot, you can click and drag the name upward to have it pop out. From there you can click on the option on the bottom left of the downward facing curve:

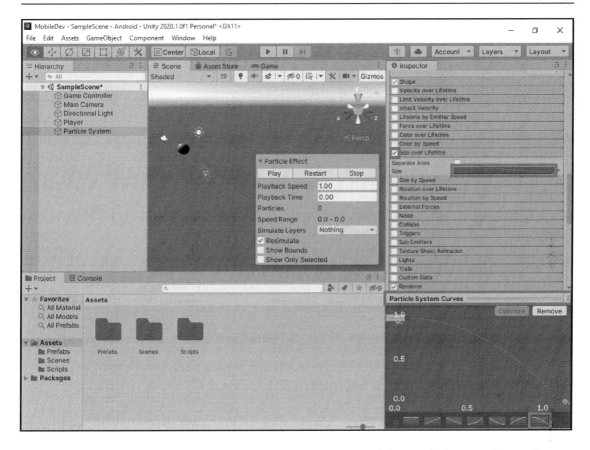

This will make the particles smaller over time, and they will destroy themselves only after they become invisible (a scale of 0).

11. Finally, check the **Collision** property and open it, setting the **Type** property to **World**. This will cause the particles to hit the ground.

12. Change the name of the particle system to Explosion. Then, make your object a prefab by dragging and dropping it from the **Hierarchy** tab into the **Project** tab in the Assets/Prefabs folder. Once the prefab is created, remove the original from the scene by selecting it and pressing the *Delete* key.

13. Next, assign it to the Explosion property of the **Obstacle Behaviour (Script)** in the **Obstacle** prefab:

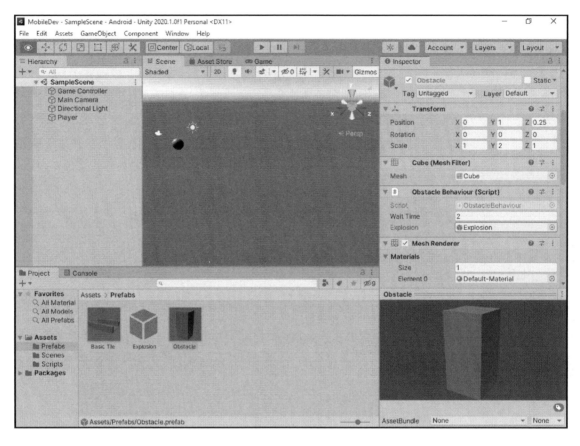

14. Save your project and export it to your mobile device:

From now on, whenever we tap on the obstacles on our mobile device, they will be destroyed.

Summary

In this chapter, we have learned the main ways in which games are controlled when working on mobile devices. We also learned how we can use mouse inputs, touch events, gestures, and the accelerometer to allow players to interact with our game.

In the next chapter, we will explore the other main way that players interact with a game by diving into the world of user interfaces and creating menus that can be enjoyed no matter what device the user is playing the game on.

4
Resolution-Independent UI

When working on mobile devices, one of the things that you'll need to spend a fair bit of time on is the **User Interface (UI)**. Unlike when developing projects for PC, where you only need to care about a single resolution or aspect ratio, there are many different devices out there with different resolutions and aspect ratios when building for mobile. For instance, we have phones, which fit in our pocket, but also tablets, which are huge. Not only that, but mobile games can also be played horizontally or vertically.

A **Graphical User Interface (GUI)** is the way that players interact with your games. You've actually been using a GUI in all of the previous chapters (the Unity Editor) and also when interacting with your operating system. Without a GUI of some sort, the only way you'd be able to interact with a computer is a command prompt, such as DOS or UNIX.

When working on GUIs, we want them to be as intuitive as possible and to only contain information that is pertinent to the player at any given time. There are people whose main job is programming and/or designing UIs, and there are college degrees on the subject as well. So, while we won't talk about everything to do with using GUIs, I do want to touch on the aspects that should be quite helpful when working on your own projects in the future.

When building for mobile, it's very important that you design your UI to be resolution-independent—that is, to ensure that the UI will scale and adjust itself to fit any screen size that is given to it. This will not only help us now but also in the future.

In this chapter, we will build the UI for our game, starting with a title screen, and then build the other menus that we will want to use for future chapters. This chapter will be split into a number of topics. The chapter is a simple step-by-step process from beginning to end. The following is the outline of our tasks:

- Creating a title screen
- Adding UI elements to the screen
- Implementing a pause menu
- Pausing the game
- Adapting GUIs for notch devices

Technical requirements

This book utilizes Unity 2020.1.0f1 and Unity Hub 2.3.1, but the steps should work with minimal changes in future versions of the editor. If you would like to download the exact version used in this book, and there is a new version out, you can visit Unity's download archive at `https://unity3d.com/get-unity/download/archive`. You can also find the system requirements for Unity at `https://docs.unity3d.com/2020.1/Documentation/Manual/system-requirements.html` in the **Unity Editor system requirements** section. You can find the code files present in this chapter on GitHub at `https://github.com/PacktPublishing/Unity-2020-Mobile-Game-Development-Second-Edition/tree/master/Chapter%2004`.

Creating a title screen

Now, before we start adding UI elements to our game, let's first set up some groundwork and foundational knowledge by creating something that we will need anyway—a title screen:

1. To start, we'll go ahead and create a new scene for us to work with by going to **File | New Scene**. When dealing with a UI, we will often want to see a visual representation of what will be drawn on the screen, so we will want to make use of 2D mode to have a better representation of what our UI will look like in the final version of the game.
2. To do that, go to the **Scene** view tab—you'll see the control bar menu with a **2D** button on it underneath that. Click on it, and you should see the camera automatically move into something that looks similar to the following screenshot:

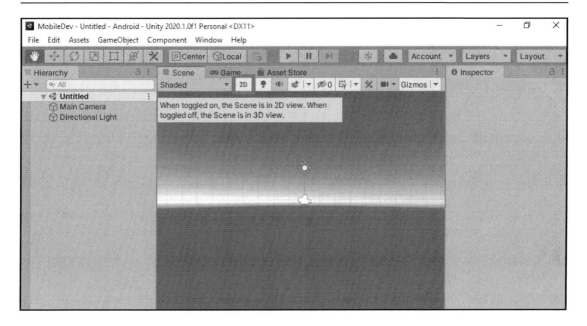

The **2D** button switches the camera between 2D and 3D views. In 2D mode, you'll note that the Scene **Gizmos** is gone due to the fact that the only option is to look perpendicularly at the XY plane (the x axis pointing to the right and the y axis pointing upward) and that our camera has changed to an orthographic view.

3. We have to create a **Text** object with the name of our game. Go to the menu and select **GameObject** | **UI** | **Text**.

Note that while this book is using the included-by-default Unity UI system and **Text** objects, the following steps also work with TextMesh Pro objects and all of the concepts in this chapter work the same with both systems. If you are interested in using TextMesh Pro with your project, you can find more information on the additional steps required to import and utilize it in your project: `https://learn.unity.com/tutorial/quickstart-to-textmesh-pro-2019-3`.

4. This will create three new objects, as you can see in the **Hierarchy** view:

- **Canvas**: This is the area where all of the UI elements will reside, and if you try to create a UI element without one already existing, Unity will create one for you like it just did here. From the **Scene** view tab, it will draw a white rectangle around itself to show you how large it is and will resize itself depending on how large the **Game** view is:

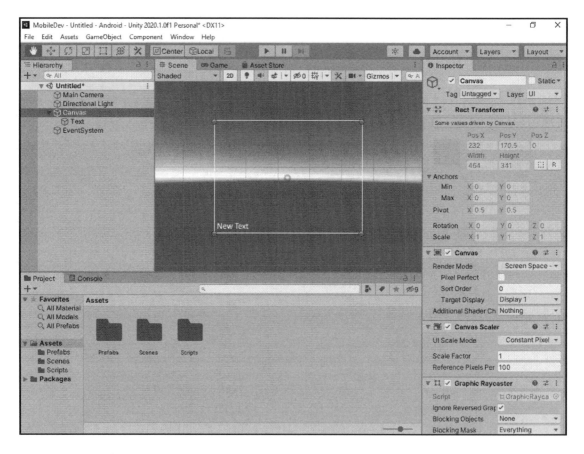

 If you double-click on an object in the **Hierarchy** window, the camera will automatically move and zoom so you can see the object within the **Scene** window.

The GameObject contains a **Canvas** component, which allows you to dictate how the image will be rendered (and a **Canvas Scaler** component to make your art scale, depending on the resolution of the device the game is running on) and the **Graphic Raycaster** component, which determines whether any objects on the **Canvas** has been hit. We will dive into the **Canvas Scaler** component later on in this section.

For more information on the **Canvas** object, check out `http://docs.unity3d.com/Manual/UICanvas.html`. In particular, the discussion of the render modes is quite useful in understanding the ways that UI elements can be rendered onto the screen.

- **Text**: This object is our actual text object, which has all of the properties that allow us to position the object anywhere on the **Canvas** object and change the text, color, size, and so on that will be displayed.

- **EventSystem**: This object allows users to send events to objects in our game based on various input types, from keyboard presses to touch events to gamepads. There are properties in this object that allow you to specify how you'd like your users to interact with your UI, and if you try to create a UI element without one existing, Unity will create one for you like it did here. If you want to have any kind of interactive material in your level using Unity's UI system, such as buttons, sliders, and so on, you must have an object with the **EventSystem** component attached within the level or the events will not trigger.

For more information on the **EventSystem** object, check out `http://docs.unity3d.com/Manual/EventSystem.html`.

5. By default, you may or may not see where our textbox was created. If you aren't able to see it, you can go to the **Hierarchy** window and then double-click on the **Text** object. If all went well, we should have something like this:

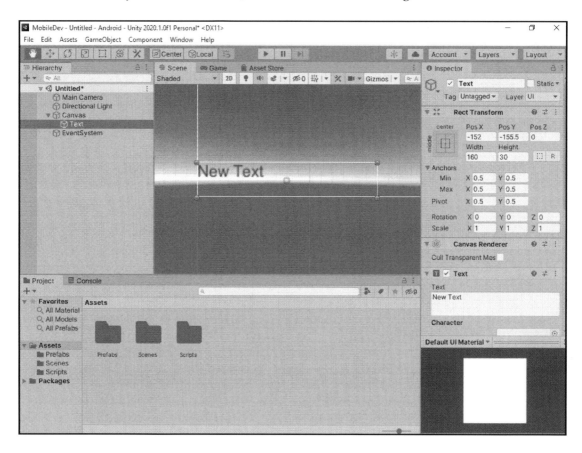

6. The next thing we will do is make it easier to tell what this object is. So, with that in mind, scroll all the way up on the **Inspector** tab with the **Text** object selected and change its name to Title Text.

We can tell whether the object is going to be visible in the game by seeing whether it is within the white box created for **Canvas**. One thing to note is that instead of the default **Transform** component that all of the game objects we've seen so far use, our **Text** object has a **Rect Transform** component in the same place.

The Rect Transform component

The **Rect Transform** component is probably the most different thing about working in the UI system, so it's a good idea to learn as much as we can about it. The Rect Transform is different than the regular Transform in that while the Transform component represents a single point, or the center of an object, the Rect Transform represents a rectangle, in which the UI element will reside. If an object with a Rect Transform has a parent, which also has a Rect Transform, the child will specify how the object should be positioned relative to its parent.

 For more information on positioning objects and information on the **Rect Transform**, check out http://docs.unity3d.com/Manual/UIBasicLayout. html.

To get a better idea of what the properties of the **Rect Transform** component mean, change the **Pos X** and **Pos Y** values to 0, which will center our object around the object's anchors; you can then double-click on the object in the **Hierarchy** tab to center the camera at its new position and can zoom in/out using the mouse wheel:

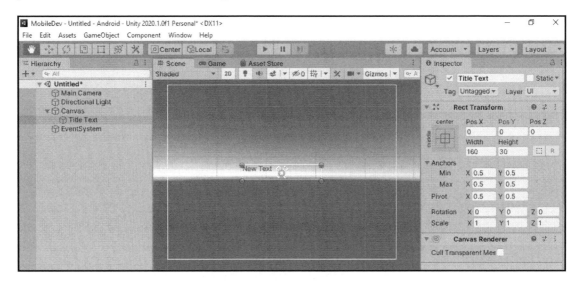

Our object's anchors are visible from the **Scene** tab via four small rectangles, creating an X shape in the center of our **Scene** tab, if you have the **Title Text** object selected (double-click on it to center the object on the screen).

 Like I mentioned previously, note that the white box that is displayed here for the **Canvas** may look different on your screen based on the aspect ratio you've set from the **Game** tab view (mine is set to **Free Aspect**, so it scales based on that to fill the space). If you go to the **Game** tab, you can select them from the drop-down menu on the left-hand side.

Next, we'll take a look at the two main elements present that work differently in the **Rect Transform** component: anchors and pivots.

Anchors

Found inside the **Rect Transform** component, anchors give you the ability to *hold on* to a corner or part of the canvas so that if the Canvas were to move and/or change, the pieces of the UI would stay in an appropriate place. These specify the edges of your element using a percentage of your parent's size. For example, if we opened the **Anchors** property from the **Rect Transform** component and set the **Min X** property to 0, the UI element would stick to the left edge of its parent.

The properties above the anchors are your position relative to the anchor that has been set. This can be quite useful when it comes to things such as supporting multiple resolutions without scaling the art assets created. In our case, we will want to have our title position itself relative to the top of the camera. Let's look at the steps to take when working with anchors:

1. Click on the **Anchor Presets** menu in the upper-left corner of the **Rect Transform** component (the box to the left of the **Pos X** and **Width** values). From there, it shows some of the most common anchor positions used in games for easy selection. In our case, we will want to pick the top-center option:

2. Note that after selecting it, the **Pos Y** value changes to another number (in my case, −170). This is saying that our object is positioned 170 units below the anchor's *y* position (in screen space, 1 unit is 1 pixel). If we change the **Pos Y** value to 0, the object would be centered along the *y-axis*' anchor, which would have the object be placed with half of it off the screen, which is not good, as you can see in the following example:

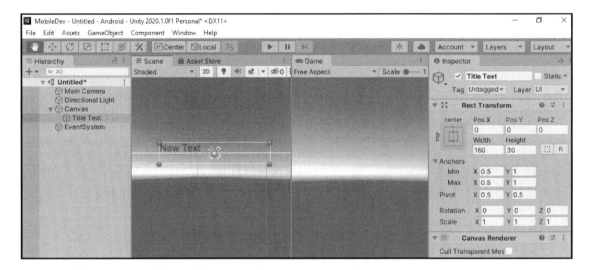

I placed the **Game** tab next to the **Scene** tab to make it easier to see the issue; you can do this by dragging and dropping the **Game** tab to the edge of the screen.

 To reset any layout changes, you may go to the **Layout** menu in the top-right part of the screen and select **Default**.

If we changed our **Title Text** object's **Pos Y** to −15 (subtracting half its **Height** value), it would be positioned correctly. However, hardcoding this value will be an issue if we decide we want to change the **Height** value later on, as we would have to remember to adjust this again. It would be a lot nicer if we had something to make **Pos Y** at 0 the edge of the map relative to our height, and, thankfully, we have the **Pivot** property to fix that.

3. Next, change the **Pivot Y** property to 1 and then change **Pos Y** to 0 if you changed it previously and it doesn't change automatically:

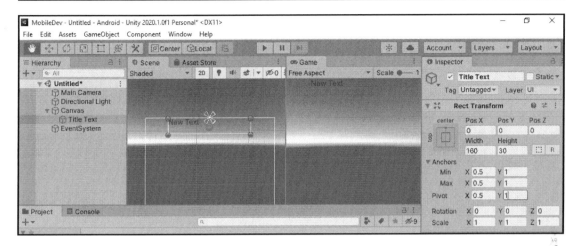

As you can see, the text is now hugging the top due to the use of the pivot setting being changed.

Pivots

Pivots are markers that note where we want things to be in relation to our object. This means that objects will be moved, rotated, and/or scaled via this position. To see how this changes the way things react, try changing the **Rotation Z** property with **Pivot Y** values of 0, 0.5, and 1, and note the differences in how things are rotated.

Note that it is possible to set the **Pivot**, **Position**, and **Anchors** of an object via the **Anchors Preset** menu I mentioned previously, if you hold down the *Alt + Shift* keys while clicking on the object. This way, all of the steps we discussed will happen all at once, but it's a good idea to get a foundation of what everything means before jumping straight into using shortcuts.

Now that we have a basic understanding of how to work within the Rect Transform space, let's start finalizing our **Title Text** object.

Adjusting and resizing the title text

Now that we have our object positioned correctly, let's give it some visual flair to our title text using the following steps:

1. Select the **Title Text** object from the **Hierarchy** tab and then move over to the **Inspector** tab and scroll down to the **Text** component. From there, change the **Text** property to `Endless Roller` and set the **Alignment** property of the object to centered vertically and horizontally. Afterward, change **Font Size** to 35. Note that now the text doesn't show up because we've made the text too big for the **Rect Transform** that we defined.

2. With that in mind, scroll up to the **Rect Transform** and change the **Width** value to 300 and **Height** to 50. We will also want it to be offset from the top of the world, so let's change **Pos Y** to −30 to give it a little offset:

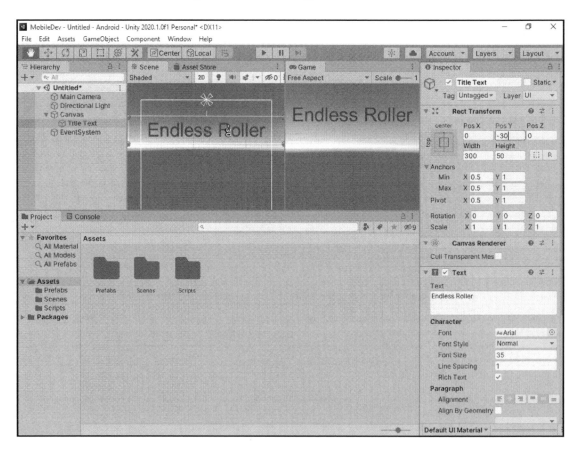

Now, this looks great for this resolution; however, if we were to play the game at a larger resolution, it may look like this:

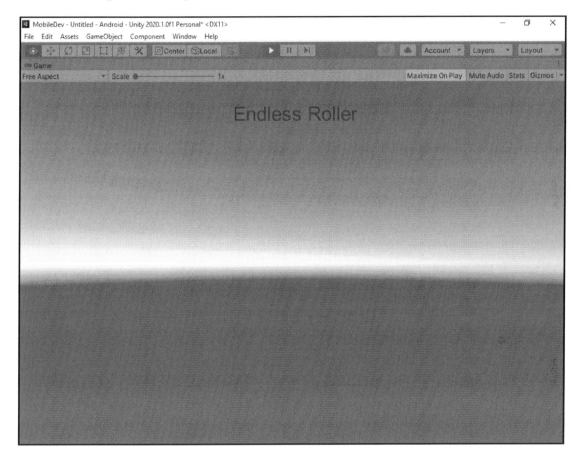

This can be good if you're trying to have a **Heads-Up Display (HUD)** in your game, but for the title screen, it's usually a good idea to have things be larger; so with that in mind, we will use the **Canvas Scaler** component to adjust how the screen will change based on the resolution we give it.

3. Select the **Canvas** object from the **Hierarchy** component and then from the **Inspector** window, go to the **Canvas Scaler** component. From there, change **UI Scale Mode** to **Scale with Screen Size**.

The key property here is **Reference Resolution**. This is the resolution that we want to base our menu on—if the resolution is made bigger, it will scale up; if it's made smaller, it will scale down. You will likely have a resolution in mind based on your mockups or an image file you've made; however, for reference, the following are some of the most common screen resolutions at the time of writing this book.

Here are some sample Apple device resolutions:

Device Name	Resolution
iPhone 11 Pro Max	2688 x 1242
iPhone 11 Pro	2436 x 1125
iPhone 11	1792 x 828
iPhone SE (2020)	1334 x 750
iPhone XS Max	1242 x 2688
iPhone XS	1125 x 2436
iPhone XR	828 x 1792
iPhone X	2436 x 1125
iPhone 7 Plus/8 Plus	1080 x 1920
iPhone 7/8	750 x 1334
iPhone 6 Plus/6S Plus	1080 x 1920
iPhone 6/6S	750 x 1334
iPhone 5	640 x 1136
iPod Touch	640 x 1136
iPad Pro	2048 x 2732
iPad 3/4	1536 x 2048
iPad Air 1 & 2	1536 x 2048
iPad Mini	768 x 1024
iPad Mini 2 & 3	1536 x 2048

Here are some sample Android device resolutions:

Device Name	Resolution
Samsung Galaxy S20 Ultra	3200 x 1440
Samsung Galaxy S20	2400 x 1080
Samsung Note 10+	2280 x1080
Google Pixel 4 XL	1440 x 2960
Google Pixel 4	2280 x 1080
Samsung Galaxy S10/S10+	3040 x 1440
Google Pixel 3 XL	2960 x 1440

Google Pixel 3/3a XL	2160 x 1080
Google Pixel 3a	2220 x 1080
Samsung Galaxy S8/S8+	2960 x 1440
Google Pixel 2 XL	2560 x 1312
Nexus 6P	1440 x 2560
Nexus 5X	1080 x 1920
Google Pixel/Pixel 2	1080 x 1920
Google Pixel XL/Pixel 2 XL	1440 x 2560
Samsung Galaxy Note 5	1440 x 2560
LG G5	1440 x 2560
One Plus 3	1080 x 1920
Samsung Galaxy S7	1440 x 2560
Samsung Galaxy S7 Edge	1440 x 2560
Nexus 7 (2013)	1200 x 1920
Nexus 9	1536 x 2048
Samsung Galaxy Tab 10	800 x 1280
Chromebook Pixel	2560 x 1700

To see a list of popular cell phone screen resolutions, check out `http://screensiz.es/phone`.

I am using a Google Pixel 3a XL, which has a resolution of 2160 x 1080, and an iPhone 6S Plus, which has a 1920 x 1080 resolution, so I think that would be a good place to start. However, if you are creating art assets, it's a good idea to create the UI at the largest resolution you plan on supporting and then build for other resolutions from there.

Unity has some of the most common resolutions built in, which can be seen/changed from the dropdown in the **Game** window view mentioned previously.

4. In the **Inspector** view, go to the **Canvas Scaler** component and change the **Reference Resolution** value to `1920 x 1080` if it isn't there already.

5. Next, under **Match**, move it all the way over to **Height**. This will ensure that when the height of our screen changes, that's when we will modify the scale of our UI.

6. Next, let's make the text a bit larger. Select the **Title Text** object and from the **Rect Transform**, change the **Width** value to 1000 and **Height** to 200, and then change the **Text** component's **Font Size** value to 130:

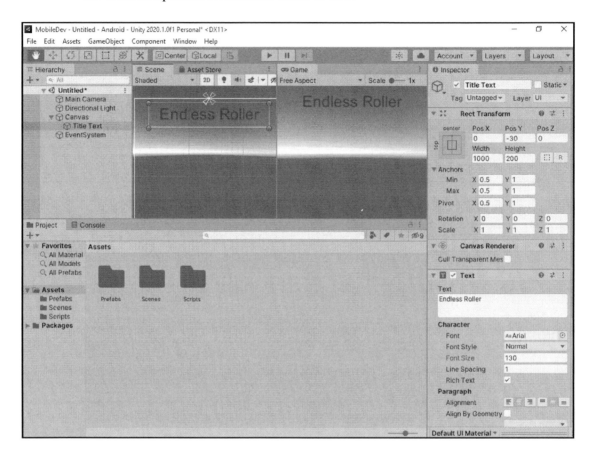

7. Now, if we play the game with a higher resolution, it will display our title nicely, scaling up to fit the larger size that we have:

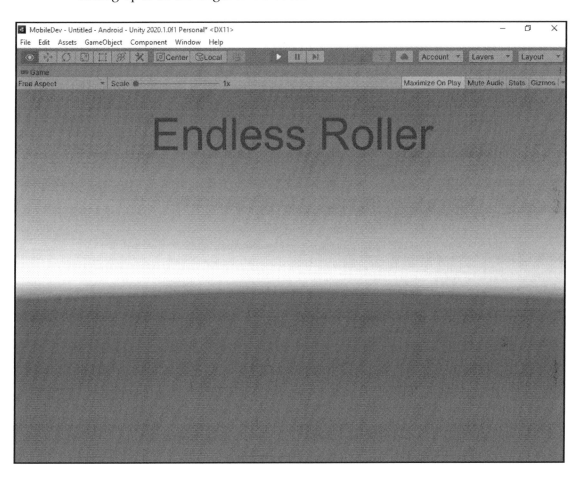

8. Go to the **Game** view control bar and pick a smaller resolution, such as **800x480 Landscape (800x480)**, and you'll note that the text will scale down to fit nicely as well:

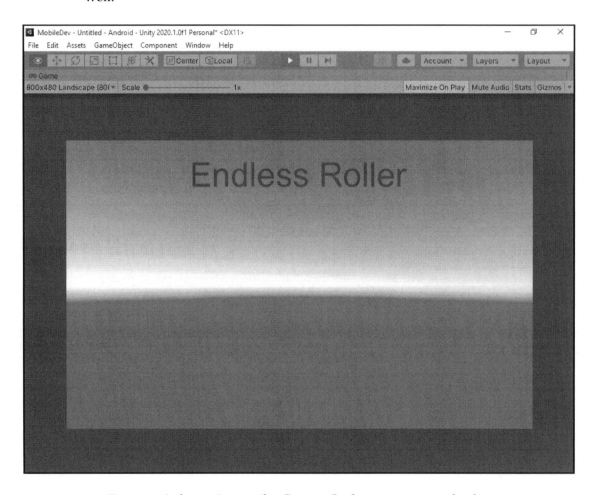

 For more information on the **Canvas Scaler** component, check out `http:/ /docs.unity3d.com/Manual/script-CanvasScaler.html`.

As you can see, the **Canvas Scaler** component will adjust the size of the text depending on the resolution of the device. Next, we will see how we can quickly test on different resolutions as well.

Selecting different aspect ratios

Like I mentioned previously, in the **Game** view, if we go to the control bar and select the first option, there is a drop-down menu where we can pick different resolutions to test our game, so we can find potential issues before exporting it to our devices:

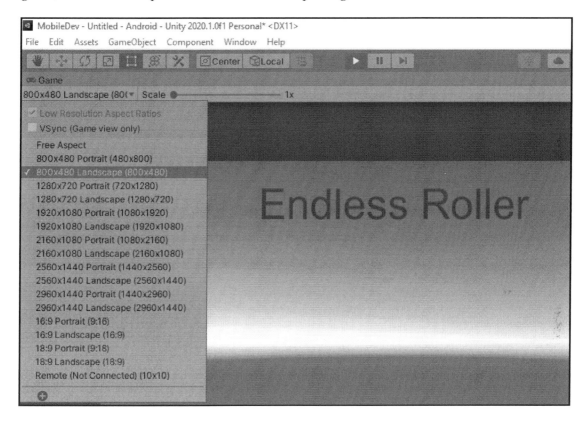

There are a number of resolutions built in for us by default, but we can also make our own using the **+** button at the bottom. I suggest that you make two new selections for your phone for landscape mode and for portrait mode at the resolutions you are trying to reach if they're not included by default (in my case, 1920 x 1080, 1080 x 1920, 2160 x 1080, and 1080 x 2160):

1. So, at this point, we can see that in a landscape ratio, it works fairly well, but let's try a portrait one:

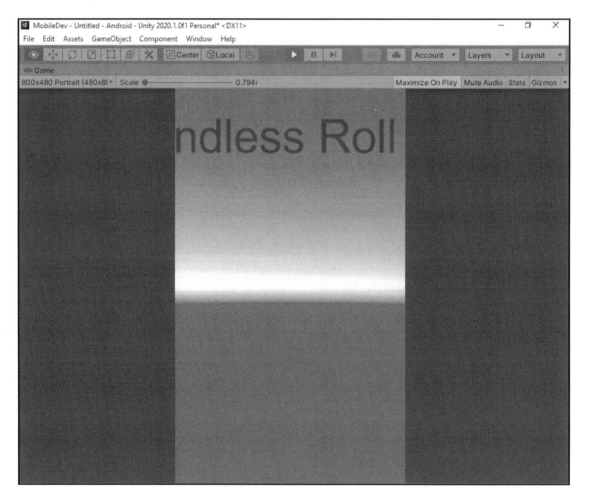

Oops! Currently, the text is overflowing past the bounds of the screen. Looks like we will have to fix that.

2. Select the **Title Text** object and check the **Best Fit** property in the **Inspector** tab under the **Text** component. This automatically scales the text to fit the space we have if the width and height were to change, which they currently don't, but we will change that next.

3. Now, go to the **Rect Transform** component, and under **Anchors**, change the **Min X** value to 0.25 and **Max X** to 0.75:

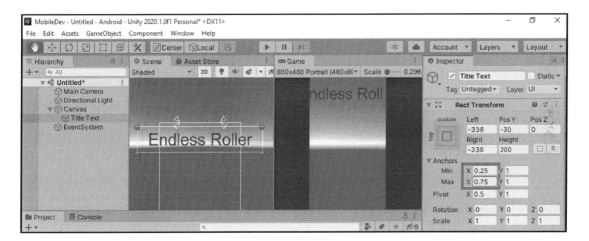

Note that now our **Rect Transform** changed the **Pos X** and **Width** values. They have now been replaced with the **Left** and **Right** properties, which are currently set to −338 and −338. This means that the area being taken up by this is −338 units away from our anchor at 25% and −338 units away from our max anchor at 75%. We want the screen to resize to be at those anchors, so we will change both the **Left** and **Right** values to 0.

4. Save our Scene as a new file inside the `Scenes` folder called `MainMenu`, and then play the game:

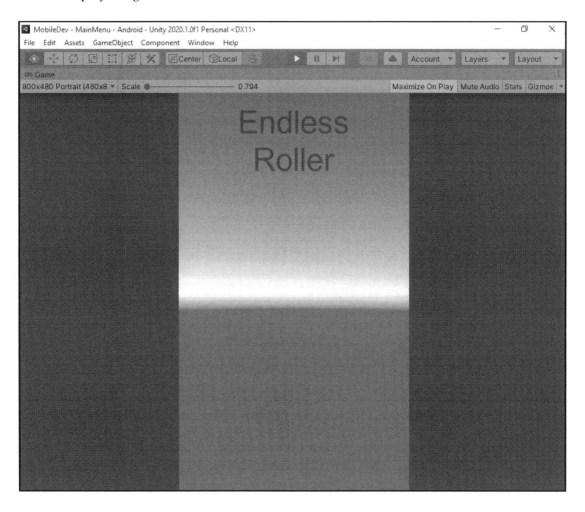

As you can see in the preceding screenshot, the text now fits a lot nicer. You'll also note that no matter what resolution we are using, this text takes up an amount of room that's fitting for a game's title. Now that we have the text displaying correctly, let's add the ability to move from the main menu into the game properly

Working with buttons

Unlike our title, for things that we want our players to touch, it's a good idea to make the buttons the same size in each device, as our fingers are the same size, no matter what device we are using. To show a possible solution for this, we will create a new Canvas using a different scaling technique:

1. Stop the game if it is currently running. We will first rename our current `Canvas` object to `Canvas - Scale w/Screen`. This way, we can easily tell whether we are using the correct Canvas for this or not.

2. Now that we have that one ready, we can create our new one. Go to the top menu bar and then select **GameObject | UI | Canvas**. Rename this new Canvas `Canvas - Scale Physical`. Then, under the **Canvas Scaler** component, change **UI Scale Mode** to **Constant Physical Size**:

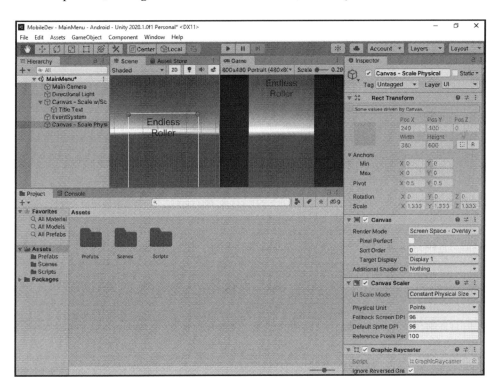

Using this method, Unity will attempt to scale the size of this Canvas so that each element has the same physical size, regardless of the resolution. Since we're going for buttons that we intend to press with our fingers, this makes a lot of sense.

3. Now, with this Canvas (`Canvas - Scale Physical`) selected in the **Hierarchy** view, go to the menu and select **GameObject | UI | Button** to create a new button inside this Canvas.

You can also do this by right-clicking on the `Canvas - Scale Physical` object from the **Hierarchy** window and selecting **UI | Button**.

At this point, you will see a new child object to **Canvas** called **Button**, and if you were to extend that object, you'd see that it has a **Text** child also:

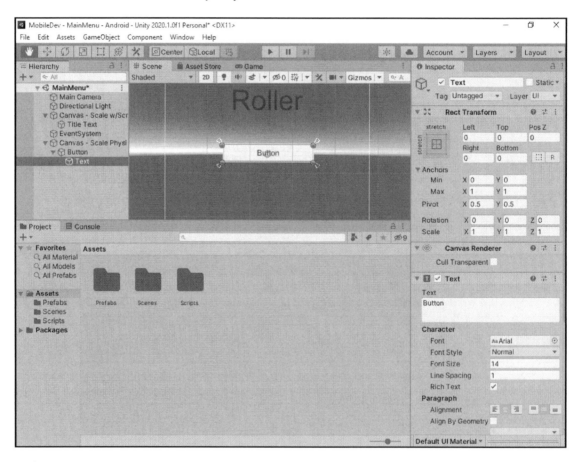

The next question is, what size should our buttons be? Google suggests in their Material guidelines for Android that at least 48 x 48 density-independent pixels should be used (dp for short), whereas Apple at their **Worldwide Developers Conference (WWDC)** recommends at least 44 dp x 44 dp. Either way, that comes somewhere around 8mm x 8mm or 0.3 inches x 0.3 inches.

To read the material guidelines, check out `https://material.io/design/layout/spacing-methods.html#touch-click-targets`.

If you were to look at the game right now and check out some of the different resolution options, you may be a bit scared due to the size of the button, depending on the resolution:

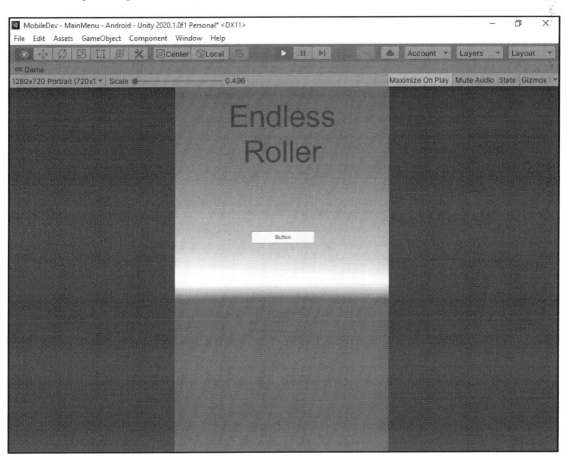

That's because our button size is assuming that the **Dots per Inch (DPI)** value is 96, when on devices such as the Google Pixel 3a XL and the iPhone 6/7/8 Plus it is around 400. For right now, I'll change the **Aspect Ratio** value to **16:9 Landscape** to see something closer to what we'll be using on our device when we play there:

If you're interested in finding out what the DPI for your device is, check out http://dpi.lv/.

4. Stop the game if it is currently running. Afterward, from the **Hierarchy** window, expand the **Button** object and from there select the **Text** child object. From there, go to the **Inspector** window and change the **Text** component's **Text** value to Play.

5. Next, let's make some adjustments to the **Button** object itself.
   From the **Hierarchy** window, select the **Button** object. Rename it `Play Button` at the top of the **Inspector** window to make it clear what the object is.

6. Next, go to the **Rect Transform** component and change the **Pos X** and **Pos Y** values to `0` to center the button in the middle of the screen. Afterward, the size of the button is quite large, so let's change the **Width** property to `75`:

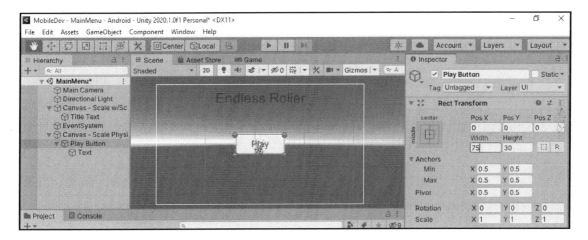

We now have a button, but it doesn't actually do anything yet. Let's fix that now.

7. Let's create a script to contain the functionality that we want. From the **Project** view, open the `Scripts` folder and let's create a new C# script called `MainMenuBehaviour`.

8. Once your IDE has opened, use the following code:

```
using UnityEngine;
using UnityEngine.SceneManagement; // LoadScene

public class MainMenuBehaviour : MonoBehaviour
{
    /// <summary>
    /// Will load a new scene upon being called
    /// </summary>
    /// <param name="levelName">The name of the level we want
    /// to go to</param>
    public void LoadLevel(string levelName)
    {
        SceneManager.LoadScene(levelName);
    }
}
```

The `LoadLevel` function will load a level based on the name that we provide to it making use of Unity's Scene Manager, which we added using a statement at the top of our code so that we would have access to that namespace.

9. Save the script and go back to the Unity editor. To call Unity's UI Events from the editor, we will need to have a game object with the `MainMenuBehaviour` component attached to it to call this function from. We could use one of the currently existing objects, but we'll just create a new object, making it easier to be found in the future.

10. With that in mind, create an empty game object (**Game Object | Create Empty...**) in your scene called `Main Menu` and then add the `MainMenuBehaviour` script to it. Then, drag and drop it to the top of the **Hierarchy** tab to make it easier to access in the future and reset its position for the sake of neatness:

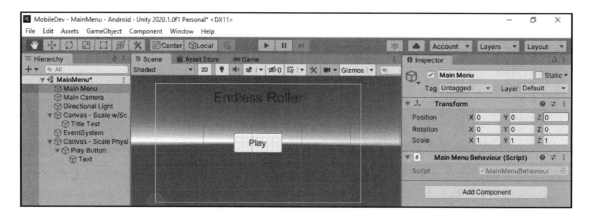

11. Select your **Play Button** object from **Hierarchy**, and go to the **Inspector** tab and scroll down to the **Button** component from there. Then, in the **On Click ()** section, click on the **+** icon to add something for our button to do.

12. Then, drag and drop the **Main Menu** object from the **Hierarchy** tab to the area that currently says **None (Object)**, which is added to the list.

13. Click on the dropdown that currently says **No Function** and then select
MainMenuBehaviour.LoadLevel. Then, in the textbox that appears below that,
type in the name of our game's level, `Gameplay`:

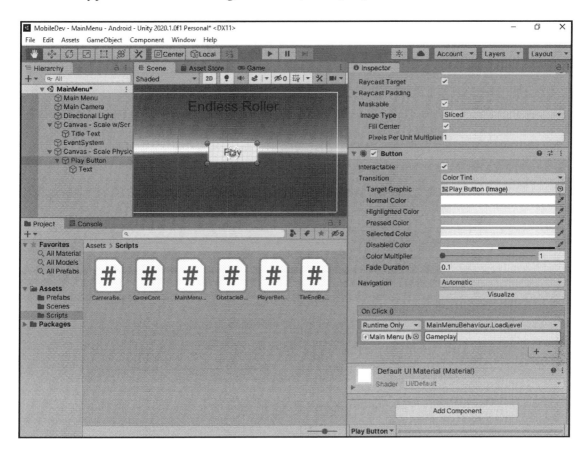

14. Save your scene by going to **File | Save**. Lastly, open **Build Settings** as we did before by going to **File | Build Settings** and add our **MainMenu** to the list at index **0** by selecting **Add Open Scenes** and then dragging the **MainMenu** level to the top, so that it will be the level that starts off when we start the game:

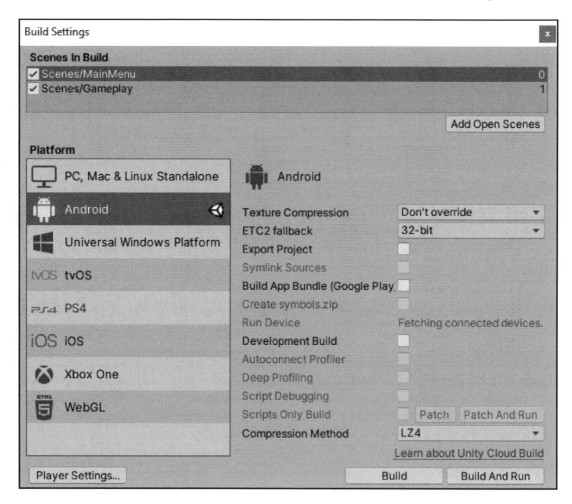

15. Save your project and Scene and click on the **Play** button:

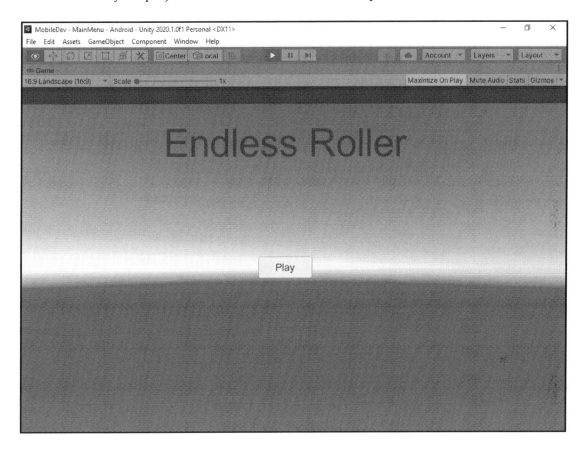

At this point, our main menu is working well, and we can get into the game without any issues by clicking on the **Play** button:

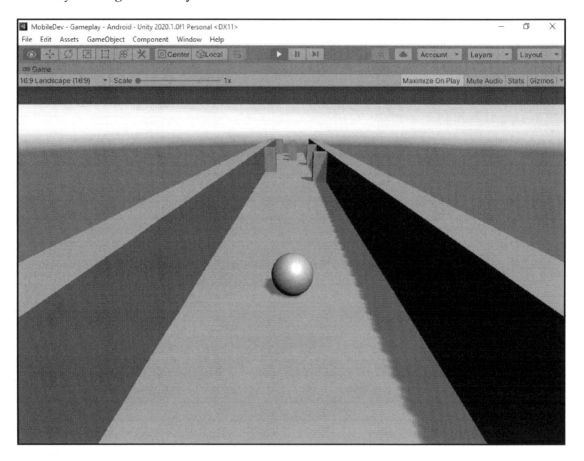

Now that we have the main menu, we will move on to building something else that most games will need: a pause menu.

Adding a pause menu

In PC games, pause menus will likely be triggered by the *Esc* key, whereas in a mobile game, it typically needs its very own button. We will make it so that this project supports both. Let's look at the steps:

1. Open up the **Gameplay** Scene by going to the **Project** window, opening the Assets/Scenes folder, and double-clicking on **Gameplay**, thus saving the **MainMenu** level if you didn't do so already:

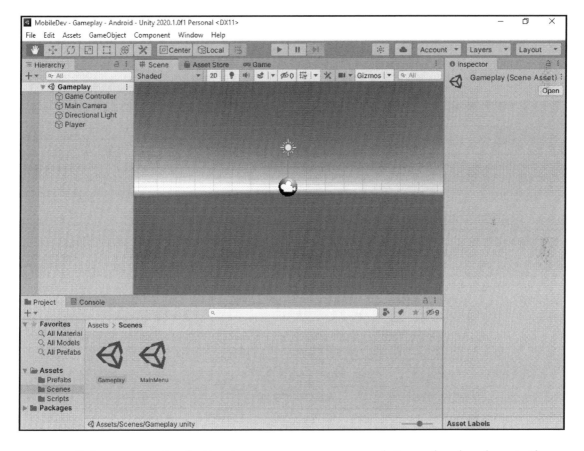

Before we create a button to open our pause menu, let's go ahead and create the pause menu that we'll be opening first.

2. The first thing we'll do is dim our screen when we enter the pause menu. An easy way to do that is having an image scale to cover our entire screen, which is what the **Panel** object does by default. We can create it by selecting **Game Object | UI | Panel**. Note that this creates a **Canvas** object and an **EventSystem** object in addition to the **Panel** object, because one doesn't exist in this Scene already.

3. Rename the **Panel** object to `Pause Menu`. Then, with the object selected from the **Inspector** window, go to the **Image** component and we will then change the **Color** property to black with a higher transparency by increasing the alpha channel (**A**) to `178`:

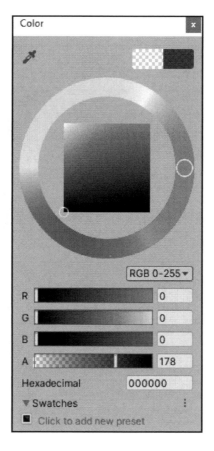

The **Image** component works in a similar manner to the **Sprite Renderer** for 2D games, with information on an image to draw and the color to use for it.

4. Switch to the **Game** window to get a better look at what the **Panel** object is doing to the screen. The current image has a thin border, which I'm not a fan of, in this case. You may keep it if you'd like, but I'm going to remove it and change the **Source Image** value to **None (Sprite)** by selecting the current one and pressing the *Delete* key:

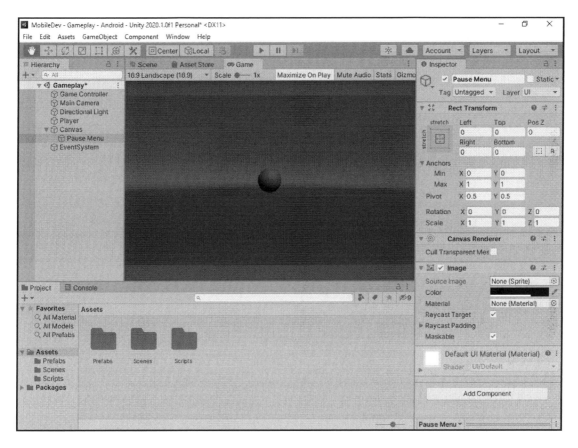

Now that we have this, we will need to populate the menu with content. In this case, we will have a **Text** object saying that the game is paused and some buttons allowing the player to resume, restart, or return to the main menu.

5. Let's create another panel to hold our pause menu contents. We want this panel to be a child of our **Pause Menu** object, so we can do this easily by going to the **Hierarchy** window, right-clicking on **Pause Menu**, and selecting **UI | Panel**:

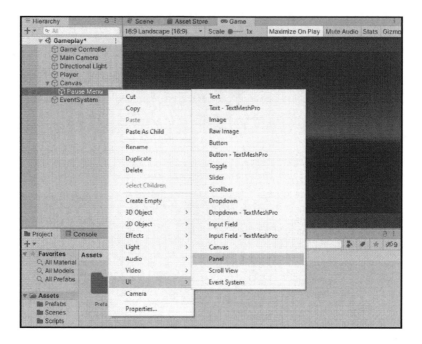

Now, for this panel, I don't want it to take up the entire screen, so I will use another component to modify its size based on the resolution we receive. In this case, I will use an **Aspect Ratio Fitter** component.

6. In the **Inspector** window, scroll all the way down and then select **Add Component** and start typing in `Aspect`. From there, select **Aspect Ratio Fitter** and then press the *Enter* key.

7. Afterward, go to our newly added component and change the **Aspect Mode** value to `Fit In Parent` to ensure that the panel will always fit within our screen and set **Aspect Ratio** to `0.5`. This means that it will be twice as high as it is wide (width over height, which means ½—`0.5`).

If you go to the **Game** window and switch aspect ratios, you'll note that the menu will stay in a similar shape.

For more information on the **Aspect Ratio Fitter** component, check out https://docs.unity3d.com/Manual/script-AspectRatioFitter.html.

8. This is good, but I don't want to have the panel stuck directly to the edge of our screen, so we will make this object invisible by clicking on the checkmark by the **Image** component. This will disable the component and stop the component's functionality.

9. Then, right-click on the **Panel** object and create another panel by going to **UI | Panel**. Rename this new object `Pause Menu Contents` and then change the **Rect Transform** component's left, right, top, and bottom values to **10** to give us a border around the screen.

10. We will use physical buttons like last time, so let's move to the **Canvas** object, and under the **Canvas Scaler** component, change **UI Scale Mode** to **Constant Physical Size**:

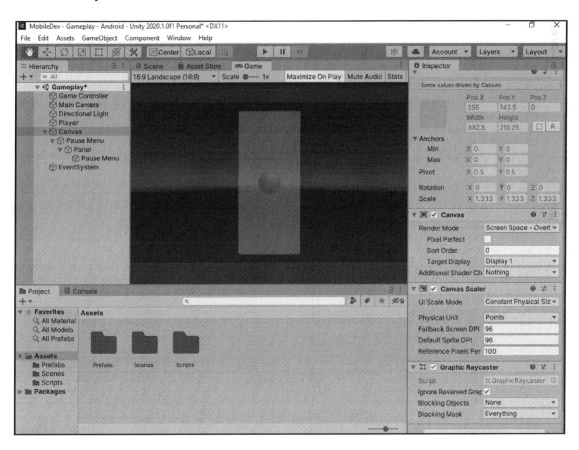

We could place everything manually as we did previously, but in this case, we may want to use another feature that Unity's UI System has: layout groups.

Layout groups will resize the children of an object so that a component will automatically fit the area of the parent. There are several different layout groups, including grid-based, horizontal, and vertical layout groups. In our case, the menu will probably be vertical.

For more information on Unity's way of automatically creating layouts, check out https://docs.unity3d.com/Manual/UIAutoLayout.html.

11. Select the **Pause Menu Contents** object in the **Hierarchy** window and then switch to the **Inspector** window. From there, scroll all the way down to the **Add Component** option and select it. Type in Vertical Layout Group and select the **Vertical Layout Group** by pressing the *Enter* key.

12. Let's create some children to fit in our menu. From the **Hierarchy** window, right-click on the **Pause Menu Contents** object and select UI | **Button**.

13. This creates a button, but you'll note that it looks pretty much like a normal button. Let's open up its child **Text** object and change the text to Resume.

14. Afterward, select the **Pause Menu Contents** object and under the **Inspector** window, go to the **Vertical Layout Group (Script)** component and change the **Child Alignment** value to **Middle Center**. Then, change the **Child Control Size** value to have **Width** toggled.

15. Then, in the **Vertical Layout Group** component, click on the arrow to the left of the **Padding** property to open it up and then set all of the sides to 5:

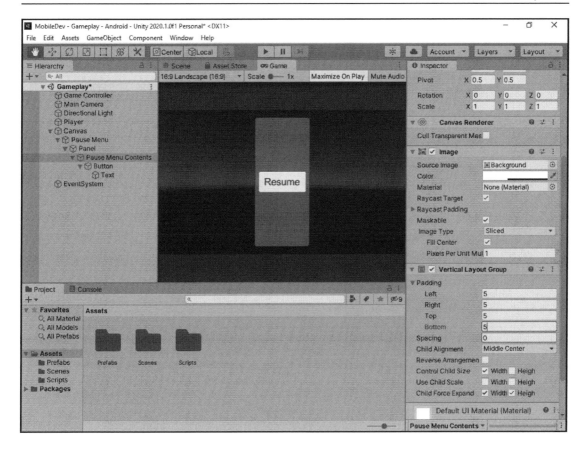

This will add 5 pixels of padding in each direction within all of the children of the layout group.

16. Now, duplicate this button twice and change the text to **Restart** and **Main Menu**. Then, to make it easy to tell the difference between them, let's change the objects' names to **Resume Button**, **Restart Button**, and **Main Menu Button**.

17. Next, right-click on the **Pause Menu Contents** object and select **UI | Text**. Change the object's text to **Paused** and change its alignment to be centered and increase the size until it's somewhere you like. Note how the order in which the children are changes the order in which they are displayed. With that in mind, drag the **Text** object to the top:

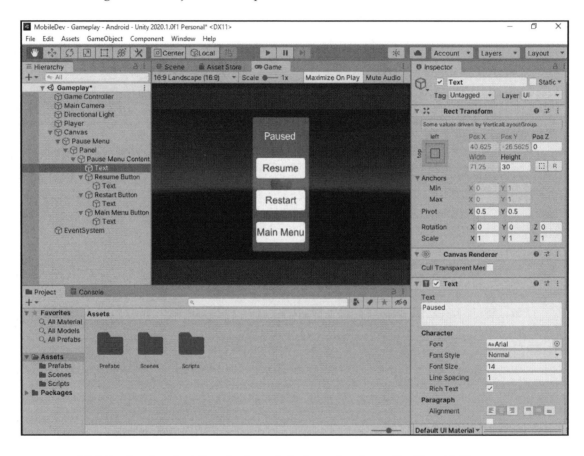

This looks nice, but there's also a lot of spacing here. So, if we'd like, we can instead condense the contents of our menu to just fit what we have there.

18. To do this, we can go to **Hierarchy** and select the **Pause Menu Contents** object and then add a **Content Size Fitter** component. Once it is added, we will change **Horizontal Fit** and **Vertical Fit** to **Preferred Size**.

19. This will scrunch all the buttons together, so we can change the **Spacing** property of **Vertical Layout Group** to 5 and add some space between the buttons:

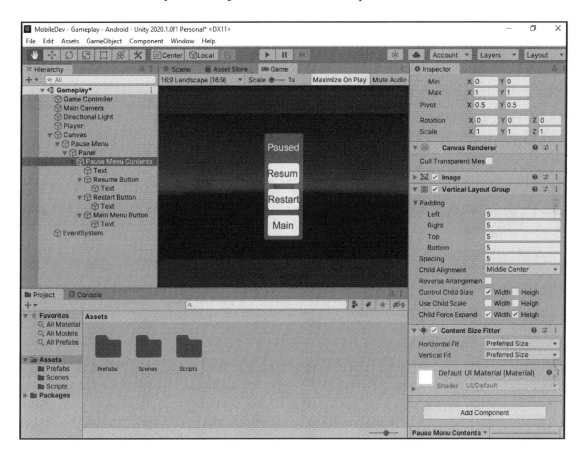

You may notice that the buttons are now all the same size and spaced out, but the individual buttons themselves are smaller than they should be.

20. To make sure that the buttons fit no matter what size we have, select each button (can be done by using *Ctrl* + clicking on each object in the **Hierarchy** window) and add a **Horizontal Layout Group (Script)** instance to them. From there, check the **Child Controls Size** value for **Width** and **Height** and add padding of 5:

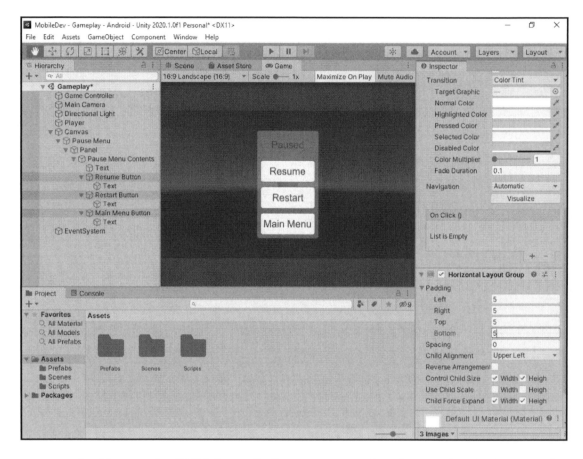

In this case, the **Child Controls Size** property will make it so that the button will increase its size to ensure that it fits the size of the text provided.

If you'd prefer not to do it all at once, after you create the first **Horizontal Layout Group (Script)** on one object, you can right-click on it and select **Copy Component**; then, go to the other two buttons, right-click on the **Inspector** tab at in the **Rect Transform** component, and then select **Paste Component As New**.

21. We will also go to the paused **Text** object and increase the **Text** component's **Font Size** value to 25 to fill out the area and emphasize that we are in the pause menu:

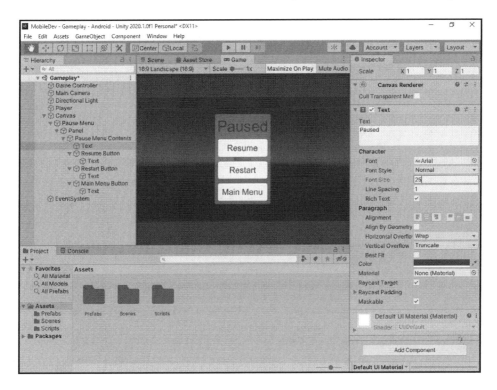

22. Now that we have the buttons themselves, let's actually make them do something. In the **Project** window, open up the `Scripts` folder and create a new C# Script called `PauseScreenBehaviour` and double-click on it to open up the IDE of your choice.

23. Once it's opened, use the following code:

```
using UnityEngine;
using UnityEngine.SceneManagement; // SceneManager

public class PauseScreenBehaviour : MainMenuBehaviour
{

    public static bool paused;

    [Tooltip("Reference to the pause menu object to turn on/off")]
    public GameObject pauseMenu;
```

```
/// <summary>
/// Reloads our current level, effectively "restarting" the
/// game
/// </summary>
public void Restart()
{
    SceneManager.LoadScene(SceneManager.GetActiveScene().name);
}

/// <summary>
/// Will turn our pause menu on or off
/// </summary>
/// <param name="isPaused"></param>
public void SetPauseMenu(bool isPaused)
{
    paused = isPaused;

    // If the game is paused, timeScale is 0, otherwise 1
    Time.timeScale = (paused) ? 0 : 1;
    pauseMenu.SetActive(paused);
}

void Start()
{
 // Must be reset in Start or else game will be paused upon
                                            // restart
    paused = false;
}
}
```

In this script, we will first use a `static` variable, which is called `paused`. When we declare a `static` variable, we ensure that there will only ever be one of those variables inside this class, which all instances will share. One of the advantages of this is that we can access the property in other scripts using the class name followed by a period and then the attribute's name (in this case, `PauseScreenBehaviour.paused`). We will use this concept later on when we want to open the menu through code.

We then have two public functions, which we will call via the UI elements. First, we have a `Restart` function, which will use Unity's Scene Manager to return us to the currently loaded level, effectively restarting the game. It is important to note that `static` variables do not reset when restarting in Unity, so that's why I set `paused` to `false` in the `Start` function to ensure that when we come to the level, it is unpaused.

Finally, we have a `SetPauseMenu` function, which will turn the pause menu on or off based on the value of `isPaused`. It also sets the `Time.timeScale` property, where 0 means that nothing will happen and 1 means normal time. This property will modify the `Time.deltaTime` variable, effectively canceling out movement that we have as long as we use it.

24. Save your script and dive back into Unity.

25. Then, we'll create a new empty game object by going to **GameObject | Create Empty**. We'll name it `Pause Screen Handler` and then attach the **Pause Screen Behaviour (Script)** component to it.

26. Next, assign the **Pause Menu** variable to the **Pause Menu** game object in the **Hierarchy** tab:

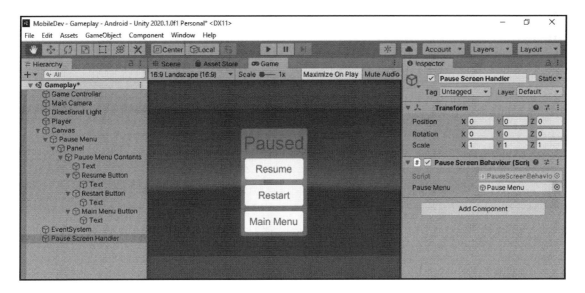

27. Now that we have the script, we can now change the buttons to actually do something. Go to the **Inspector** window with the **Resume Button** object selected, go to the **Button** component's **On Click ()** section, and click on the + button to add an action to occur.

28. Drag and drop the **Pause Menu Handler** object from the **Hierarchy** window into the box on the bottom-left side of the **On Click ()** action in the **Inspector** window. Next, go to the dropdown and select **Pause Screen Behaviour | SetPauseMenu**. By default, it's on false due to not being checked, so this should work for us:

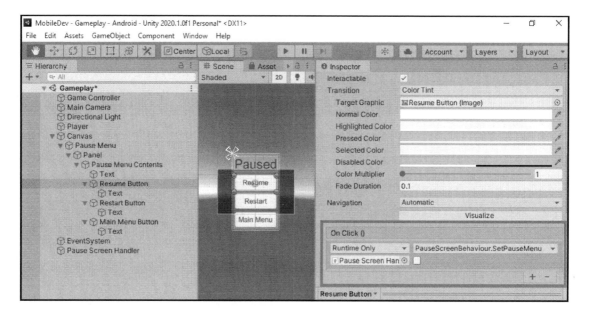

29. Likewise, do the same for the **Restart** button object, this time calling the `Restart` function.

30. Next, do the same for the **Main Menu Button** object, except call `LoadLevel` and put the name of our main menu level in the string place (`MainMenu`, in my case).

Note that the `PauseScreenHandler` script already contains `LoadLevel` due to the fact that we are inheriting from the `MainMenuBehaviour` class.

31. Save our game and go ahead and run it:

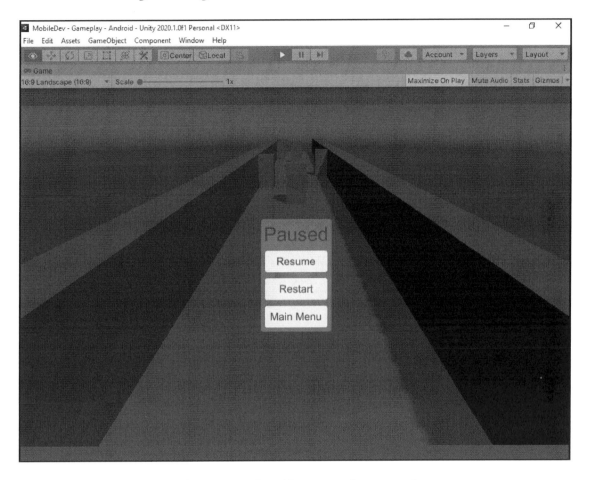

As you can see in the preceding screenshot, if we start the game, the menu appears correctly—we can click **Main Menu** button to get to the main menu and **Resume** continues the game.

At this point, we have some issues: once the menu is gone, there is no way to get it back; the game should start unpaused; and the game should actually pause. Let's tackle these issues next.

Pausing the game

To get the game to pause correctly, we will tweak some scripts we've written previously using the following steps:

1. Open the `PlayerBehaviour` script and add the code highlighted in bold to the `FixedUpdate` function:

```
/// <summary>
/// FixedUpdate is called at a fixed framerate and is a prime place
///     to put
/// Anything based on time.
/// </summary>
void FixedUpdate()
{
    // If the game is paused, don't do anything
    if (PauseScreenBehaviour.paused)
    {
        return;
    }

    // Check if we're moving to the side
    var horizontalSpeed = Input.GetAxis("Horizontal") * dodgeSpeed;

    // Rest of FixedUpdate function...
```

The added code makes it so that if the game is paused, we will not do anything within the function.

2. We then also need to add the same script to the top of the `Update` function as well:

```
/// <summary>
/// Update is called once per frame
/// </summary>
private void Update()
{
    // If the game is paused, don't do anything
    if (PauseScreenBehaviour.paused)
    {
        return;
    }

    // Check if we are running on a mobile device
    #if UNITY_IOS || UNITY_ANDROID

    // Rest of Update function...
```

3. Now, the game, by default, should be unpaused, so let's go ahead and select the **Pause Menu** object in the **Hierarchy** view and then click on the active button in the **Inspector** view to disable it:

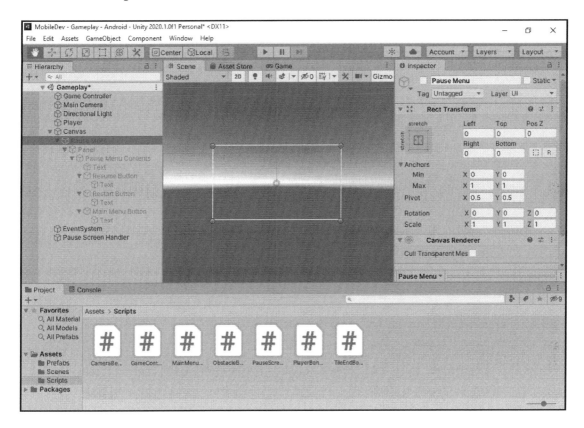

4. In addition to this, we will need a way to turn it on. On PC games, this is usually the *Esc* button, but, for mobile, we will instead have a button that players can click to turn on the menu. Go ahead and right-click on the **Canvas** object in the **Hierarchy** view and select **UI | Button**.

5. Rename the new object `Show Pause Button` and use the **Anchor Presets** menu to place the object at the bottom left of the screen (use *Alt + Shift* to set **Pivot** and **Position** as well).

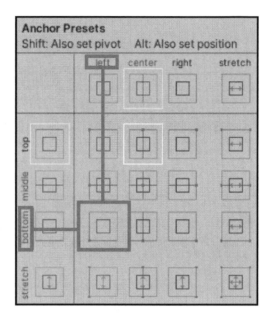

6. Then, still on the **RectTransform** component, change the **Width** value to 30, as it won't need to be that large.

7. Open up the **Text** component and change the **Text** property to | | to make it look like a pause button.

8. Go back and select the **Show Pause Button** object and create an **On Click ()** event using the **SetPauseMenu** function on the **Pause Screen Behaviour** component on the **Pause Screen Handler** object. Then, click on the checkbox to set it to pause.

9. Now, we want to remove this pause button when we click. We could do this through code, but just to show that we can also do this via the editor, go ahead and click on **+** again to add another action to **On Click ()**.

10. Next, drag and drop the actual **Show Pause Button** and then call the **GameObject | SetActive** function. Then, uncheck it to turn the object off:

11. Go back to the **Resume Button** and add another event to its button to turn the **Show Pause Menu** button back on when we leave using **SetActive** as we used in the previous step.

As mentioned previously, one problem that won't be apparent now unless you restart the level is the fact that `static` variables will keep their values each time we reload the game. In our case, we set `paused`, which turns our `Time.timeScale` to 0. Thankfully, we can fix this fairly easily.

12. Lastly, open the `PauseScreenBehaviour` script and update the `Start` function to have the following, replacing the original line:

```
void Start()
{
    // Must be reset in Start or else game will be paused upon
                                                    // restart
    SetPauseMenu(false);
}
```

13. Save your script and the Scene, and then play the game:

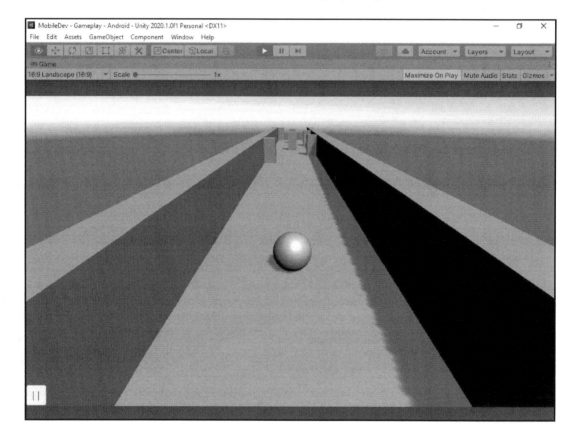

The pause menu now works correctly. At this point, our UI should work for the vast majority of cell phones. However, there are certain phones that contain "notches." We will see how to adjust our UI for that in the next section.

Adapting GUI for notch devices

Since the first edition of this book, there have been many phones that have come out with sensor housings, more commonly known as "notches." Made popular with the iPhone X, this has grown to be a part of many phones that are out right now, such as the iPhone XS, XR, Google Pixel XL, One Plus 7, Huawei P20, Xiaomi Mi 8, Vivo V9, and Samsung Galaxy S10. While some people online state that entire-screen displays are the future, iOS devices, Android devices running 9.0 and above, and Unity have added in support for notches built into devices, and we can use the `Screen.safeArea` property in Unity to ensure that all of our content is visible.

To get started, we will first go to the main menu to tweak the menu text:

1. Go to the **Project** view and open up the `MainMenu` Scene in the `Scenes` folder. In the *Adding a pause menu* section, we saw how we can use the **Panel** object in order to hold the contents we want to display. We will use this concept to account for the safe area.

2. With the level opened, go to the **Hierarchy** view and create a child panel for our title screen to be inside by right-clicking on the **Canvas - Scale w/Screen** object and selecting **UI | Panel**.

3. Afterward, make **Title Text** a child of the newly created panel by dragging and dropping the object on top of the newly created **Panel** object:

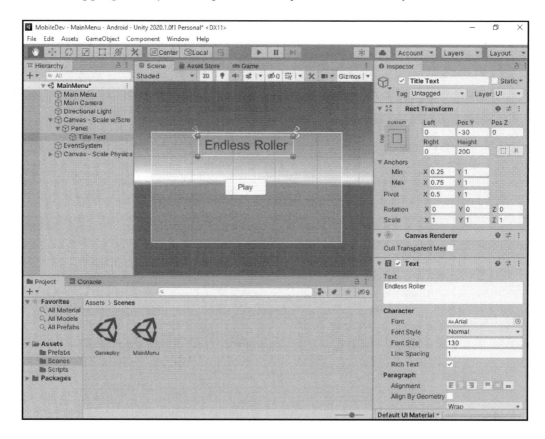

4. From the **Project** view, go to the `Scripts` folder and create a new C# Script called `UISafeAreaHandler`. Double-click on it to open your code editor and use the following code:

```
using UnityEngine;

public class UISafeAreaHandler : MonoBehaviour
{
    RectTransform panel;

    // Start is called before the first frame update
    void Start()
    {
        panel = GetComponent<RectTransform>();
    }
```

```
// Update is called once per frame
void Update()
{
    Rect area = Screen.safeArea;

    // Pixel size in screen space of the whole screen
    Vector2 screenSize = new Vector2(Screen.width,
                            Screen.height);

    // Set anchors to percentages of the screen used.
    panel.anchorMin = area.position / screenSize;
    panel.anchorMax = (area.position + area.size) / screenSize;

}
}
```

The `Screen.safeArea` property returns a variable of the `Rect` type, which contains an X and Y position and a width and height, just like the **Rect Transform** component we worked with previously in this chapter. This Rect Transform gives a box containing the safe area that doesn't have notches inside it. Note that this property is in screen space and so will be given in pixels. For those Android phones running 8.1 or lower, `Screen.safeArea` will just return `Rect(0, 0, Screen.width, Screen.height)`, which will work due to the lack of a notch.

`Screen.safeArea` will change depending on the orientation that the device is currently in. Since we want to support all orientations (landscape and portrait mode), we'll have to check for the safe area changing at runtime, which is why we use the `Update` function to do modifications.

We previously saw that anchors can be used to specify the size of a panel. Anchors work in viewport space, which is to say that the values go from (0, 0) to (1, 1). Since the `Rect` given by `Screen.safeArea` is in screen (pixel) space, we divide by the screen size in pixels to convert to the points to viewport space.

5. Save the script and return to the Unity Editor. Then, attach the **UI Safe Area Handler** component to the **Panel** object that we just created.

6. Update the `UISafeAreaHandler` script by adding the following:

```
// Update is called once per frame
void Update()
{
    Rect area = Screen.safeArea;

    // Pixel size in screen space of the whole screen
```

```
Vector2 screenSize = new Vector2(Screen.width, Screen.height);

//For testing purposes
if (Application.isEditor && Input.GetButton("Jump"))
{
    // Use the notch properties of the iPhone XS Max
    if(Screen.height > Screen.width)
    {
        // Portrait
        area = new Rect(0f, 0.038f, 1f, 0.913f);
    }
    else
    {
        // Landscape
        area = new Rect(0.049f, 0.051f, 0.902f, 0.949f);
    }

    panel.anchorMin = area.position;
    panel.anchorMax = (area.position + area.size);

    return;
}

// set anchors to percentages of the screen used.
panel.anchorMin = area.position / screenSize;
panel.anchorMax = (area.position + area.size) / screenSize;

}
```

In this script, we added the ability, if we are inside the Unity Editor, to press the spacebar to change the value of the area and set the panel's anchor values to something different. In this case, we are using the values given by the iPhone XS Max if calling `Screen.safeArea`. Since the editor doesn't set orientation properties in Unity, we check the screen size to determine whether we are in landscape or portrait mode.

7. Save the script and return to the editor. Play the game and you should notice that when you press the spacebar, you will see the panel tweak its size appropriately:

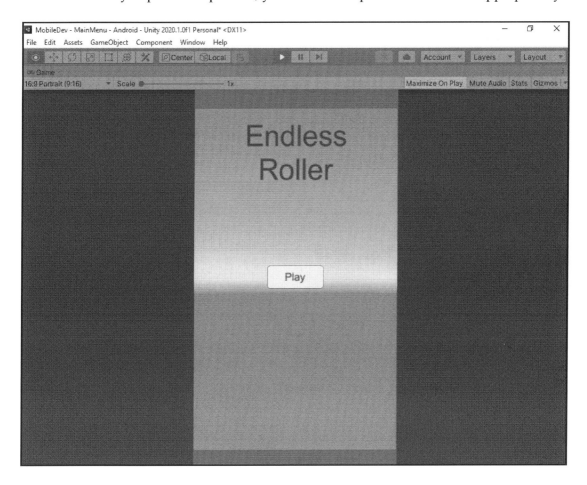

In portrait mode, the top portion of the screen is cut off for the notch and the bottom is cut off for the home button:

Switching to landscape, we lose the left/right side for the notch and on iOS, it cuts off the other side as well. Just as in portrait, the top is cut off for the home key.

With this, we see that the menu adjusts itself correctly! However, there is a chance that the **Play** button no longer works. This is because both of our Canvas objects are drawn in the same sort order, which means either can be on top of the other, similar to the concept of z-fighting you may know of if you've worked on 2D games in the past. Thankfully, we can fix that pretty easily.

8. Select the **Canvas - Scale w/Screen** object. From the **Inspector** window, go to the **Canvas** component and set **Sort Order** to −1. The button with a **Sort Order** value of 0 will always be on top of the contents of this Canvas.

While the semi-transparent white panel is useful in illustrating the concept, we don't actually want our users to see it when the game is being played. With that in mind, let's turn off the image.

9. Select the **Panel** object. From the **Image** component, uncheck the checkbox to the left of the component's name to disable it.

If you wanted to still have the image visible and have the button still work, you can instead uncheck the **Raycast Target** property.

Now that the first Canvas is completed, we can now do the same actions for the other one.

10. Go to the **Canvas - Scale Physical** component and create another **Panel** object with the **UI Safe Area Handler** component attached to it, making sure to disable the **Image** component. Next, make the **Play** button a child of it:

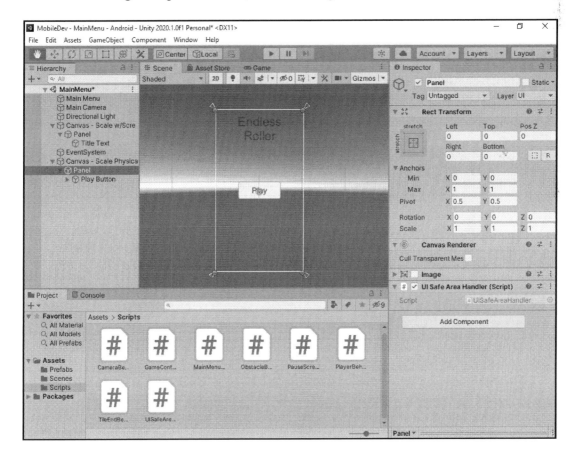

11. Save your Scene. Now that we have the main menu completed, we can tweak the `Gameplay` Scene as well.

12. Open the `Gameplay` Scene, then make a child panel of the **Canvas** to hold **Show Pause Button**. From there, attach the **UI Safe Area Handler** component and disable the **Image** component on it:

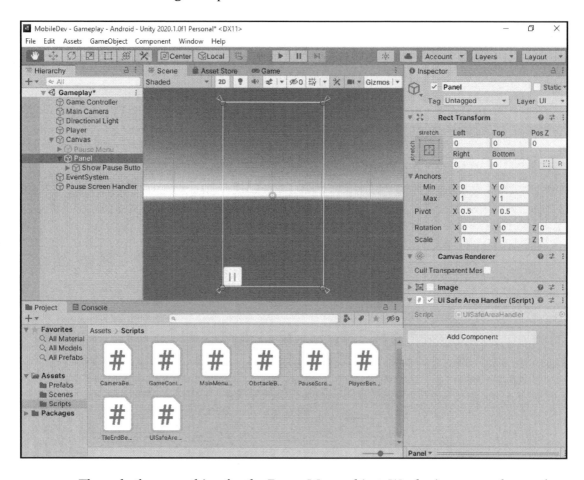

Then, do the same thing for the **Pause Menu** object. We don't want to change the **Pause Menu** object as we want the black screen even in the notch areas. We have previously created a panel to hold the content of the pause menu, but that object is using the Aspect Ratio Fitter, which will overwrite any anchor changes we would make in code. To keep this functionality as well as the Content Size Fitters in the child objects, we can just create a parent panel to act as a holder.

13. Make the **Pause Menu** object active again by selecting it in the **Hierarchy** window and then clicking on the checkbox by its name in the **Inspector** window. Right-click on the **Pause Menu** object and create a **Panel** object by right-clicking and selecting **UI | Panel**. Drag and drop the previously created panel that was a child of **Pause Menu** to become a child of our new panel. In the new panel, add the **UI Safe Area Handler** component and disable the **Image** component:

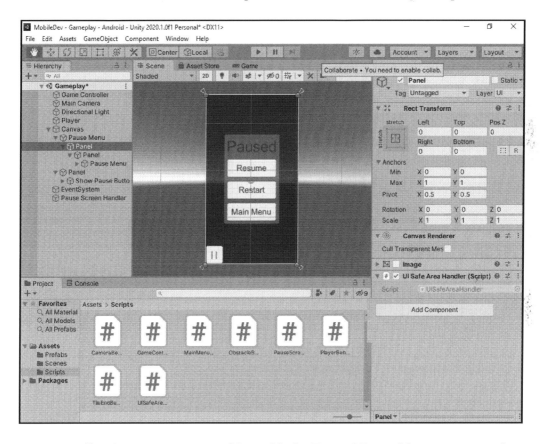

14. Finally, since we are not working with the **Pause Menu** object anymore, select the **Pause Menu** object from the **Hierarchy** window and in the **Inspector** window, uncheck the checkbox by the name to disable the object.

15. Save your Scene and play the game:

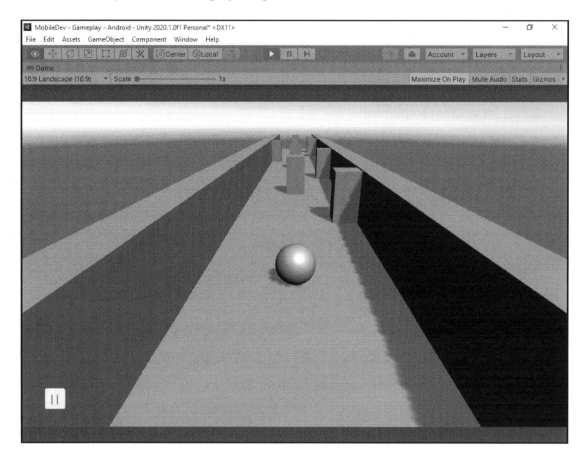

As you can see, if we hold down the spacebar, we can see both menus working correctly!

Summary

With that, we've got a good foundation to build on when creating UI elements for a mobile game. We first covered how to create a title screen, making use of buttons and **Text** objects. We then covered how to use panels, buttons, text, and layout groups to make your menus adapt to the size of your elements. We also touched on how layout groups can arrange our objects to fit in a pleasing manner.

We integrated the pause menu into our game itself and made it work with everything in our project. Finally, we saw how to have our project automatically adapt to fit within the allotted safe areas to handle the notches found on phones. We will be revisiting these concepts in later chapters, so keep these explanations in mind.

 One in-development tool to keep an eye on is Device Simulator. This is a tool that aims to allow developers to see what their game will look like on many devices. For more information on it, check out `https://docs.` `unity3d.com/Packages/com.unity.device-simulator@2.2/manual/` `index.html`.

In the next chapter, we will dive into monetization and take a look at just how we can add Unity ads to our project.

Advertising Using Unity Ads 5

When working on mobile titles, you need to think about how you are going to sell your game. Deciding on how to best sell a game can be difficult. Of course, you can sell your game for a price, and there is a possibility that it will be successful, but you'll be limiting your audience numbers to a much lower amount. This could work well for a niche game, but if you're trying to make a game with broad appeal where you want to get as many players as possible to play your title, you may have some issues.

Having a price on the game can be a major hurdle in getting those initial customers who can share the game via word of mouth and contribute to having more people play your game. To solve this potential issue, you do have the option of making your game free. Afterward, you can give players the opportunity to purchase things or show advertisements when playing the project.

That's not to say that having a bunch of advertisements in a free game is the best option either. Having too many ads, or even the wrong kind of ads, can drive users away, which can be even worse. Many developers have their own opinions on whether it's a good idea to use ads or not, but that's not the purpose of this chapter. In this chapter, we will look into different options available to us for advertising over the course of our game and show how to implement them, should you choose to add the content to your game.

In this chapter, we will integrate the Unity Ads framework into our project and learn how to create both simple and complex versions of advertisements. This is done by first setting up Unity's Ads system, then creating a simple ad before adding additional callback options. We then see how we can give additional incentives to view ads utilizing opt-in rewards and adding a cooldown timer to prevent the players from watching too many ads.

This chapter will be split into a number of topics. It will contain a simple step-by-step process, from beginning to end. The following is the outline of our tasks:

- Setting up Unity Ads
- Creating a simple ad
- Adding in ad callback methods
- Opt-in advertisements with rewards
- Integrating a cooldown timer

Technical requirements

This book utilizes Unity 2020.1.0f1 and Unity Hub 2.3.1 but the steps should work with minimal changes in future versions of the editor. If you would like to download the exact version used in this book, and there is a new version out, you can visit Unity's download archive at `https://unity3d.com/get-unity/download/archive`. You can also find the system requirements for Unity at `https://docs.unity3d.com/2020.1/Documentation/Manual/system-requirements.html` in the **Unity Editor system requirements** section. You can find the code files present in this chapter on GitHub at `https://github.com/PacktPublishing/Unity-2020-Mobile-Game-Development-Second-Edition/tree/master/Chapter%2005`.

Setting up Unity Ads

Unity Ads is a video ad network for iOS and Android that can monetize your existing player base by showing ads. Unity Ads offers video ads that can be shown as either rewarded or non-rewarded placements. As the name suggests, rewarded ads will give the users a reward or incentive that will help them while playing the game. Before we can enable Unity Ads, we must first enable Unity's Services suite. To activate Unity Services, you have to link your project to a Unity Services Project ID, which is how Unity can tell the difference between the different projects you are creating, so let's see how to do that:

1. Open the **Services** window by going to **Window** | **General** | **Services**, pressing *Ctrl + O*, or by clicking on the button that has a cloud on it in the toolbar on the right-hand side:

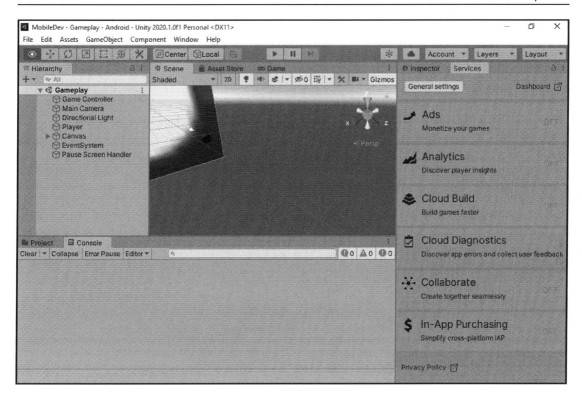

2. At the top left, you'll see a button that says **General Settings**. Click on it and a new window will pop up and you should see something similar to the following:

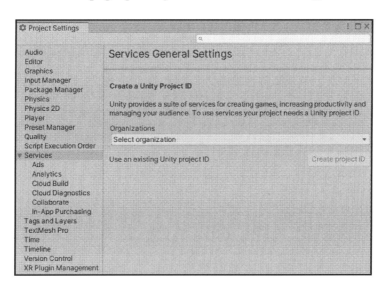

Assuming that you haven't worked with Unity Services before, you will need to create an **Organization** and **Project Name**.

3. Click on the dropdown and select your username and then click on the **Create project ID** button. The project name is automatically created according to the name of your project when you first created it, but you can change this in the **Settings** section of the **Services** window.

> Unity automatically creates an organization using your account username; however, if you need to make another one, you can do so at `https://id.unity.com/organizations`.

You can now access the analytics services either by clicking on the inner sections of the menu that popped up, or through the **Services** window in the Unity Editor, which contains a number of sections that we will be using over the course of this book.

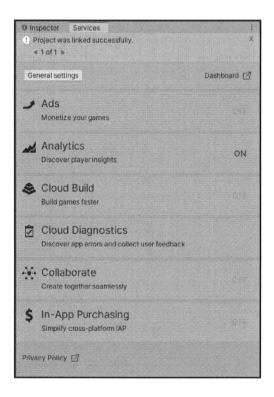

4. At the top of the menu that pops up, you'll see a button called **Ads**. Go ahead and click on it to enter the menu. From there, click on the toggle in the top-right corner to turn Ads on. You'll then be asked questions about your game. If your game is not directed toward children, go ahead and select **No** from the drop-down menu and then click on the **Save** button, otherwise select **Yes** and then click on **Save**:

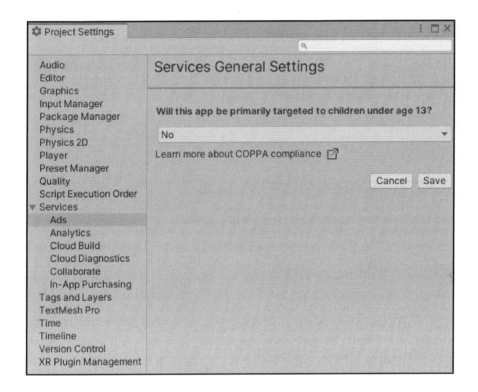

When you indicate whether your game is designed for children under the age of 13 years, ads will not be behaviorally targeted to users in your game. Behavioral targeting can yield higher **effective cost per thousand impressions (eCPMs)** by showing ads that are more relevant to your users, but its use is prohibited with users under the age of 13 due to **Children's Online Privacy Protection Rule Act (COPPA)** regulations. For more info on this, check out `https://forum.unity.com/threads/age-designation.326930/`.

5. Then, when brought to the **Ads** menu, click on the **Off** button to turn it on. Ads should be toggled on at this point. Then, click on the checkbox for **Enable test mode**. This will ensure that the ads displayed are just for testing:

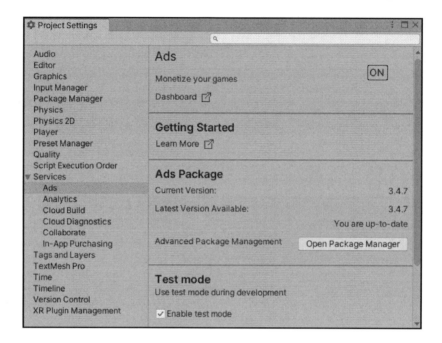

 It is against Unity Ads' terms of service to distribute live ads to beta testers. If they were to click on or install any of the advertised games, their activity would be monetized and the automated fraud system would flag the game for fraud and disable it. That's why we keep test mode enabled until the game is ready to launch.

6. When you are ready to deploy your game to an app store, make sure to uncheck the **Enable test mode** option. If you scroll down, you'll see a property called the Game Id; note down those values as we will need them in order to initialize Unity Ads at the start of the game.

7. To get started, it would be a good idea for us to have all of the ad-related behavior to share a script, so we will create a new class called `UnityAd Controller` by going to the **Project** window, opening the `Assets/ Scripts` folder, and selecting **Create | C# Script**.

8. Open up the file in the IDE of your choice, and use the following code:

```
using UnityEngine;

using UnityEngine.Advertisements; // Advertisement class

public class UnityAdController : MonoBehaviour
{
    /// <summary>
    /// If we should show ads or not
    /// </summary>
    public static bool showAds = true;

    /// <summary>
    /// Replace with your actual gameId
    /// </summary>
    private string gameId = "1234567";

    /// <summary>
    /// If the game is in test mode or not
    /// </summary>
    private bool testMode = true;

    /// <summary>
    /// Unity Ads must be initialized or else ads will not work
    ///     /// properly
    /// </summary>
    private void Start()
    {
        // No need to initialize if it already is done
        if(!Advertisement.isInitialized)
        {
            Advertisement.Initialize(gameId, testMode);
        }
    }

}
```

The preceding code does a number of things. We first state that we are using the `UnityEngine.Advertisments` namespace to get access to the `Advertisement` class. If you only intend to implement video, interstitial, and banner ads for your monetization strategy, this is the API that Unity suggests be used. In addition to this, in order to use Unity Ads you must call the `Advertisement.Initialize` function, which I do inside of the `Start` function of this object.

9. From the Project window, open up the **MainMenu** scene and once inside, create an empty GameObject (**GameObject | Create Empty**) and name it `Unity Ad Manager`. Once created, attach the **Unity Ad Controller** script to it:

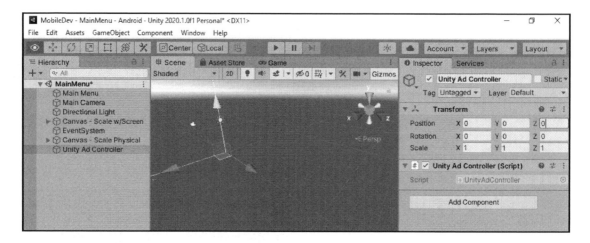

Because this object is spawned at the **MainMenu** level, it is loaded at the beginning of the game, which is perfect for what we will use it for.

At this point, we have finished the setup process required to utilize Unity Ads by enabling Unity Analytics and then turning the Ads menu on. With the setup process complete, we can now proceed to actually adding a simple ad to our project.

Displaying a simple ad

Advertisements are a possible way to generate revenue from players playing your game. As mentioned previously, Unity Ads has two different types of ads that we can display: simple and rewarded. Simple ads are easy to use, hence the name, and allow users to have simple full-screen interstitial ads. This can be really useful for when moving between levels or perhaps for when the player wants to restart the game. Let's see how we can implement that feature now. Implement the following steps:

1. To get started, we will need to add a new function to the `UnityAdController` class:

```
public static void ShowAd()
{
    if (Advertisement.IsReady())
    {
```

```
            Advertisement.Show();
        }
    }
```

Here, we created a static method called ShowAd. We made this static so that we can access the function without actually having to create an instance of this class in order to call this function. We then check whether an advertisement is ready, and if it is, we will call the Show() function to display it on the screen.

2. Save your script and then open up the MainMenuBehaviour file and add the following highlighted code:

```
/// <summary>
/// Will load a new scene upon being called
/// </summary>
/// <param name="levelName">The name of the level we want
/// to go to</param>
public void LoadLevel(string levelName)
{
    SceneManager.LoadScene(levelName);

    if (UnityAdController.showAds)
    {
        // Show an ad
        UnityAdController.ShowAd();
    }
}
```

This will have an advertisement play each time we call the LoadLevel function if it is supported. We also added a new parameter with a default value. The nice thing about this is that we can optionally decide when we want to show an ad. For instance, we may want to make it so that when we restart the game we don't play an ad.

3. Now let's see this in action. Play the game and then click on the **Play** button:

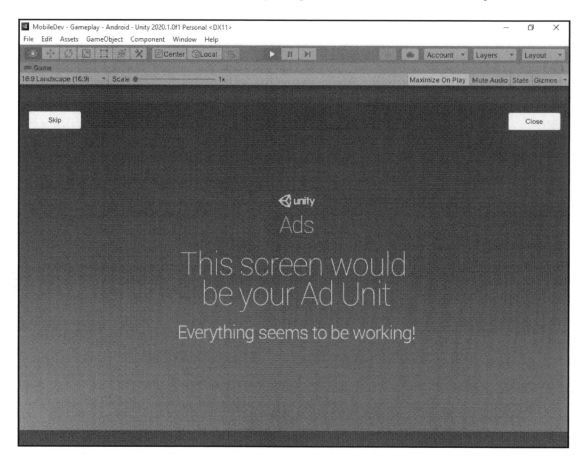

As you can note in the preceding screenshot, the ad works correctly. This screen is what is shown when playing the game in the editor. It has buttons to allow us to test whether a player skips or watches a video in full. When we disable test mode, we will then see live video ads.

You'll also see this happen if, once in the game, you open the pause menu and click on the **Main Menu** button.

If this does not work and/or show up, check the **Player Settings** menu you learned about previously and ensure that your current platform is set to Android or iOS.

This provides us with the easiest way of getting an ad to show up in our game, but there are still a number of things we need to do to ensure our ads work properly, which we will be looking at next.

Another type of ad that can be used is banner ads. These work similarly to default ads but you'd call `Advertisement.Banner.Show` instead of `Advertisement.Show`. For more information on that, check out `https://docs.unity3d.com/Packages/com.unity.ads@3.2/manual/MonetizationBannerAdsUnity.html`.

Utilizing ad callback methods

The code we wrote for the `LoadLevel` function works perfectly fine when we go to the main menu of the game; however, if we dive into the game itself from the main menu, the game will still be going on in the background with the ad blocking the player from playing the game.

When running your app on an actual mobile device, the Unity Player will pause while Unity Ads are shown. However, if you are testing in the Unity Editor, the game is not paused while the placeholder ads are shown. However, we can simulate that behavior ourselves using the `Advertisement.ShowOptions` class.

We will pause the game when an ad is shown and then resume the game once the ad is finished. To do so, perform the following steps:

1. Let's first open up the `UnityAdController` class and update the `Start` function to the following:

```
/// <summary>
/// Unity Ads must be initialized or else ads will not work
   /// properly
/// </summary>
private void Start()
{
    // No need to initialize if it already is done
    if(!Advertisement.isInitialized)
    {
        // Use the functions provided by this to allow custom
```

```
        // behavior
        // on the ads
        Advertisement.AddListener(this);
        Advertisement.Initialize(gameId, testMode);
    }
}
```

The `Advertisement.AddListener` function takes in an `IUnityAdsListener` object. The `I` at the start of the name here indicates that this type is an interface. This is a keyword in C# designating something like a contract, promising that whatever you provide to this function contains the functionalities required by the interface.

2. Now update the class definition to the following:

```
public class UnityAdController : MonoBehaviour, IUnityAdsListener
```

By adding the comma and then `IUnityAdsListener`, we are stating that we will implement the methods provided by the `IUnityAdsListener` interface. To see what those methods are, from your IDE, you may be able to right-click on the `IUnityAdsListener` option and select **Go to Definition**. From there, you may see something like the following:

```
#region Assembly UnityEngine.Advertisements, Version=3.4.6.0,
Culture=neutral, PublicKeyToken=null
//
C:\Users\Desktop\MobileDev\Library\ScriptAssemblies\UnityEngine.Adv
e
    rtisements.dll
#endregion

using UnityEngine.Advertisements;

namespace UnityEngine.Advertisements
{
    public interface IUnityAdsListener
    {
        void OnUnityAdsDidError(string message);
        void OnUnityAdsDidFinish(string placementId, ShowResult
            showResult);
        void OnUnityAdsDidStart(string placementId);
        void OnUnityAdsReady(string placementId);
    }
}
```

So we will need to create four methods inside our own class with the exact same names, parameters, and return types.

For more information on interfaces and how they work in C#, check out `https://www.tutorialsteacher.com/csharp/csharp-interface`.

3. After doing this, we need to implement the functions used by the interface:

```
#region IUnityAdsListener Methods
public void OnUnityAdsReady(string placementId)
{
    // Actions to take when an Ad is ready to display, such as
    // enabling a rewards button
}

public void OnUnityAdsDidError(string message)
{
    // If there was an error, display it
    Debug.LogError(message);
}

public void OnUnityAdsDidStart(string placementId)
{
    // Pause game while ad is shown
    PauseScreenBehaviour.paused = true;
    Time.timeScale = 0f;
}

public void OnUnityAdsDidFinish(string placementId, ShowResult
    showResult)
{
    // Unpause when ad is over
    PauseScreenBehaviour.paused = false;
    Time.timeScale = 1f;
}
#endregion
```

Each of these four functions does something when we are creating ads. Of note is the `OnUnityAdsDidStart` method, where we pause the game, and then the `OnUnityAdsDidFinish` method where we unpause. We utilize a region here in order to make it easier to compartmentalize our code.

For more information on the `#region` block, check out `https://docs.microsoft.com/en-us/dotnet/csharp/language-reference/preprocessor-directives/preprocessor-region`.

4. Next, we will make it so that `PauseScreenBehaviour` doesn't override this new change. So, we will replace the `Start()` function with the following:

```
private void Start()
{
    if(!UnityAdController.showAds)
    {
        // If not showing ads, just start the game
        SetPauseMenu(false);
    }
}
```

Performing the preceding snippet is important because otherwise the game will immediately be turned off when the level loads in the `Start` function after we tell the game to pause, which is called after the level loads. This is needed for the PC version of the game, as there is nothing else to unpause the static value.

5. Save our scripts and start the game up again:

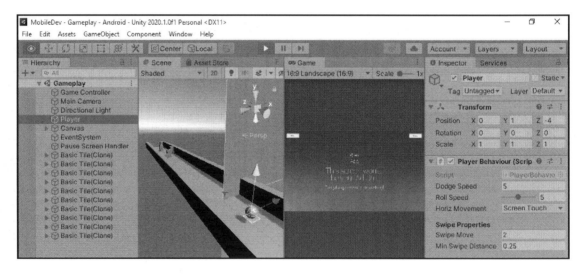

With that, when we transition from the main menu to the game, we will pause the game until we are ready to jump in. Now that we can see how to work basic advertisements that aren't optional, let's give players the opportunity to see an ad for some kind of benefit.

Opt-in advertisements with rewards

According to AdColony, the most recommended form of mobile game ads by 58% of mobile developers is the rewarded video ad. By that, we're referring to making ads an opt-in experience where players choose to see an ad and receive some kind of bonus in return. That way, users feel it's a choice for them whether or not to watch the ad, and they feel more compelled to watch it because they will get something out of it.

Rewarded ad placements typically yield higher **effective Cost Per 1000 Impressions (eCPMs)** since they offer more engagement from users by allowing them to opt in before watching an ad in exchange for some in-game reward.

 If you're interested in learning more about why reward ads are recommended, check out `https://www.adcolony.com/blog/2016/04/26/ the-top-ads-recommended-by-mobile-game-developers/`.

In our game, we could add the choice of restarting the game or seeing an ad to continue the game. This means that we will need to create some kind of menu in order for the player to select whether or not to see the ad, so let's add that in next:

1. Stop the game if you haven't done so already, and then open up the `Gameplay` scene. Afterward, let's create a **Game Over** menu by first going to the **Hierarchy** window and expanding the **Canvas** game object if you have not done so already. Then, select the `Pause Menu` object and duplicate it by pressing *Ctrl + D*. Rename this new object `Game Over` and then toggle it on so that we can see it. To make it easier to see, feel free to toggle to the 2D mode we used previously when creating the UI elements of our game.

2. Next, expand the `Game Over` object and both of the **Panel** children, then change the **Pause Menu Contents** object's name to `Game Over Contents` and change the child **Text** object's **Text** component to say `Game Over` instead.

3. Now, change the **Resume** button to say `Continue (Play Ad)` and change the button object's name to `Continue Button`:

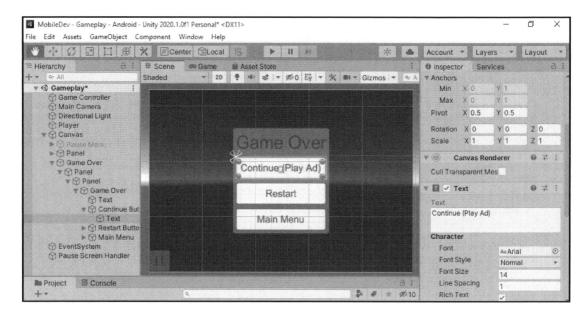

4. We'll first need to update the `ObstacleBehaviour` script to handle it; add the following highlighted code:

```
using UnityEngine;
using UnityEngine.UI; // Button

public class ObstacleBehaviour : MonoBehaviour
{

    [Tooltip("How long to wait before restarting the game")]
    public float waitTime = 2.0f;

    public GameObject explosion;

    private GameObject player;

    private void OnCollisionEnter(Collision collision)
    {
        // First check if we collided with the player
        if (collision.gameObject.GetComponent<PlayerBehaviour>())
        {
            // Destroy (Hide) the player
            collision.gameObject.SetActive(false);
```

```
        player = collision.gameObject;

        // Call the function ResetGame after waitTime
            // has passed
        Invoke("ResetGame", waitTime);
    }
}

/// <summary>
/// Will restart the currently loaded level
/// </summary>
private void ResetGame()
{
    //Bring up restart menu
    var go = GetGameOverMenu();
    go.SetActive(true);

    // Get our continue button
    var buttons = go.transform.GetComponentsInChildren<Button>
        ();
    Button continueButton = null;

    foreach (var button in buttons)
    {
        if (button.gameObject.name == "Continue Button")
        {
            continueButton = button;
            break;
        }
    }

    // If we found the button we can use it
    if (continueButton)
    {
        if (UnityAdController.showAds)
        {
            // If player clicks on button we want to play ad
                // and then continue
            continueButton.onClick.AddListener
                (UnityAdController.ShowAd);
            UnityAdController.obstacle = this;
        }
        else
        {
            // If can't play an ad, no need for continue button
            continueButton.gameObject.SetActive(false);
        }
```

```
        }
    }

    /// <summary>
    /// If the object is tapped, we spawn an explosion and
    /// destroy this object
    /// </summary>
    private void PlayerTouch()
    {
        if (explosion != null)
        {
            var particles = Instantiate(explosion,
                transform.position,
            Quaternion.identity);
            Destroy(particles, 1.0f);
        }

        Destroy(this.gameObject);
    }

    /// <summary>
    /// Retrieves the Game Over menu game object
    /// </summary>
    /// <returns>The Game Over menu object</returns>
    GameObject GetGameOverMenu()
    {
        var canvas = GameObject.Find("Canvas").transform;
        return canvas.Find("Game Over").gameObject;
    }

    /// <summary>
    /// Handles resetting the game if needed
    /// </summary>
    public void Continue()
    {
        var go = GetGameOverMenu();
        go.SetActive(false);
        player.SetActive(true);

        // Explode this as well (So if we respawn player can
            // continue)
        PlayerTouch();
    }

}
```

In this instance, we remove the destruction of our player and we hide them instead. The reason we do this is so that if the player decides to play the ad, we can then unhide it and resume the game as normal. We also destroy what the player hit. So, if we do restart the game, then the player will be able to start off from right where they initially began. With that in mind, we also created a Continue function that will set up the game to be continued if we need to do so.

5. Open up the UnityAdController script and add the following variable declaration at the top of the file:

```
// For holding the obstacle for continuing the game
public static ObstacleBehaviour obstacle;
```

6. Afterward, staying in the UnityAdController script, update the OnUnityAdsDidFinish function to the following:

```
public void OnUnityAdsDidFinish(string placementId, ShowResult
showResult)
{
    // If there is an obstacle, we can remove it to continue the
    // game
    if (obstacle != null && showResult == ShowResult.Finished)
    {
        obstacle.Continue();
    }

    // Unpause when ad is over
    PauseScreenBehaviour.paused = false;
    Time.timeScale = 1f;
}
```

Our additions first check whether there is an obstacle that our player hit. If there is, we then check the value of the showResult variable that is provided by the function. We utilize the ShowResult enum to verify that the player actually completed the ad and did not click on the **Skip** button.

7. We want to make sure that Unity's Advertisement system works in both scenes — so we can copy paste the **Unity Ad Manager** object from the **Main Menu** and we could also add it through code. To do so, open up the GameController script and add the following highlighted code to the Start function:

```
Private void Start ()
// If there is no UnityAdController, we can add it through code

if(!GameObject.FindObjectOfType<UnityAdController>())
 {
     var adController = new GameObject("Unity Ad Manager");
     adController.AddComponent<UnityAdController>();
 }
// Set our starting point
    nextTileLocation = startPoint;
```

8. Save your scripts and return to the Unity Editor.

9. Click on the Game Over object and disable it, save our scene, and then open the **Main Menu** scene and dive into the game.

If you do not see the ads there, it may be due to the fact that Unity Ads were not initialized. This is done in the **Main Menu** scene so you'll need to go there first before you see the ads.

At this point, when we die in the game, we'll be given a **Game Over** screen:

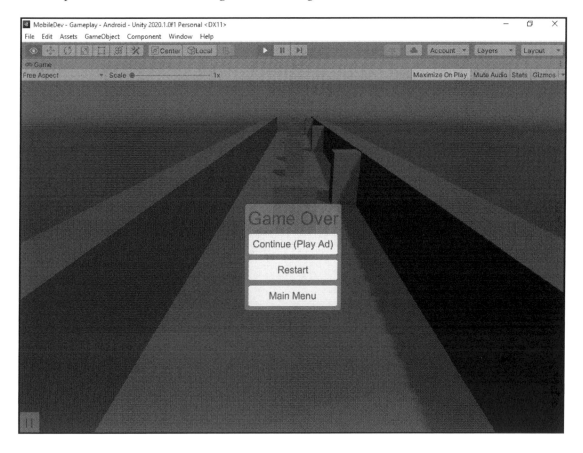

If we click on **Continue (Play Ad)**, we will have an ad play. If the player skips it, nothing will happen, but if they watch all the way through, it should bring us back into the game as if nothing happened:

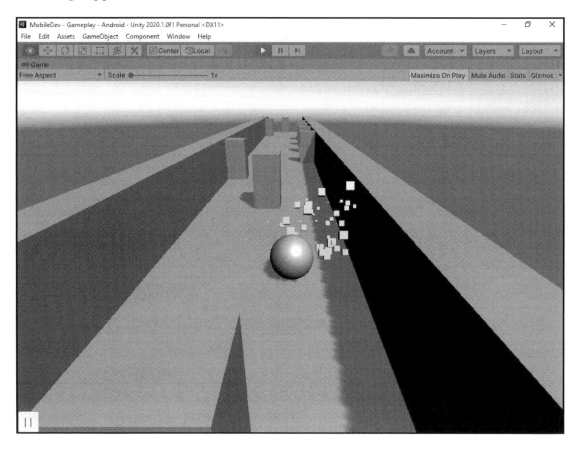

With that, our ad system is working correctly. We now have seen how we can integrate the use of ads into our gameplay and provide a reason for players to actually want to see this content.

Adding in a cooldown timer

Ads are great for developers; however, according to Unity's Monetization FAQs, each user is only able to view 25 ads per day. With that in mind, we will likely want to make it so that players can only trigger ads every once in a while. This also has the benefit of making players want to come back to our game after a period of time.

For more information on Unity's Monetization FAQs, check
out `https://unityads.unity3d.com/help/faq/monetization`.

We will now program it so that our **Continue** option will only work once in a while with a
short delay that we can easily customize if we like:

1. To get started, go back to the `UnityAdController` script and add the following
   new variable to it, shown in the highlighted code:

```
using System; // DateTime
using UnityEngine;
using UnityEngine.Advertisements; // Advertisement class

public class UnityAdController : MonoBehaviour, IUnityAdsListener
{
    /// <summary>
    /// If we should show ads or not
    /// </summary>
    public static bool showAds = true;

    // Nullable type
    public static DateTime? nextRewardTime = null;

    // For holding the obstacle for continuing the game
    public static ObstacleBehaviour obstacle;

    // Rest of UnityAdController...
```

The `nextRewardTime` variable is of the `DateTime` type, which we haven't talked
about previously. Basically, it's a structure that represents a point in time that we
can compare to other points in time, and is built into .NET Framework. We'll use
this to store the time (if any) that needs to pass before the player is able to play
another ad. Note that `DateTime` is part of the `System` namespace. That is why we
added the `using System;` line in the preceding code as well.

 For more information on the `DateTime` class, check
out `https://msdn.microsoft.com/en-us/library/system.datetime(v=v
s.110).aspx`.

You may notice the ? next to the type of this variable. When we do this, we create what's called a nullable type. The advantage of using them is that they can be null in addition to having normal values. We do this so that we don't have to fill in a default value just for the sake of having one.

 For more information on nullable types, check out https://www.tutorialspoint.com/csharp/csharp_nullables.htm.

2. To add a time delay between ad showings, we will create a new function for this purpose:

```
public static void ShowRewardAd()
{
    nextRewardTime = DateTime.Now.AddSeconds(15);

    ShowAd();
}
```

Now when we show a reward ad, we set nextRewardTime to 15 seconds from when the function is called. Of course, we can just as easily set this to minutes or hours using the AddMinutes and AddHours functions.

3. Save your script and then open up the ObstacleBehaviour script. At the top of the script, add the following new using statements:

```
using System; // DateTime
using System.Collections; // IEnumerator
```

4. Afterward, we will need to modify the bottom part of the ResetGame() function to have the following changes highlighted in bold:

```
// Rest of ResetGame above...

// If we found the button we can use it
if (continueButton)
{
    if (UnityAdController.showAds)
    {
        // If player clicks on button we want to play ad and
        // then continue
        StartCoroutine(ShowContinue(continueButton));
    }
    else
    {
```

```
        // If can't play an ad, no need for continue button
        continueButton.gameObject.SetActive(false);
        }
    }
}
```

Now, instead of just adding a listener to this button, we have replaced it with a call to the `StartCoroutine` function, which takes in a function that we haven't written yet. I think it's probably a good idea to talk a little bit about coroutines before we actually write one.

A coroutine is like a function that has the ability to pause execution and continue where it left off after a period of time. By default, a coroutine is resumed on the frame after we start to `yield`, but it is also possible to introduce a time delay using the `WaitForSeconds` function to specify how long you want to wait for before it's called again.

5. Next, use the following script for the `ShowContinue` function:

```
public IEnumerator ShowContinue(Button contButton)
{
    while (true)
    {
        var btnText = contButton.GetComponentInChildren<Text>();

        // Check if we haven't reached the next reward time yet
        // (if one exists)
        var rewardTime = UnityAdController.nextRewardTime;

        bool validTime = rewardTime.HasValue;
        bool timePassed = true;

        if (validTime)
        {
            timePassed = DateTime.Now > rewardTime.Value;
        }

        if (!timePassed)
        {
            // Unable to click on the button
            contButton.interactable = false;

            // Get the time remaining until we get to the next
            //   reward time
            TimeSpan remaining = rewardTime.Value - DateTime.Now;

            // Get the time left in the following format 99:99
```

```
        var countdownText = string.Format("{0:D2}:{1:D2}",
                            remaining.Minutes,
                            remaining.Seconds);

        // Set our button's text to reflect the new time
        btnText.text = countdownText;

        // Come back after 1 second and check again
        yield return new WaitForSeconds(1f);
    }
    else
    {
        // It's valid to click the button now
        contButton.interactable = true;

        // If player clicks on button we want to play ad and
          // then continue
        contButton.onClick.AddListener
                    (UnityAdController.ShowRewardAd);
        UnityAdController.obstacle = this;

        // Change text to its original version
        btnText.text = "Continue (Play Ad)";

        // We can now leave the coroutine
        break;
    }
}
```

This coroutine will do a number of things, starting off by entering a `while` (`true`) loop. Now, usually, this is a very bad thing, as it would cause an infinite loop, but we break out of the loop if we have no reward time set or if we've passed the time set in the `nextRewardTime` variable. If not, we will figure out how much time is left before that time has passed and will change the button's text to display it. We then use the `WaitForSeconds` function to pause execution and come back after 1 second has passed.

 If you're interested in learning more about the behind-the-scenes aspects of how coroutines work, Drew Campbell has written a neat article on it at https://gamedevunboxed.com/unity-coroutines-how-do-they-work/.

6. Save all of our scripts and dive back into Unity and play the game:

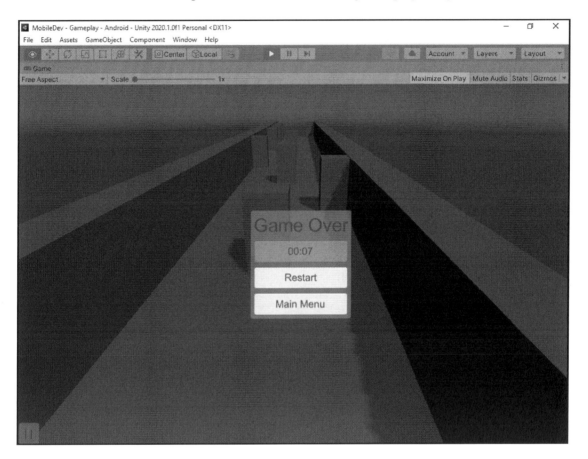

Upon restarting the game once, you'll see that if we try to do so again, we are brought to a delay screen. After the time gets down to 0, the player will then be able to continue once again.

 For additional information on the best practices for rewarded ads like this, check out https://docs.unity3d.com/Packages/com.unity.ads@3.2/ manual/MonetizationResourcesBestPracticesAds.html.

Summary

With that, we've got a good foundation on how to add ads to our game. Hopefully, you can see how easy it is to implement and can think of new ways to engage players to have the best experience possible. Over the course of this chapter, we discovered how to set up Unity Ads. We then saw how we could create simple ads and learned how to react to the player's actions by implementing the `IUnityAdsListener` interface. Afterward, we saw how we can add rewards for players using opt-in advertisements in the game, and we added a cooldown to the system to make the game less annoying for players. With these newly acquired skills, you should be able to add advertisements and gain additional revenue from your own games that you create in the future.

While this is a valid way to monetize our games, we will dive into the other more popular form of in-game monetization in the next chapter: in-app purchases.

6
Implementing In-App Purchases

As mentioned in Chapter 5, *Advertising Using Unity Ads*, there are many options out there when it comes to selling your game on a mobile platform. If you decide to go free-to-play, in addition to showing ads, there is also the ability to sell people additional content and/or advantages through the use of **In-App Purchases (IAP)**. This can be a way to engage users of your game and convert them from a free player to a paid one.

Typically, these can be options such as removing ads or offering themes to players, but you can also do things such as unlock new levels and add additional content so that people addicted to your game will be clamoring to give you more of their time. Alternatively, you can also think of your IAPs as items that players will want to buy in order to enhance their gameplay experiences, such as power-ups and upgrades.

In this chapter, we will integrate Unity's In-App Purchasing system into our project and take a look at how to create an IAP that is for consumable content as well as permanent unlocks. By the end of the chapter, we will see how to set up Unity's IAP system, create our first possible purchasable item, and then we will see how to restore purchases on certain devices before seeing additional resources for the various app stores that exist.

This chapter is split into a number of topics. It contains a simple step-by-step process from beginning to end. The following is the outline of our tasks:

- Setting up Unity IAP
- Creating our first purchase

- Adding a button to restore purchases
- Configuring purchases for the stores of your choice

Technical requirements

This book utilizes Unity 2020.1.0f1 and Unity Hub 2.3.1, but the steps should work with minimal changes in future versions of the editor. If you would like to download the exact version used in this book, and there is a new version out, you can visit Unity's download archive at `https://unity3d.com/get-unity/download/archive`. You can also find the system requirements for Unity at `https://docs.unity3d.com/2020.1/Documentation/Manual/system-requirements.html` in the **Unity Editor system requirements** section.

You can find the code files present in this chapter on GitHub at `https://github.com/PacktPublishing/Unity-2020-Mobile-Game-Development-Second-Edition/tree/master/Chapter%2006`.

Setting up Unity IAP

Unity IAP is a service that allows us to sell a variety of different items to players within our game projects and is currently supported by the iOS App Store, Mac App Store, Google Play, Windows Store, Amazon Appstore, and more, by default. So, using this, we can easily sell our items in many different places. We have already set up Unity Services in Chapter 5, *Advertising Using Unity Ads*, so this will be a lot easier to get going. Perform the following steps to add Unity IAP:

1. Open the **Services** window by going to **Window** | **Services** or by clicking on the **Cloud** button in the toolbar.

 Assuming that you are following along from the preceding chapter, we should already have services set up. If not, check out the *Setting up Unity Ads* section in Chapter 5, *Advertising Using Unity Ads*, for an explanation on how to do so.

2. From the **Services** menu, scroll down to the **In-App Purchasing** item. You will note that it's currently off:

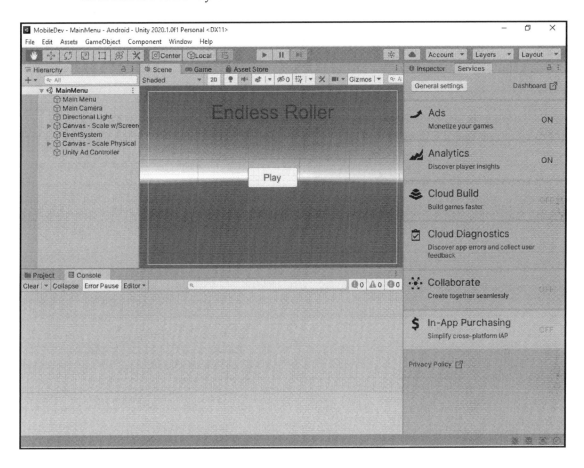

3. Click on the **In-App Purchasing** button to open the menu up and then click on the **Off** button to turn it on. If all went well, you should see the menu change to something similar to the following:

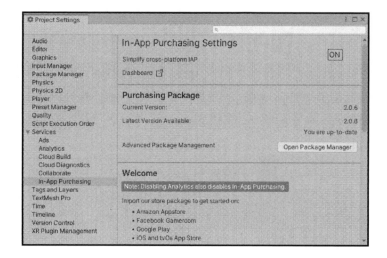

4. Scroll down and you should be able to see, at the end of the **Welcome** section, a button that says **Import**. Unity IAP requires us to import a package for us to create IAPs, so let's go ahead and click on the **Import** button and wait for it to finish:

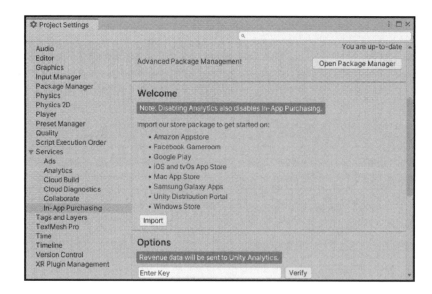

5. At this point, we get a popup saying that it needs to determine whether our project is configured properly and asking whether we want to install it:

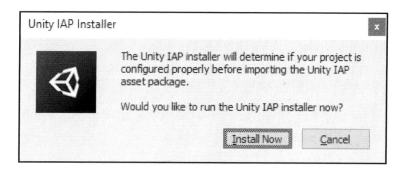

6. Go ahead and click on the **Install Now** function. You'll see a new window pop up called the **Unity IAP Installer**. Read through the instructions and then press the **Next >>** button:

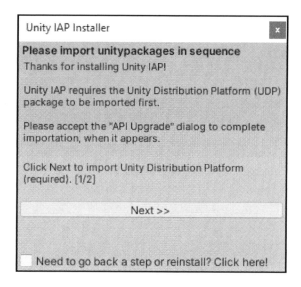

7. You'll then see an **Import Unity Package** dialog for the **UDP** system. Go ahead and click **Import**:

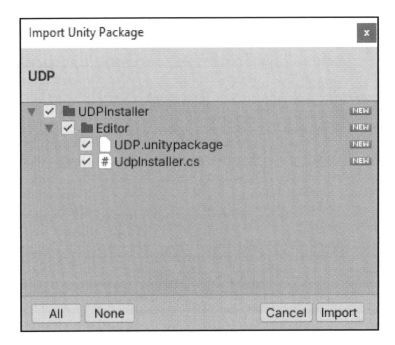

When importing either of these upcoming packages, it may say that an API update is required. This is likely because the version of Unity that you're using is newer than the last update of the Unity IAP API. Go ahead and click on the **I Made a Backup. Go ahead!** button and wait for it to finish.

8. If all goes well, you can move on to the next step. Once you continue, you should see an **Import Unity Package** window come up. Click on **Import** and wait for it to finish:

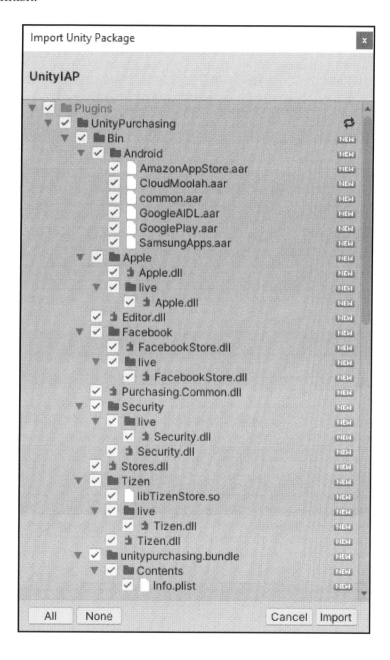

9. If all went well, you can then click on the **Close, and clean up installer scripts >>** option to end the installation process:

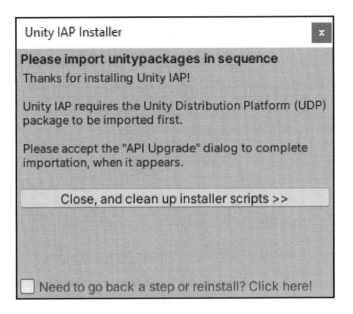

 If you encounter an issue with installing the Unity IAP system (Unity crashed on me the first time I attempted to do so), when you come up to the first window, check the **Need to go back a step or reinstall? Click here!** option and install that way instead, going through both packages in order.

You'll note that when it finishes, you'll have a new folder named Plugins that has been created along with some additional folders. At this point, you may see a window asking to install the Unity IAP package.

 If, for some reason, you encounter any errors at this point in the Console window, try to first close and then open the Services window again and check whether **Unity IAP** is enabled. If that doesn't work, disconnect and reconnect it to the internet and then sign back into Unity Services and then re-enable Unity IAP.

Once you come back, you should note that both **Analytics** and **In-App Purchasing** are now set to **ON** and the Unity IAP is up to date:

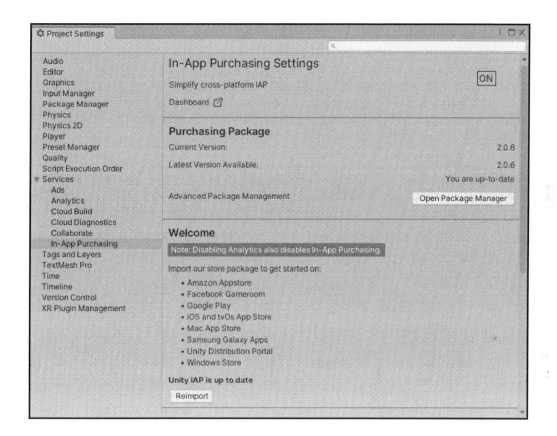

 The IAP package is created externally from the main engine itself because the code is meant to be extremely flexible and can be updated to fit any policies that are needed. We can then just update the package instead of having to update it to the latest version of Unity, which can be very important when working on a large project.

Now that we have the IAP system brought into our project, we can now utilize it to create your first purchasable object for your players.

Creating our first purchase

To make our first in-app purchase, we will make use of a feature of Unity that was just added to our project, Codeless IAP. It is called Codeless IAP because you do not need to write any code for the actual IAP transaction, just the script that defines what users get if they make the purchase. It's by far the easiest way to integrate in-app purchases in Unity games and a great way to start trying IAPs in our project.

One of the most common in-app purchases is the ability to disable advertisements in mobile games. Using the following steps, let's add that functionality by creating a button that, when clicked, will disable advertisements:

1. Open up our Main Menu level by going to the **Project** window, opening the Assets/Scenes folder, and then double-clicking on the MainMenu file.

2. From there, return to the **Scene** window if not there already and then click on the **2D** button to go into 2D mode since we'll be working with UI.

3. We will first need to have something to sell and to do that, we will use the IAP Catalog, which we can access by going to **Window** | **Unity IAP** | **IAP Catalog**:

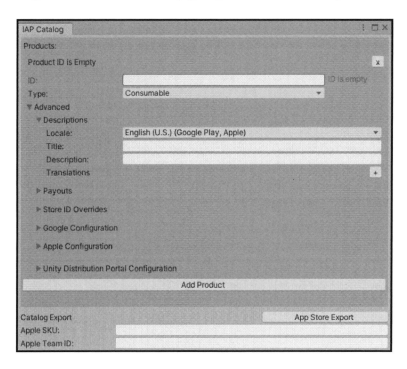

4. Now, the first thing we'll need to do is create an ID for our product, which is how we identify our product in different app stores. In our case, let's go with removeAds. Then, under **Type**, change it to **Non Consumable**:

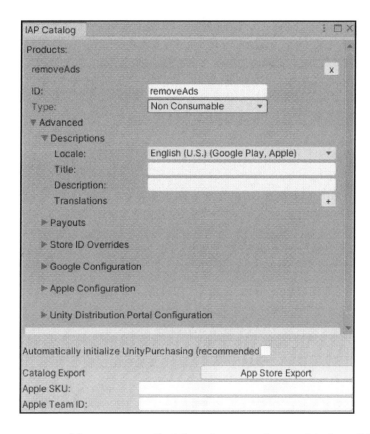

By non-consumable, we mean that the players only need to buy this once, and the game will keep that in mind for later. The others are consumable, meaning that they are used for things that can be bought over and over again, such as special power-ups and subscriptions. These give access to some kind of content for a period of time, possibly recurring until a user cancels them.

5. Next, we can close out of the **IAP Catalog** by clicking on **X** in the top-right corner of the window.

6. Select the **Canvas - Scale Physical** object in the **Hierarchy** window. From there, select **Window | Unity IAP | Create IAP Button**, and you should see a new button created in our scene:

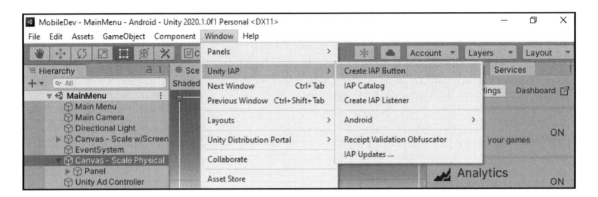

This button will be used to perform an in-app purchase to remove the ads in the game. To ensure that both the **Start** and **Remove Ads** buttons show up correctly on the screen, we will create a menu that can hold both of them. This means creating another panel as a child of our Safe Area panel.

7. From the Hierarchy window, select our **Panel** object and, in the **Inspector** window, rename it to SafeAreaHolder.

8. Afterward, create a child **Panel** object of SafeAreaHolder and have it fill the entire screen as we did before. Add a **Vertical Layout Group** component to it. From there, change the **Child Alignment** to **Middle Center** and set all of the **Padding** and **Spacing** to 10.

9. Then, add a **Content Size Fitter** component and set the **Vertical Fit** and **Horizontal Fit** field to **Preferred Size**:

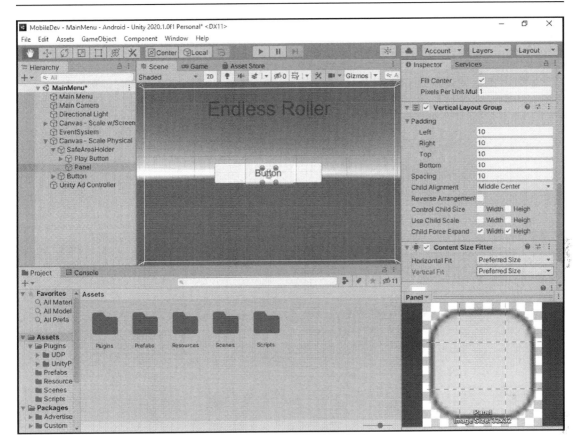

10. Rename the newly added button to `Remove Ads Button` and then add a **Horiztonal Layout Group** component to it with all of the **Padding** set to `10` and check **Width** and **Height** to the **Child Controls Size** property. Also, add a **Content Size Fitter** component to it with both **Fits** set to **Preferred Size**. Then, in the child **Text** object's **Text** component, change the **Text** property to show `Remove Ads` instead.

For a reminder on what these instructions mean and what each step does, check out `Chapter 4`, *Resolution-Independent UI*.

11. Finally, drag and drop the two buttons onto the Panel object, with the **Play** button in the top half and the **Remove Ads** button below it, as follows:

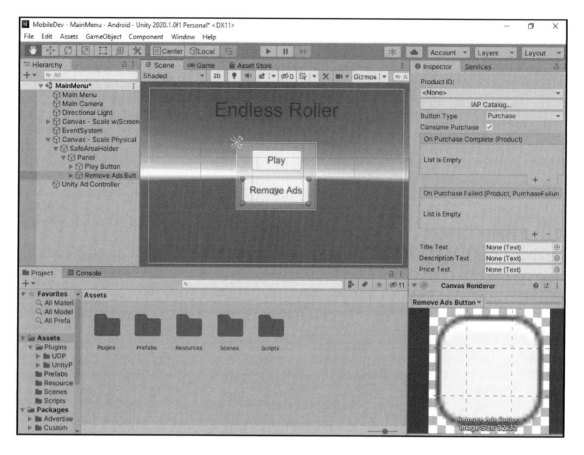

12. Next, with the **Remove Ads** object selected, move to the **Inspector** tab and scroll down to the **IAP Button** component. Under **Product ID:** click the dropdown, and select **removeAds**. You'll note that the IAP Button class has an **On Purchase Complete (Product)** function that works similar to **On Click** that we've used with Button components in the past. With that in mind, we will need to create a function that we would like to call when the player presses the button.

In Chapter 5, *Advertising Using Unity Ads*, we created a static variable inside the UnityAdController class called showAds. We will use this variable to check whether we should show ads.

13. We will need to open up the `MainMenuBehaviour` script and add the following functions to the class:

```
public void DisableAds()
{
    UnityAdController.showAds = false;

    // Used to store that we shouldn't show ads
    PlayerPrefs.SetInt("Show Ads", 0);
}

protected virtual void Start()
{
    // Initialize the showAds variable
    UnityAdController.showAds = (PlayerPrefs.GetInt("Show Ads", 1)
        == 1);
}
```

Here we are using Unity's `PlayerPrefs` system in order to save if a player should be shown ads or not. `PlayerPrefs` are cool because they save information between playthroughs of the game and are used often for things such as high scores and player preferences (hence the name). To reset the properties for testing, you can go to **Edit | Clear All PlayerPrefs**.

For more information on PlayerPrefs, check out `https://docs.unity3d.com/ScriptReference/PlayerPrefs.html`.

Note that I made the `Start` function `virtual`, which means that inherited classes can also use this as a foundation for their own scripts. We also marked the function as `protected`, which works the same as a `private` function but it also is accessible in child classes.

14. With that in mind, we will also need to update the `Start` function of `PauseScreenBehaviour` to the following:

```
protected override void Start()
{
    // Initalize Ads if needed
    base.Start();

    if (!UnityAdController.showAds)
    {
        // If not showing ads, just start the game
        SetPauseMenu(false);
```

```
        }
    }
```

The override keyword makes it so that it will replace the default behavior of Start. However, when we call base.Start(), we are ensuring that the preceding content from MainMenuBehaviour will be called—in this case, we ensure that the UnityAdController has the correct value set.

15. Finally, we will need to adjust the ObstacleBehaviour script to handle not playing ads as well. Update the ShowContinue function to use the following:

```
// Other code above...

        // Come back after 1 second and check again
        yield return new WaitForSeconds(1f);
    }
    else if (!UnityAdController.showAds)
    {
        // It's valid to click the button now
        contButton.interactable = true;

        // If player clicks on button we want to just continue
        contButton.onClick.AddListener(Continue);

        UnityAdController.obstacle = this;

        // Change text to allow continue
        btnText.text = "Free Continue";

        // We can now leave the coroutine
        break;
    }
    else
    {
        // It's valid to click the button now
        contButton.interactable = true;

    // More code below...
```

16. We will also need to make a slight adjustment to the ResetGame method by removing or commenting out the following lines:

```
// If we found the button we can use it
if (continueButton)
{
    //if (UnityAdController.showAds)
    //{
```

```
                    // If player clicks on button we want to play ad and
                    // then continue
                    StartCoroutine(ShowContinue(continueButton));
        //}
        //else
        //{
        // // If can't play an ad, no need for continue button
        // continueButton.gameObject.SetActive(false);
        //}
    }
```

17. Save your script and dive into Unity.

18. From the **Hierarchy** window, select the **Remove Ads** button. Go into the **Inspector** tab and then scroll down to the **IAP Button** component. Go ahead and click on the plus button underneath the **On Purchase Complete (Product)** option, and then add the `Main Menu` object in the little box on the bottom of the side below the **Runtime Only** dropdown. Then, select **Main Menu Behaviour | DisableAds** from the dropdown to the right:

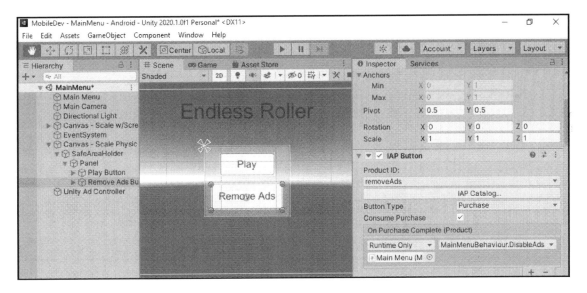

19. Now, save our scene and start the game:

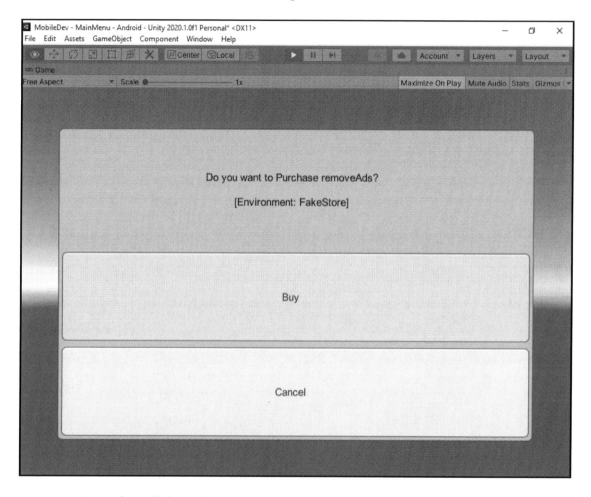

Now, if we click on the **Remove Ads** button, it will ask whether we want to make the purchase. If we do, it will then make it so when we go into the game, there are no ads. Likewise, when we now die, it will display a **Free Continue** button:

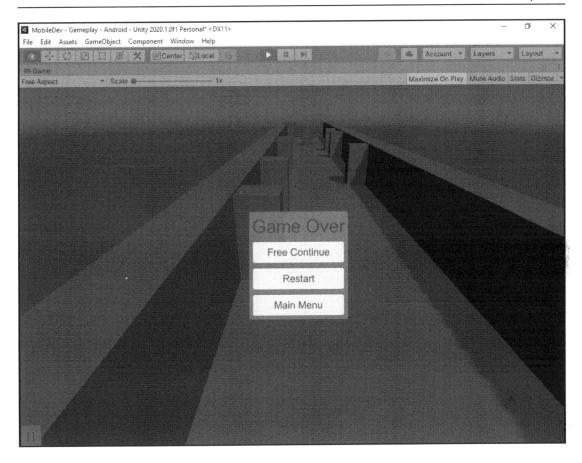

With that, we now have the Unity aspect of creating a simple purchase completed.

If you're interested in learning more about Codeless IAP, check out `https://docs.unity3d.com/Manual/UnityIAPCodelessIAP.html`. If you'd like to dive into more customizable forms of IAPs, you can access the library directly. Information on that can be found at `https://unity3d.com/learn/tutorials/topics/ads-analytics/integrating-unity-iap-your-game`.

With this, you can now build as many products as you'd like to have in your game. However, certain platforms also have requirements with regard to the functionality to restore previous purchases. In the next section, we will see how to do that.

Adding a button to restore purchases

On platforms that support it (Google Play and Universal Windows Applications, most notably), if you purchase something, uninstall, and then reinstall a game using Unity IAP, it automatically restores any products the user owns during the first initialization following reinstallation.

For those on iOS, users must have the ability to restore their purchases via a button due to Apple requiring them to reauthenticate their password before it happens. Not doing so will prevent our game from being accepted on the iOS App Store, so it's a good idea to include this functionality if we wish to deploy there. Let's look at the steps to do just that:

1. Go to the **Hierarchy** window and select the **Remove Ads Button** object. Once selected, duplicate it by pressing *Ctrl + D*.
2. Change the duplicate's name by selecting it and changing its name to `Restore Button` in the **Inspector** window.
3. From the **Hierarchy** window, open up the **Text** object and change the text to say `Restore Purchases` as well.
4. Now, select the **Restore** object, and then, in the **IAP Button** component, go to **Button Type** and select **Restore**:

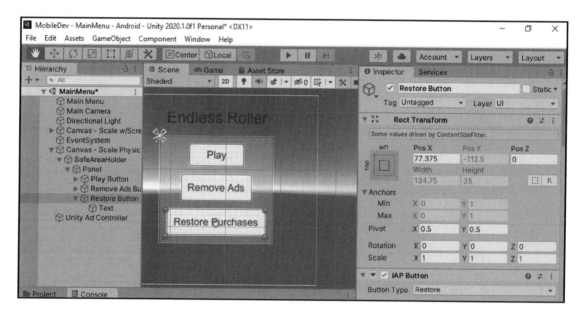

You should note that the properties of the **IAP Button** component change and now only allow you to set the **Button Type** as there is nothing left to customize.

5. Save your scene and jump into Unity.

6. When you start the game and try to click on the **Restore** Purchases, you'll get a warning in the **Console** window stating that this isn't a supported platform:

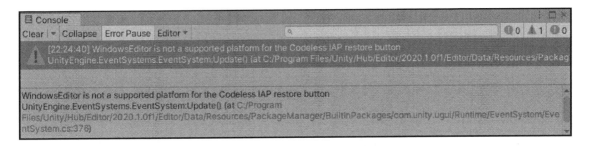

So, with that in mind, we can adjust our game so that the button will only show up if we are currently running on a supported platform.

7. Go to the `Scripts` folder and create a C# script called `RestoreAdsChecker`. Once it's opened, use the following script for it:

```csharp
using UnityEngine;
using UnityEngine.Purchasing;

/// <summary>
/// Will show or remove a button depending on if we can restore
    /// ads or not
/// </summary>
public class RestoreAdsChecker : MonoBehaviour
{

    // Use this for initialization
    void Start()
    {
        bool canRestore = false;

        switch (Application.platform)
        {
            // Windows Store
            case RuntimePlatform.WSAPlayerX86:
            case RuntimePlatform.WSAPlayerX64:
            case RuntimePlatform.WSAPlayerARM:

            // iOS, OSX, tvOS
            case RuntimePlatform.IPhonePlayer:
            case RuntimePlatform.OSXPlayer:
            case RuntimePlatform.tvOS:
```

```
                        canRestore = true;
                        break;

                // Android
                case RuntimePlatform.Android:
                    switch (StandardPurchasingModule.Instance().appStore)
                    {
                        case AppStore.SamsungApps:
                        case AppStore.CloudMoolah:
                            canRestore = true;
                            break;

                    }
                    break;
            }

        gameObject.SetActive(canRestore);
        }

    }
```

This script goes through all of the stores listed in Unity's `IAPButton` class, and if they are something that can be restored, we set `canRestore` to `true`, otherwise, it will stay as `false`. Finally, we will remove the object if we cannot restore it, without having to create specific things for different builds.

8. Save the script and dive back into Unity.

9. Attach our newly created `RestoreAdsChecker` component to our **Restore Button** object:

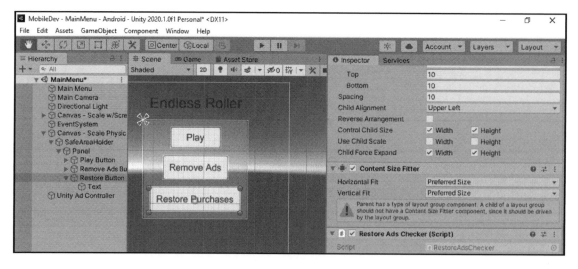

10. Save your project and start up the game:

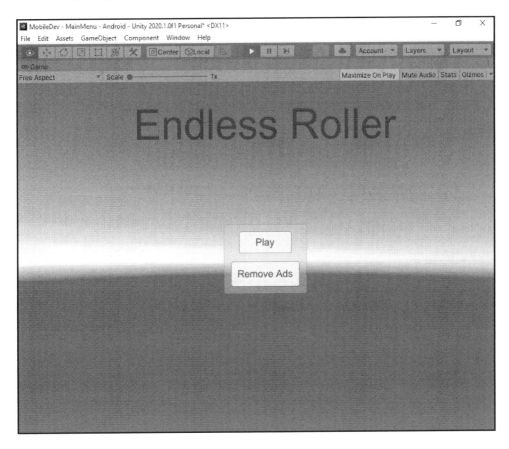

Now due to the **RestoreAdsChecker** component that we added on our PC build of the game, the Restore button doesn't show up, but if we export for iOS, it will show up on our device!

For more information on restoring transactions and how this functionally works, check out `https://docs.unity3d.com/Manual/UnityIAPRestoringTransactions.html`.

This ensures that our game has this particular feature on each of the different platforms that support it. With that in mind, we will next look at some of the specific stores and places you may wish to add support for IAPs in your game.

Configuring purchases for the stores of your choice

Unfortunately, we do not have enough room in the book to go step by step through the process for every store, but I do have pages that you can reference to go through the entire process for the following stores:

- **The Apple App Store and Mac App Store:** `https://docs.unity3d.com/Manual/UnityIAPAppleConfiguration.html`
- **Google Play Store:** `https://docs.unity3d.com/Manual/UnityIAPGoogleConfiguration.html`
- **The Windows Store:** `https://docs.unity3d.com/Manual/UnityIAPWindowsConfiguration.html`
- **Amazon Appstore and Amazon Underground:** `https://docs.unity3d.com/Manual/UnityIAPAmazonConfiguration.html`
- **Samsung Galaxy:** `https://docs.unity3d.com/Manual/UnityIAPSamsungConfiguration.html`
- **CloudMoolah Moo Store:** `https://docs.unity3d.com/Manual/UnityIAPMoolahMooStore.html`

There are some potential issues when trying to publish to multiple Android IAP stores (such as Samsung and Google) with the same build. You can find information on resolving those issues

at `https://docs.unity3d.com/Manual/UnityIAPCrossStoreInstallationIssues.html`.

Summary

In this chapter, we covered how to create in-app purchases, making use of Unity in your project. We first covered how to set up Unity's IAP system and then dived into using Codeless IAP to easily add a purchasable item to your game. We then created the functionality to restore our purchase if we uninstall and reinstall our game and went over where we can go to set up our purchases depending on the store we want to target. These new skills give you the ability to make additional revenue from your game, while also allowing you to target multiple stores and platforms, making it possible for even more people to see your title.

Now, of course, having all these ways to make money isn't going to help us if no one is playing our game. In the next chapter, we will get social, learning how we can make use of social media to share our score and get other players interested in our title.

Further reading

For more tips and tricks on improving your freemium strategy, I suggest that you check out the following article by *Pepe Agell* at `https://webcache.googleusercontent.com/search?q=cache:n1mjnyG4P6IJ:https://www.chartboost.com/blog/inapp-purchases-for-indie-mobile-games-freemium-strategy/+cd=1hl=enct=clnkgl=us.`

7
Getting Social

We now have all of the foundational things needed to get our game out into the world; it's mechanically working, and we've set up all of the monetization. Having all of the features that we have added to our project is great, but if no one is playing your game, there's no reason to have them.

Word-of-mouth marketing is the most reliable way to get others to try your game. Providing people with opportunities to share the game helps others discover the project and it's something that we should really try to do, as marketing and getting your game out there is one of the hardest things to do as an indie developer.

In this chapter, you will learn some of the different ways to integrate social media into your projects. We will start off by adding something to share – a score. Afterward, we will see how we can share the score to Twitter. Then we will see how we can have our game connect to Facebook and use content from Facebook within our game itself.

This chapter will be split into a number of topics. It will contain a simple step-by-step process from beginning to end. The following is the outline of our tasks:

- Adding a scoring system
- Sharing high scores via Twitter
- Downloading and installing Facebook's SDK
- Logging in to our game via Facebook
- Displaying a Facebook name and profile picture

Technical requirements

This book utilizes Unity 2020.1.0f1 and Unity Hub 2.3.1, but the steps should work with minimal changes in future versions of the editor. If you would like to download the exact version used in this book, and there is a new version out, you can visit Unity's download archive at `https://unity3d.com/get-unity/download/archive`. You can also find the system requirements for Unity at `https://docs.unity3d.com/2020.1/Documentation/Manual/system-requirements.html` in the **Unity Editor system requirements** section. To deploy your project, you will need an Android or iOS device.

You can find the code files present in this chapter on GitHub at `https://github.com/PacktPublishing/Unity-2020-Mobile-Game-Development-Second-Edition/tree/master/Chapter%2007`.

Adding a scoring system

In order to provide an incentive for players to share our game with others, we need to provide a compelling reason to do so. Some people are very competitive and wish to be the best at playing a game, challenging others to do better than them. To help with that, we can allow our players to share a score value via social media. However, to do that, we'll first need to have a scoring system. Thankfully, it's not too difficult to do that, so let's add that in real quick using the following steps:

1. Start off by opening the `Gameplay.scene` file located in the `Assets/Scenes` folder of the project. To show our players what their score is, we'll need to have some way to display it on the screen. In our case, the easiest way would be with a text object.

2. From the **Hierarchy** window, select the **Panel** object that is a child of the **Canvas** object and rename it to `SafeAreaHolder`, as we did with the panel with the **UI Safe Area Handler** component in the Title Screen scene. Afterward, right-click on the `SafeAreaHolder` object and select **UI | Text** as shown in the following screenshot:

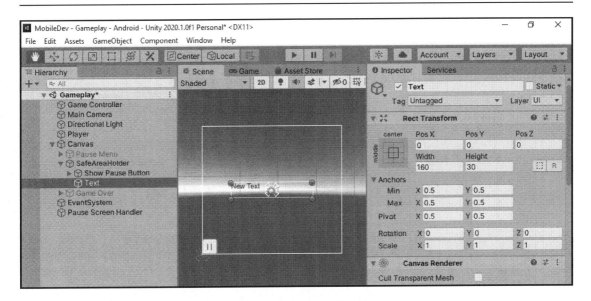

This will make the **Text** object a child of the **Panel** object, which in turn will automatically resize itself to fit within a notch if there is one in the devices.

3. Rename this object `Score Text` and use the **Anchors Preset** menu at the top center, holding down *Shift + Alt* to set the pivot and position as well.

4. Afterward, let's set the **RectTransform** component's **Height** property on the object to `50` to ensure that we have space to hold the score when we increase the size.

5. Next, in **Text component**, change **Text** property to `0` and set **Alignment** to centered. Afterward, set **Font Size** to `40` so that it's easy to see.

6. To improve its readability, let's add another component, **Outline**, by going to **Add Component** and then typing in `Outline` and pressing **Enter**.

7. From there, set the **Effect Color** field to White as shown here:

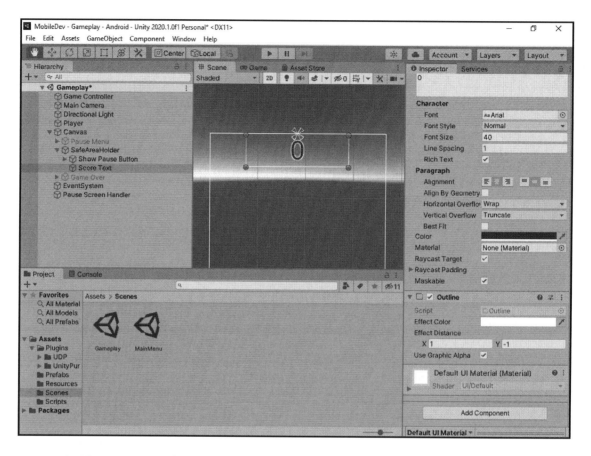

8. Next, open up the `PlayerBehaviour` script and add the following line at the top of the file:

```
using UnityEngine.UI; // Text
```

9. Next, add the following code inside the class:

```
[Header("Object References")]
public Text scoreText;

private float score = 0;

public float Score
{
    get { return score; }
```

```
        set
        {
            score = value;

            // Check if scoreText has been assigned
            if (scoreText == null)
            {
                Debug.LogError("Score Text is not set. " +
                    "Please go to the Inspector and assign it");
                // If not assigned, don't try to update it.
                return;
            }

            // Update the text to display the whole number portion
            // of the score
            scoreText.text = string.Format("{0:0}", score);
        }
    }
```

We first have a reference to the scoreText object, which we will need to set in the **Inspector**. This is of the **Text** class, which contains properties relating to the text displayed on the object.

This makes use of C#'s get/set functions, which are implicit getters and setters. Basically, any time we get or set the Score variable, we will execute whatever is located between {}. In our case, any time we set the Score variable, it will update our text for us.

For those who opted to use TextMeshPro, you can set the text property much like with the Unity Text class' built-in text property. For more info on that, check out http://digitalnativestudios.com/textmeshpro/docs/ScriptReference/TextMeshPro-text.html.

This has an advantage over what a number of my students do, which is to update the value of the text every frame, which doesn't need to happen. We only need to update the text when the value changes, which makes it perfect for us to use in this situation.

For more information on the get/set accessors, check out https://docs.microsoft.com/en-us/dotnet/csharp/programming-guide/classes-and-structs/using-properties.

10. Then, update the `PlayerBehaviour` class to have the following highlighted changes:

```
// Start is called before the first frame update
private void Start()
{
    // Get access to our Rigidbody component
    rb = GetComponent<Rigidbody>();

    minSwipeDistancePixels = minSwipeDistance * Screen.dpi;

    Score = 0;
}


/// <summary>
/// Update is called once per frame
/// </summary>
private void Update()
{
    // If the game is paused, don't do anything
    if (PauseScreenBehaviour.paused)
    {
        return;
    }

    Score += Time.deltaTime;

    // Rest of Update here...
```

What we are doing here is resetting our score whenever the player is created and increasing the value while the game isn't paused.

11. Save the script and dive back into Unity.

12. Select the **Player** object and drag and drop our **Score Text** object into the **Score Text** variable on the **Player Behaviour** component:

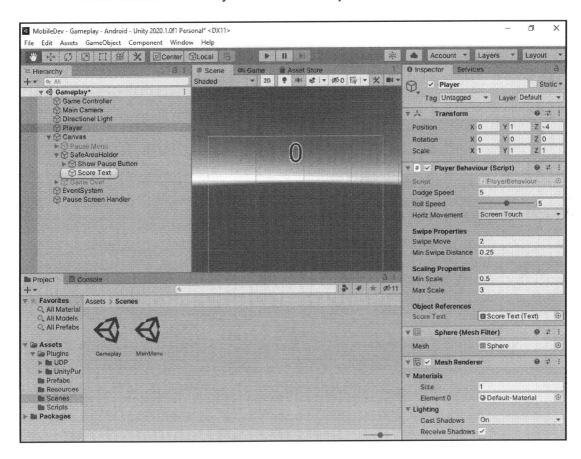

13. Once assigned, go ahead and play the game. The game's interface is shown in the following screenshot:

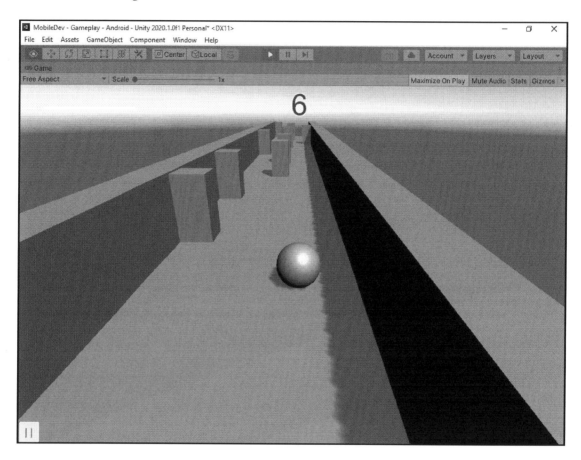

Now, as you can see, we have a score for our game, which updates as we play. This will allow players to easily know what their competency with the game is and give them some information that they can share with others. Now that we have a scoring system, let's take a look at how we can share a high score using Twitter.

Sharing high scores via Twitter

Twitter is an online news and social networking service where users post and interact with each other through messages that they call *tweets*, which are limited to 280 characters. Many indie game developers use Twitter as a way to attract others to play their games.

Twitter is a great option to start off with because we can add it very easily to our project by simply opening a specific URL. Let's look at the steps to do just that:

1. Open the `PauseScreenBehaviour` script. Once inside, we will add the following code inside the `PlayerScreenBehaviour` class:

```
#region Share Score via Twitter

/// <summary>
/// Web address in order to create a tweet
/// </summary>
private const string tweetTextAddress =
        "http://twitter.com/intent/tweet?text=";

/// <summary>
/// Where we want players to visit
/// </summary>
private string appStoreLink = "http://johnpdoran.com/";

[Tooltip("Reference to the player for the score")]
public PlayerBehaviour player;

/// <summary>
/// Will open Twitter with a prebuilt tweet. When called on iOS or
/// Android will open up Twitter app if installed
/// </summary>
public void TweetScore()
{
    // Create contents of the tweet
    string tweet = "I got " + string.Format("{0:0}", player.Score)
            + " points in Endless Roller! Can you do better?";

    // Create the entire message
    string message = tweet + "\n" + appStoreLink;

    //Ensures string is URL friendly
    string url =
        UnityEngine.Networking.UnityWebRequest.EscapeURL(message);

    // Open the URL to create the tweet
    Application.OpenURL(tweetTextAddress + url);
```

```
}

#endregion
```

First of all, we will use a number of new things. You'll note that the preceding block of code starts and ends with `#region` and `#endregion`, respectively. What this does is allow us to expand and collapse this portion of code inside Visual Studio. When we introduce longer code files, it can be convenient to be able to collapse or hide certain parts of your script so that you can focus only on the part of the file you're working on. Since this portion of code has nothing to do with the rest of the script, this is a good place for us to use it.

To open URLs inside Unity, we will need to make use of the `Application.OpenURL` function and the `UnityWebRequest` class.

 For more information on Twitter's Web Intents and the ways you can use them, check out `https://dev.twitter.com/web/intents`.

The `UnityWebRequest` class is typically used to load content at runtime, but it also has the `EscapeURL` function, which will convert a string into a format that web browsers are comfortable with. For instance, the newline character will not be displayed by itself.

 For more information on the `EscapeURL` function, check out `https://docs.unity3d.com/ScriptReference/Networking.UnityWebRequest.EscapeURL.html`.

2. Save the script and dive back into Unity. From the **Hierarchy** window, select the **Pause Screen Handler** object and then set the **Player** property in the **Inspector** tab to our `Player` object by dragging and dropping the **Player** game object from the **Hierarchy** window onto the **Player** property in the **Inspector** window:

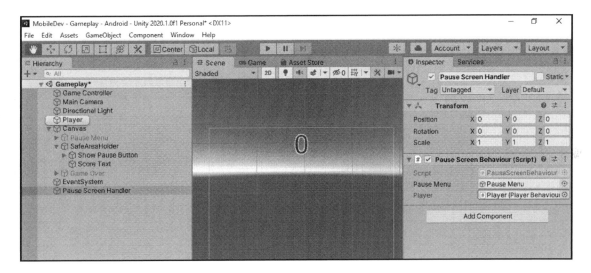

3. Now, we need to have a button for our **Game Over** screen to allow us to share our score.

4. Open up the **Canvas** object and toggle the **Game Over** object to **ON** by clicking on the check mark beside its name in the **Inspector** window.

5. From there, expand the two **Panel** child objects and the **Game Over Contents** object. Select the **Main Menu Button** object and duplicate it by pressing *Ctrl + D*. Next, change the name to `Tweet Score Button` and also update the text in the child object to display `Tweet Score` as well.

6. Afterward, select the **Tweet Score** button object and scroll down to the **Button** component. From there, change the function we are calling to the **PauseScreenBehaviour** | **Tweet Score** function:

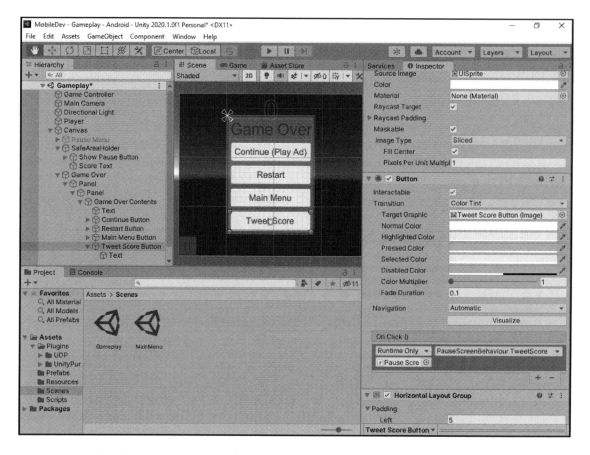

7. Select the **Game Over** object in the **Hierarchy** and disable it again. Next, save your scene and start the game.

8. Now when we fail the game, we can click on the **Tweet Score** button and our browser will open on our PC:

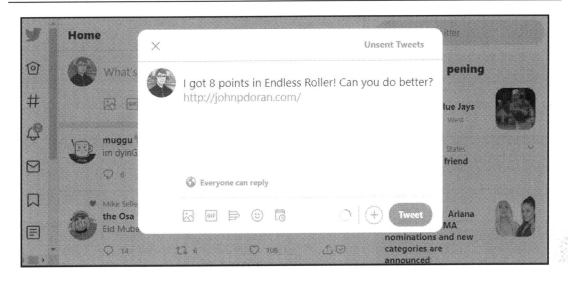

However, on our mobile devices, it will open up the Twitter app:

With that, you learned just how easy it is to share something using Twitter.

For those who are interested in doing more than this with Twitter, they do have their own API for Unity, which will allow you to let users log in to your game using Twitter if you'd like to do that instead of Facebook, which we will be doing later on. If you're interested in looking into it, you can find more information at `https://dev.twitter.com/twitterkit/unity/overview`.

Of course, there are other social networks that exist as well, some of which have their very own **software development kit (SDK)**, which allows you to access the information that they have. In the next section, we will explore how to utilize this.

Downloading and installing Facebook's SDK

We couldn't have a chapter on social networking without mentioning Facebook. Facebook has its own SDK that can be used with Unity. This can allow us to use the information that Facebook already has, including the user's name and profile image within our game experience. Let's look at the steps to incorporate them:

1. Open up your web browser and visit `https://developers.facebook.com/docs/unity/`:

2. Click on the **Download the SDK** button and wait for it to finish downloading. Once it is downloaded, unzip it and then open up the `facebook-unity-sdk-7.21.1` folder. Then, open up the `FacebookSDK` folder and you'll see a single file, `facebook-unity-sdk-7.21.1.unitypackage`.

3. Double-click on the `unitypackage` file, and you should have a window pop up as shown here:

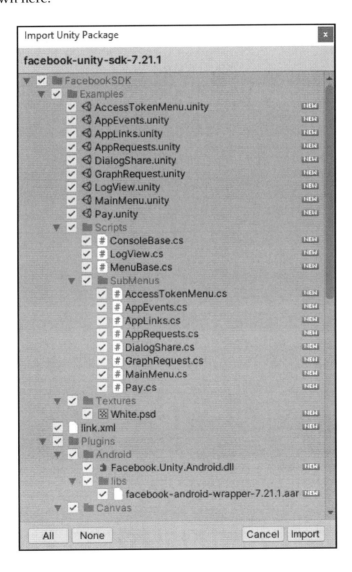

If this does not work, you can also go to **Assets** | **Import Package** | **Custom Package** and then find the folder that you unzipped the file to and open it that way.

4. Click on the **Import** button and wait for it to finish loading. From here, you'll get a popup noting the project may contain obsolete APIs. Go ahead and click on the **I Made a Backup. Go Ahead!** button and wait for it to finish.

   You may get an error at the moment, but we will resolve this in *Step 10*.

   Now, in order to use the Facebook API, we will first need to have a Facebook App ID, so let's do that next.

5. Go back to your web browser and go to `https://developers.facebook.com/` and click on the **Log In** button in the top-right corner of the screen. Once you login to your Facebook account, you should see something similar to the following screenshot:

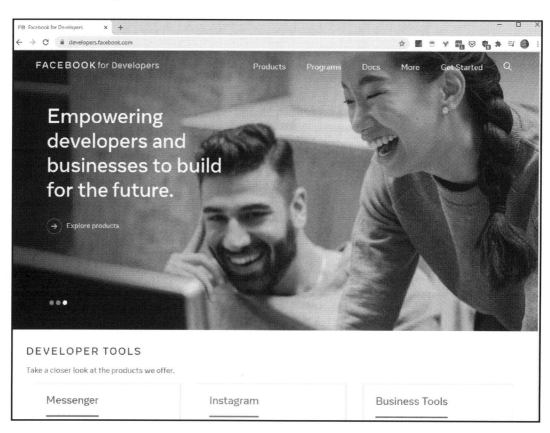

6. From the preceding page, click on the **Get Started** button in the top-right corner of the screen. From there, you'll be brought to a screen where you need to click **Next** and then you'll be asked your role. Click on **Developer** and, from the next screen, click on the **Create First App** button.

7. Afterward, add a **Display Name** for your game (I used `Endless Roller`) and your **Contact E-mail** and then select **Create App ID**.

8. Once you're brought to your app's page, click on the **Dashboard** option to the left of the default info for your game. Note the **App ID** and copy it by clicking on it or by highlighting it and then pressing *Ctrl + C*:

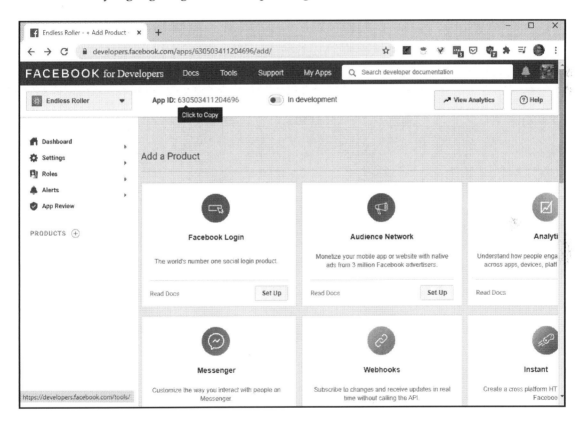

9. Return to Unity, and you will note a new Facebook option on the top bar. Select it and then select **Edit Settings**. Once there, click on **Inspector** if you need to and you'll see a number of options. Set **Facebook App Id (?)** to our created app's ID and then set the name to our game's name:

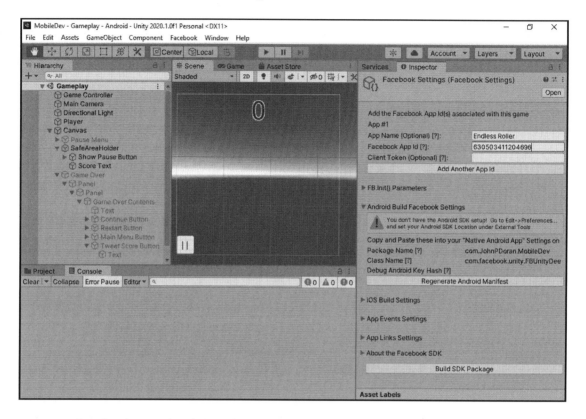

Lastly, the Facebook SDK has an error that will cause you to not be able to export your games onto Android devices because it does not support Unity automatically finding the SDK.

10. In order to fix this, go into **Edit | Preferences**. From there, go to the **External Tools** section. Uncheck the **Android SDK Tools Installed with Unity (recommended)** option. Then, click the **Browse** button to select the SDK location, as shown in the following screenshot:

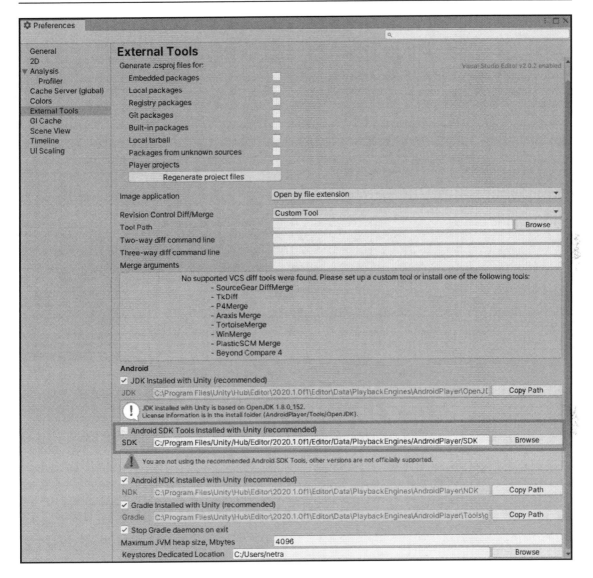

11. Facebook also requires one more program in the path, which is part of the JDK. To add this, uncheck the **JDK Installed with Unity (recommended)** option and add the JDK path to it. In my case, it was `C:\Program Files\Unity\Hub\Editor\2020.1.0f1\Editor\Data\PlaybackEngines\AndroidPlayer\OpenJDK`.

12. Next, you can close the **Preferences** menu.

There is a possibility that you may get an error the next time that you try to export your game to Android due to changing the SDK location. If this is the case, close your Unity project and then go to the project folder and delete the `Temp` folder. Upon restarting the project, the error should go away.

13. Return to the **Facebook Settings** menu by going to **Facebook | Edit Settings....** Now, you'll notice that under **Android Build Facebook Settings**, there is a new error stating that OpenSSL is not found. See the following screenshot:

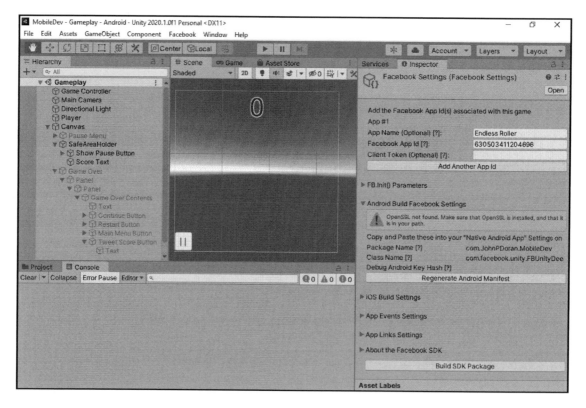

For those on a Mac, you can follow the instructions given here in order to install OpenSSL and add it to your path: https://developers.facebook.com/docs/facebook-login/android/advanced

14. To fix this, we will first need to download OpenSSL by going to `http://slproweb.com/products/Win32OpenSSL.html`. From there, select the **EXE** link below the **Win64 OpenSSL v1.1.1g** option as shown here:

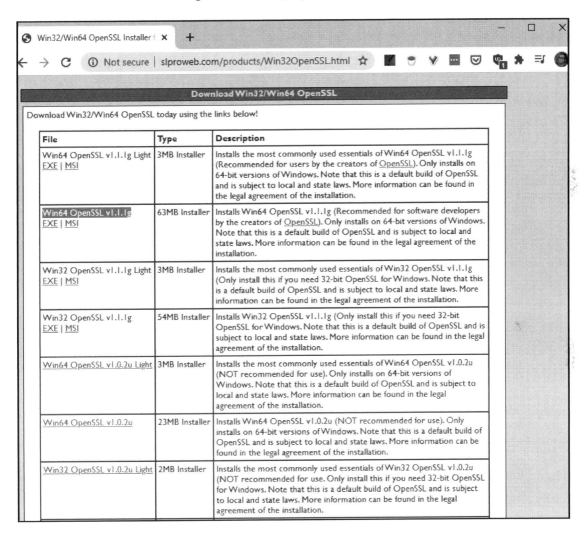

15. Once downloaded, install the program with the default options as shown in the following screenshot:

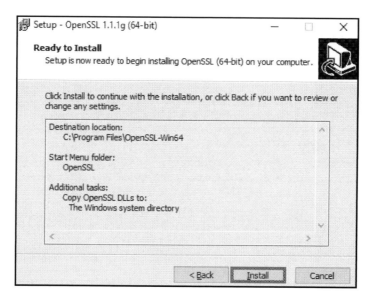

16. Once completed, you may uncheck the donation option and click on the **Finish** button.

17. We then need to add the location of OpenSSL to the path. To do this, press the Windows key on your keyboard and start typing in Env, and then select the **Edit the system environment variables** option, as shown in the following screenshot:

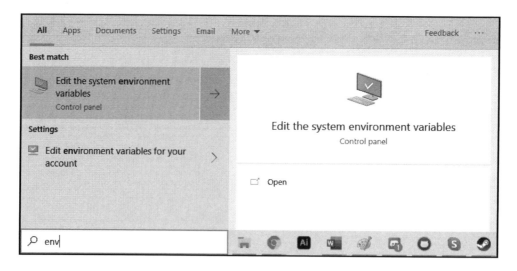

18. From the window that pops up, click the **Environment Variables...** option at the bottom right. Double-click on the **Path** option in the **System variables** section and then, from that menu, click on **New**. From there, put in the location of OpenSSL. For me, it was `C:\Program Files\OpenSSL-Win64\bin`:

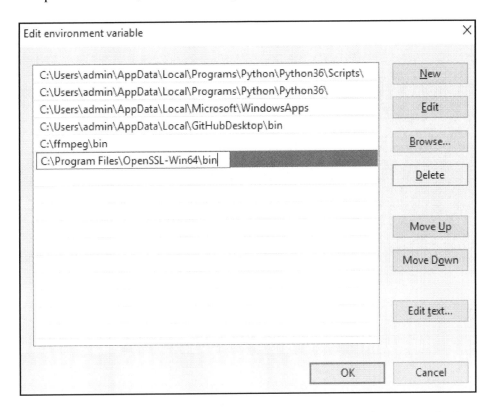

19. Then, click on **New** one more time and add the path to the JDK tools. In my case, it was `C:\Program Files\Unity\Hub\Editor\2020.1.0f1\Editor\Data\PlaybackEngines\AndroidPlayer\OpenJDK\bin`.

20. Click on the **OK** button and then the **OK** button on the **Environmental Variables** window.

21. Once both options are added, close your Unity project and restart your computer. Once Unity reopens, you may have to wait for the **Resolving Android Dependencies** menu to complete, but once it finishes, you should be able to see the **Facebook Settings (Facebook | Edit Settings)** menu working correctly and giving us a value under **Debug Android Key Hash [?]**:

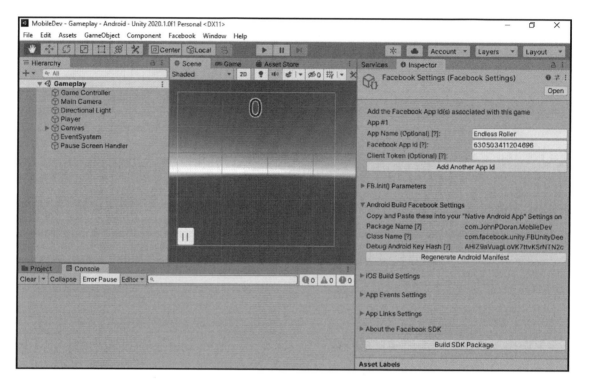

This means that our setup of the Facebook SDK is complete!

22. Depending on the platform you wish to deploy to, go to the following websites and complete the tasks listed:
    - For Android, check out https://developers.facebook.com/docs/unity/getting-started/android.
    - For iOS, check out https://developers.facebook.com/docs/unity/getting-started/ios.

Now that we have set that up, we can start adding to it by first allowing our game to be logged in to using Facebook.

Logging in to our game via Facebook

One of the things we can do when using the Facebook API is to allow our users to log in to the game using their Facebook account. Then, we can use their name and image automatically within our project. The following steps show us how to achieve this:

1. Let's first open up our **Main Menu** level by going to the **Project** window, open the Assets/Scenes folder, and then double-click on the MainMenu file.

2. From there, let's click on the **2D** button to go into 2D mode if you haven't done so previously. What we will do is remove the original menu and instead have a button for players to log in via Facebook or play as a guest when the game starts.

3. Go to the **Hierarchy** window, select the **Canvas - Scale Physical** object, and expand it and the **SafeAreaHolder** child. Select the **Panel** child and rename it Menu Options.

4. Then, select the Menu Options object in the **Hierarchy** window and duplicate it by pressing *Ctrl + D*. Then, rename the newly created Facebook Login object. Select the **Menu Options** game object again and then disable it by going to the **Inspector** tab and clicking on the check mark beside its name:

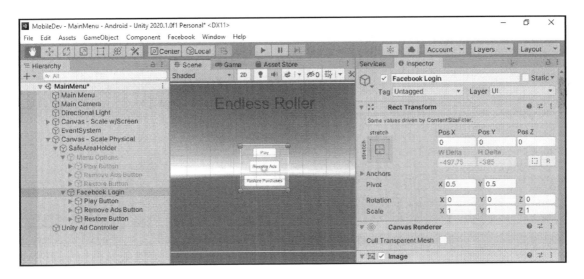

We will have the Facebook Login object turn the menu on when needed.

5. Next, open the **Facebook Login** options and remove the **Restore Button** and **Play Button** objects. Click on the **Remove Ads Button**, right-click on the **IAP Button** component, and then select the **Remove** component.

6. Duplicate the **Remove Ads** button by pressing the *Ctrl + D* keys. Then, name those two buttons `Facebook Login Button` and `Continue as Guest Button`. Also, change the **Text** property of both of these buttons as `Facebook Login` and `Continue as Guest`:

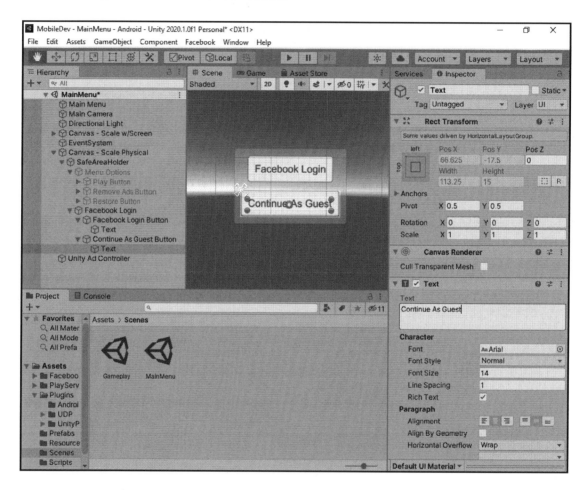

7. Now that we have the buttons working correctly, we need to write the script that will allow us to log in. Go to the `Scripts` folder and open our `MainMenuBehaviour` script. We will use the `List` class to hold the permissions we want in order to access Facebook and the content of the `FB` class in the Facebook SDK.

8. So, to do that, we'll first add the following to the top of the `MainMenuBehaviour` script:

```
using UnityEngine;
using UnityEngine.SceneManagement; // LoadScene
using System.Collections.Generic; // List
using Facebook.Unity; // FB
```

9. Then add the following variables to the `MainMenuBehaviour` class:

```
[Header("Object References")]
public GameObject mainMenu;
public GameObject facebookLogin;
```

10. Now, add the following code within the `MainMenuBehaviour` class:

```
#region Facebook

public void Awake()
{
    // We only call FB Init once, so check if it has been called
    // already
    if (!FB.IsInitialized)
    {
        FB.Init(OnInitComplete, OnHideUnity);
    }
}

/// <summary>
/// Once initialized, will inform if logged in on Facebook
/// </summary>
private void OnInitComplete()
{
    if (FB.IsLoggedIn)
    {
        print("Logged into Facebook");

        // Close Login and open Main Menu
        ShowMainMenu();
    }
}

/// <summary>
/// Called whenever Unity loses focus
/// </summary>
/// <param name="active">If the gmae is currently active</param>
private void OnHideUnity(bool active)
{
```

```
        // Set TimeScale based on if the game is paused
        Time.timeScale = (active) ? 1 : 0;
    }

    /// <summary>
    /// Attempts to log in on Facebook
    /// </summary>
    public void FacebookLogin()
    {
        List<string> permissions = new List<string>();

        // Add permissions we want to have here
        permissions.Add("public_profile");

        FB.LogInWithReadPermissions(permissions, FacebookCallback);
    }

    /// <summary>
    /// Called once facebook has logged in, or not
    /// </summary>
    /// <param name="result">The result of our login request</param>
    private void FacebookCallback(IResult result)
    {
        if (result.Error == null)
        {
            OnInitComplete();
        }
        else
        {
            print(result.Error);
        }
    }

    public void ShowMainMenu()
    {
        if (facebookLogin != null && mainMenu != null)
        {
            facebookLogin.SetActive(false);
            mainMenu.SetActive(true);
        }
    }

    #endregion
```

In this case, we are accessing the player's public profile, which contains information such as their name and their profile picture.

For all of the properties that we can get access to, check out `https://developers.facebook.com/docs/facebook-login/permissions#reference-public_profile`.

11. Save your script and go to the **Facebook Login** button and change the button's **OnClick()** action to now call your function by clicking on the + button and then dragging and dropping the **Main Menu** object in and then selecting **Main Menu Behaviour | Facebook Login** instead:

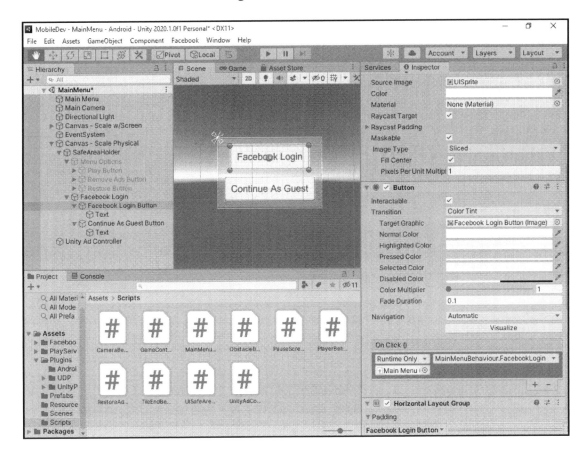

12. Then, on the **Continue as Guest Button** under the **Button** component, go to the **On Click ()** section and then click on the + button. Drag and drop the **Main Menu** object

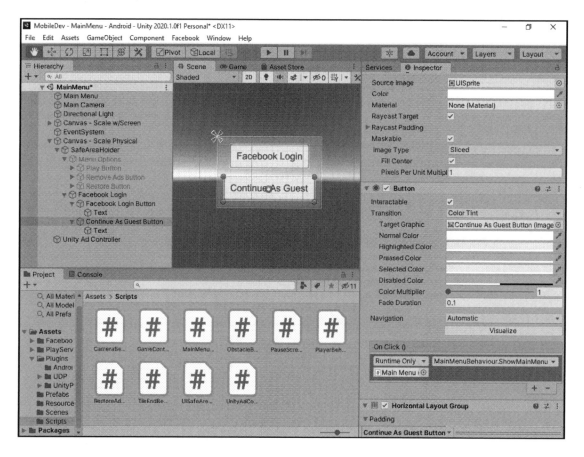

13. Finally, we will need to set the variables we created. Select the **Main Menu** object in the **Hierarchy** window and then set the **Main Menu** and **Facebook Login** properties:

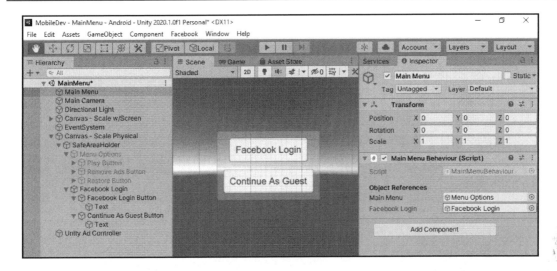

Ensure that the **Facebook Login** is set to the panel object holding both buttons.

14. Save your scene, start the game, and then click on the **Facebook Login** button:

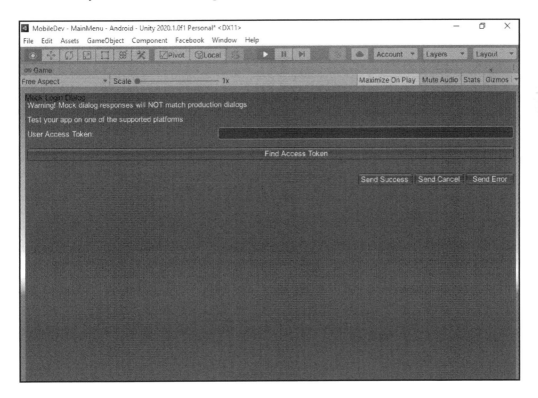

To see everything properly within the editor, it's a good idea to maximize the **Game** tab, which you can do by right-clicking on the **Game** tab and selecting **Maximize** or by checking the **Maximize On Play** option on the toolbar.

Now, you should see a menu, which is asking for a user access token, a value that every profile has that we can associate with. We'll need to go to Facebook to get that, so that's what we'll do next.

15. Click on the **Find Access Token** page, and a web browser will open with a new page:

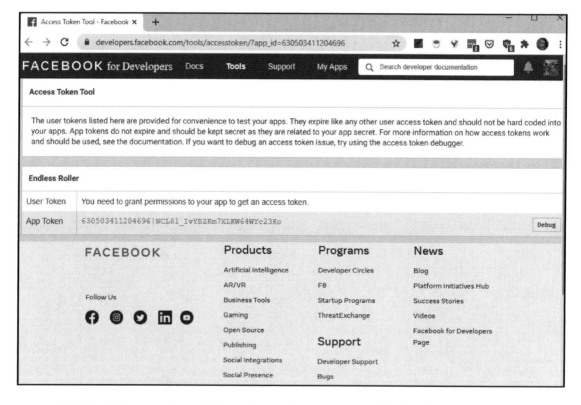

16. You'll then need to click on the **need to grant permissions** link and then on **Continue** and you'll see a string of characters under **User Token**. Copy that and then paste it into **User Access Token** property in Unity and then click on the **Send Success** button.

If you get an error when granting permissions stating "**Future off-Facebook activity for this app is off**" that means that your Facebook settings are not allowing the use of your Facebook profile to be used off of Facebook. In order to use Facebook to log in, your account must have Off-Facebook tracking enabled. To do so you can go to `https://www.facebook.com/off_facebook_activity` and ensure the **Future off-Facebook Activity** value is set to ON to be able to log in. We will be allowing users to log in as a guest, if you'd prefer not to be tracked.

Now, you'll note that the **Console** has printed that we've logged in to Facebook and that the menu has closed when we've sent the key:

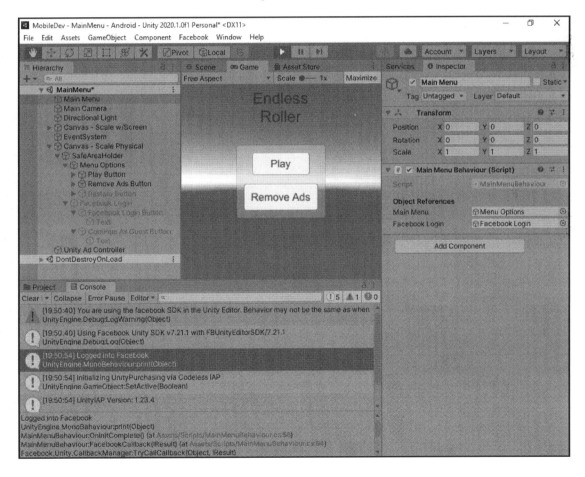

For more information on user access tokens, check out `https://developers.facebook.com/docs/facebook-login/access-tokens/#usertokens`.

Now that we have the ability to log in to Facebook, we can now use the information that we get from Facebook in order to customize our game, which is what we will be doing next.

Displaying a Facebook name and profile picture

A good thing to do is to personalize our game to fit our players. So, with that, once the player logs in, we will welcome them and display their image on the screen by following these steps:

1. Go to the `MainMenuBehaviour` script once again. From there, we'll need to add a new `using` statement to display an image and change the text we need in order to use Unity's UI system:

   ```
   using UnityEngine.UI; // Text / Image
   ```

2. We will then need to add two new variables:

   ```
   [Tooltip("Will display the user's Facebook profile pic")]
   public Image profilePic;

   [Tooltip("The text object used to display the greeting")]
   public Text greeting;
   ```

   These will hold the information that we wish to display once we get it from Facebook.

3. Afterward, we will update the `ShowMainMenu` function and add some new functions to use:

```
public void ShowMainMenu()
{
    if (facebookLogin != null && mainMenu != null)
    {
        facebookLogin.SetActive(false);
        mainMenu.SetActive(true);

        if (FB.IsLoggedIn)
        {
            // Get information from Facebook profile
            FB.API("/me?fields=name", HttpMethod.GET, SetName);
            FB.API("/me/picture?width=256&height=256",
            HttpMethod.GET, SetProfilePic);
        }
    }

}
```

The `FB.API` function makes a call to Facebook's Graph API to get data or take an action on the user's behalf and allows us to get the information that we have permission to as defined earlier. In our case, we are looking for the name and the profile picture of the user and calling the `SetName` and `SetProfilePic` functions, respectively, once we have obtained that data.

However, we currently do not have `SetName` and `SetProfilePic` functions, so we will go ahead and add them now.

4. Add the following additional code within the `Facebook` region of the script:

```
private void SetName(IResult result)
{
    if (result.Error != null)
    {
        print(result.Error);
        return;
    }

    string playerName = result.ResultDictionary["name"].ToString();

    if(greeting != null)
    {
        greeting.text = "Hello, " + playerName + "!";
```

```
                greeting.gameObject.SetActive(true);
        }

    }

    private void SetProfilePic(IGraphResult result)
    {
        if (result.Error != null)
        {
            print(result.Error);
            return;
        }

        Sprite fbImage = Sprite.Create(result.Texture,
            new Rect(0, 0, 256, 256), Vector2.zero);
        if(profilePic != null)
        {
            profilePic.sprite = fbImage;

            profilePic.gameObject.SetActive(true);
        }
    }
```

After getting the data, we will modify the image or string to display the new data that we retrieved.

For more information on the FB.API function, check out https://developers.facebook.com/docs/unity/reference/current /FB.API.

5. Now, we will need to actually create the text and image we want to display. Open up the **Canvas - Scale w/Screen** object in the **Hierarchy** tab and then rename the **Panel** child object SafeAreaHolder. Then, right-click on the **SafeAreaHolder** child object and select **UI | Panel**. Rename this object Welcome Profile:

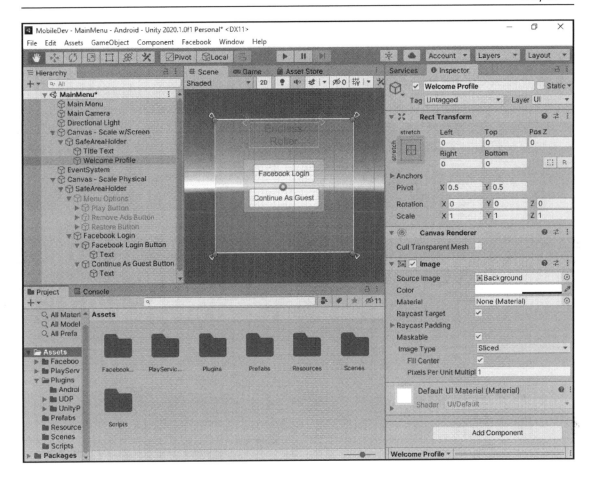

This will act as a container for all of our information for the player.

6. With the **Welcome Profile** object still selected, add a **Horizontal Layout Group** with **Padding** and **Spacing** both set to 10. From there, change **Child Alignment** to **Lower Center** and then check **Width** and **Height** under the **Control Child Size** property. Then, add a **Content Size Fitter** component and change the **Horizontal Fit** and **Vertical Fit** size to **Preferred Size**. Finally, in the **Anchor Presets** menu, hold down *Alt + Shift* and select **Bottom-center**.

7. Now, select the **Welcome Profile** object in the **Hierarchy** tab, right-click on it, and select **UI | Text**.

8. Rename the next **Text** object Greeting.

9. Then, adjust the **Text** to `Welcome` and the size to something larger, such as `50`, and then adjust **Alignment** to be centered vertically and horizontally:

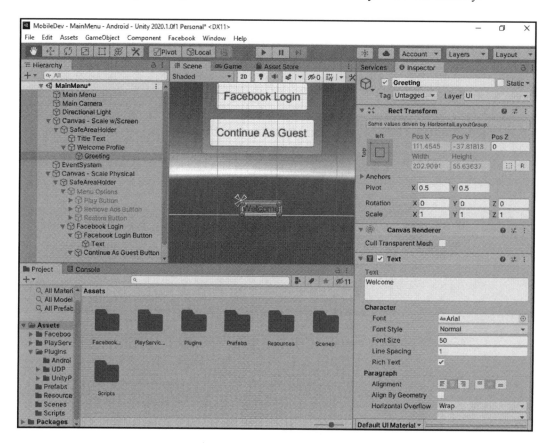

10. Likewise, let's next right-click on **Welcome Profile** again, and this time select **UI | Image**. You may notice that, by default, we are unable to set the image size due to the parent object having a **Horizontal Layout Group**. To override this default, select the image object and add a **Layout Element** component to it. From there, set **Min Width** and **Min Height** to `256`. The **Layout Element (Script)** component is great for allowing you to override things that **LayoutGroups** will do by default and can be useful if you're not getting exactly what you want with the default behavior.

For more information on the **Layout Element (Script)** component, check out `https://docs.unity3d.com/Manual/script-LayoutElement.html`.

11. Next, change the name of the **Image** object to `Profile Pic` and then reorder it so it is above the **Greeting** object in the **Hierarchy**:

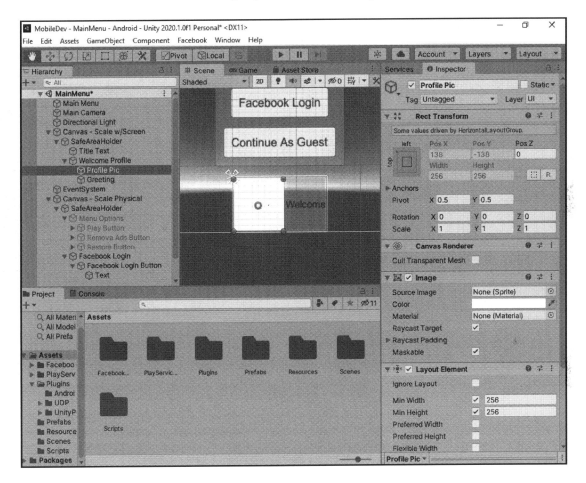

Reordering objects with a **Horizontal Layout Group** modifies their placement order.

If you change the resolution to much smaller sizes, the image is drawn on top of our menu. This is possible due to both canvases being told that they have the same priority in being drawn, similar to how Z-fighting works for 2D games. To fix potential problems in the future, we will instead put the scaling canvas as the background element.

12. To do this, we will select **Canvas - Scale Physical**, and under the **Canvas** component, change **Sort Order** to 1.

13. Now, dive back into the **Main Menu** object and set the **Greeting** and **Profile Pic** properties in the **MainMenuBehaviour** component.

14. Finally, since we don't want them visible when the game starts, let's turn off **Greeting** and our **Profile Pic** objects as well.

15. Save our game, and then start it up again by going through the appropriate login information:

As you can see in the preceding screenshot, I retrieved my actual Facebook info once I logged in.

For more information on the Facebook SDK for Unity and additional examples on what you can do with it, check out `https://developers.facebook.com/docs/unity`.

Facebook is still an incredibly useful platform for game developers and can help personalize a user's gameplay experience. This can be easily expanded to utilize several other pieces of data that Facebook has and share content with all of your user's friends.

Summary

In this chapter, we were introduced to some of the potential ways that we can share our game with others, as well as personalizing our game experiences, utilizing social media and the functionality that it provides us with. We started off by adding in a simple score system and then allowed users to share their scores via Twitter. We then set up the Facebook SDK, making it so that we can log in to it to play our game and retrieve information about our users, which we can use to customize their gameplay experience.

Now that we have people playing our game, we want them to keep coming back and playing over time. One of the easiest ways to do this is through the use of notifications, which we will be looking at in the next chapter.

Keeping Players Involved with Notifications

8

One of the best ways to keep users coming back to your game is through the use of push notifications. This allows you to stay in contact with your users even when they're not using your game. Used wisely, this can keep users playing your game for a long period of time. Using notifications too often or poorly will cause users to mute your app's notifications, which is not an ideal situation.

In this chapter, we will explore how to create notifications for both Android and iOS devices. We will then learn how to schedule notifications to keep players returning to the game later on as well as ways that we can customize them.

The chapter is split into a number of topics. It contains a simple, step-by-step process from beginning to end. Here is the outline of our tasks:

- Setting up notifications
- Scheduling notifications ahead of time
- Customizing notifications

Technical requirements

This book utilizes Unity 2020.1.0f1 and Unity Hub 2.3.1, but the steps should work with minimal changes in future versions of the editor. If you would like to download the exact version used in this book, and there is a new version out, you can visit Unity's download archive at `https://unity3d.com/get-unity/download/archive`. You can also find the system requirements for Unity at `https://docs.unity3d.com/2020.1/Documentation/Manual/system-requirements.html` in the **Unity Editor system requirements** section. To deploy your project, you will need an Android or iOS device.

You can find the code files present in this chapter on GitHub at `https://github.com/` `PacktPublishing/Unity-2020-Mobile-Game-Development-Second-Edition/tree/master/` `Chapter%2008`.

Setting up notifications

Before we can start adding notifications to our project, we will need to add a special preview package that Unity makes available. Follow the steps given here:

1. From the Unity Editor, go to **Window** | **Package Manager**.
2. From there, click on the **In Project** drop-down menu from the toolbar of the **Packages** menu and select **Unity Registry**.
3. Scroll down the available options until you reach **Mobile Notifications** and select it. Once there, click on the arrow to the side of it and select **See All Versions** and then select the latest version (in my case, it was **Version 1.3.0**). From there, click the **Install** button and you'll see the following screenshot:

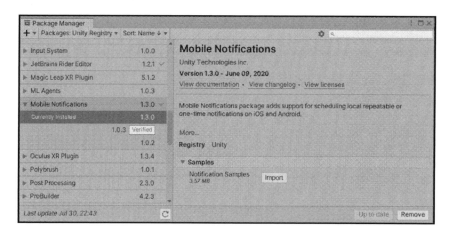

 It's important to note that this package requires your game to use Android 4.4 (API 19) and iOS 10 or above in order to function properly.

We will also be using a cross-platform wrapper also written by Unity in order to get notifications working quickly and remove the requirement of writing platform-specific code.

4. After this, open up the **Samples** section and then click on the **Import** button next to the **Notification Samples** button.
This project, created by Unity, is used to show how you can use Unity's Mobile Notifications API in some real-world examples. We are using it for the cross-platform wrapper, which will allow us to create a notification once and it will work on both Android and iOS without us doing any additional work.

5. After installing this, you may close the **Package Manager** window. To ensure that we can export our project, we need to ensure that our project has the correct Minimum API level.

6. Next, go to our **Project Settings** menu by going to **Edit | Project Settings**. From there, go to the **Player** options and scroll down to **Minimum API Level** and verify that it is set to **Android 4.4 'KitKat' (API level 19)** or higher. Afterward, you can close the **Project Settings** window:

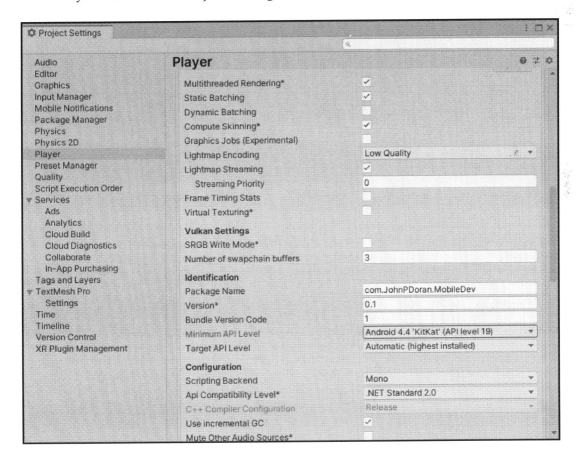

7. You should see that there are a number of folders that are part of the project. The files that we care about are located in the `Assets\Samples\Mobile Notifications\1.3.0\Notification Samples\Scripts` folder. See the following screenshot:

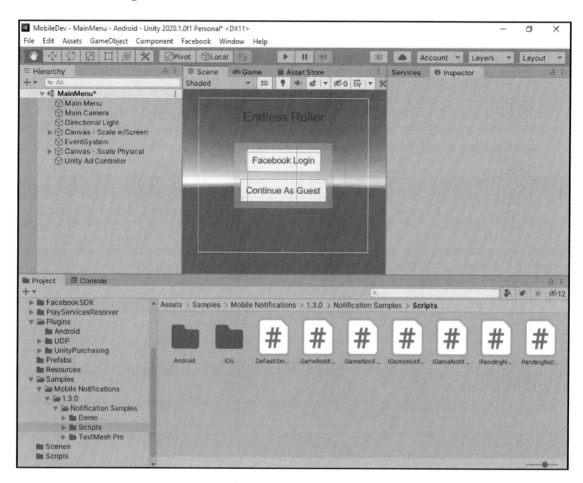

This gives us the code needed – in particular, the `GameNotificationManager` class – to be added to our script. At this point, we could move these scripts into a subfolder of our `Scripts` folder and delete the other files, or keep the files where they are.

To begin displaying notifications on our screen, we first need to add a new object to our level that will contain the Game Notifications Manager:

1. Open the **MainMenu** scene if it isn't already open. From there, create a new game object by going to **GameObject | Create Empty**.

2. From the **Inspector** window, change the name of the object to `Notifications Manager` and for the sake of neatness reset the **Transform** component's **Position** property by right-clicking on the **Transform** component and selecting the **Reset Position** option.

3. Afterward, attach the **Game Notifications Manager** component to the **Notifications Manager** object by clicking on the **Add Component** button and then typing in `gamen` and then selecting **Game Notifications Manager** from the list. It should look something like the following screenshot:

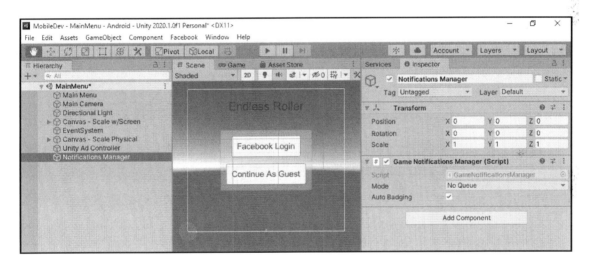

After the component has been placed, we can do the setup needed to create our first notification. Due to the implementation of the `GameNotificationsManager` class, we will need to have another script to send the notifications, which we will call `NotificationsController`.

4. From the **Project** window, open the `Assets/Scripts` folder and create a new C# script called `NotificationsController`. Double-click on the newly created file to open up your code editor of choice.

5. Next, add the following code for the class:

```
using UnityEngine;
using NotificationSamples; // GameNotificationManager

public class NotificationsController : MonoBehaviour
{
    private GameNotificationsManager notificationsManager;

    // Start is called before the first frame update
    private void Start()
    {
        // Get access to the notifications manager
        notificationsManager =
                    GetComponent<GameNotificationsManager>();


        // Create a channel to use for it (required for Android)
        GameNotificationChannel channel = new
            GameNotificationChannel("channel0","Default Channel",
                "Generic Notifications");

        // Initialize the manager so it can be used.
        notificationsManager.Initialize(channel);
    }

}
```

In the preceding code, we are first getting access to the
GameNotificationsManager class through the component. Since we are
attaching this script to the same game object that contains this script, we can use
the GetComponent function. Afterward, we create a channel to post our
notifications on. Lastly, we initialize the GameNotificationsManager
component using the channel.

6. Save your script and go back to the Unity Editor. From the **Inspector** window,
   attach the **Notifications Controller** script onto the Notifications Manager
   object as shown in the following screenshot:

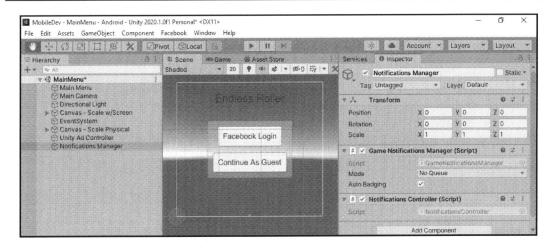

Now that we have the setup taken care of, let's see how we can actually schedule a notification to happen.

Scheduling notifications ahead of time

One of the most common forms of creating a notification is asking players to come back and play the game at a later time. This encourages users to continue playing our game and to come back multiple times. We can do this by setting a delivery time in the future using the following steps:

1. Open up the `NotificationsController` script and add the following function to it:

```
public void ShowNotification(string title, string body,
                             DateTime deliveryTime)
{
    IGameNotification notification =
            notificationsManager.CreateNotification();

    if (notification != null)
    {
        notification.Title = title;
        notification.Body = body;
        notification.DeliveryTime = deliveryTime;

        notificationsManager.ScheduleNotification(notification);
    }
}
```

This function takes in three parameters – the title, the body, and the time at which to send the notification.

2. This function requires the use of the `System` namespace for the `DateTime` class, so at the top of the `NotificationsController` file, add the following line:

```
using System; // DateTime
```

3. Creating the function doesn't do anything, so for the sake of testing that everything has been set up correctly, let's call the function within our `Start` function by adding the following highlighted code:

```
// Start is called before the first frame update
private void Start()
{
    // Get access to the notifications manager
    notificationsManager =
GetComponent<GameNotificationsManager>();


    // Create a channel to use for it (required for Android)
    GameNotificationChannel channel = new GameNotificationChannel
        ("channel0","Default Channel", "Generic Notifications");

    // Initalize the manager so it can be used.
    notificationsManager.Initialize(channel);

    ShowNotification("Endless Runner", "Come back and try to beat your
                                                        score!!",
    DateTime.Now.AddSeconds(5));
}
```

In this example, we are passing in `"Endless Runner"` as the title, `"Come back!"` as the body, and for the third parameter, we are getting the current time by using `DateTime.Now` and then asking to add 5 seconds by using the `AddSeconds` method, passing in `5`.

4. Save the script and return to the Unity Editor. Unfortunately, you won't be able to test whether notifications work on your PC. We'll have to export the game to see if it works correctly.

5. Export your game to your device and start the game. As you can see, our notifications are working correctly!

6. Generally, these kinds of notifications should be sent a day after the player has last played. We can do that by modifying the function to the following:

```
// Start is called before the first frame update
private void Start()
{
    // Get access to the notifications manager
    notificationsManager =
GetComponent<GameNotificationsManager>();

    // Create a channel to use for it (required for Android)
    GameNotificationChannel channel = new
        GameNotificationChannel("channel0", "Default Channel",
            "Generic Notifications");


    // Initalize the manager so it can be used.
    notificationsManager.Initialize(channel);

    // Remind the player to come back tomorrow to play the game
```

```
                    ShowNotification("Endless Roller",
                                "Come back and try to beat your score!",
                                DateTime.Now.AddDays(1));
            }
```

This will make it so that when we reach a level, we will display the notification after a day, but this will also happen every time we go to the main menu. To prevent this, we can add a `static bool` variable that will turn on when adding the notification. In Unity, when a variable is marked as `static`, it will be consistent throughout the running of the program. To add this variable, follow the steps given here:

1. Update the script to add the following code highlighted in bold:

```
private static bool addedReminder = false;

// Start is called before the first frame update
void Start()
{
    // Get access to the notifications manager
    notificationsManager = GetComponent<GameNotificationsManager>
                                                                ();

    // Create a channel to use for it (required for Android)
    GameNotificationChannel channel = new
        GameNotificationChannel("channel0",
            "Default Channel", "Generic Notifications");


    // Initalize the manager so it can be used.
    notificationsManager.Initialize(channel);

    // Check if the notification hasn't been added yet
    if(!addedReminder)
    {
        // Remind the player to come back tomorrow to play the game
        ShowNotification("Endless Runner",
                        "Come back and try to beat your score!",
                        DateTime.Now.AddDays(1));

        // Cannot be added again until the user comes back
        addedReminder = true;
    }
}
```

2. Save your script.

You can also cancel a notification by using the `CancelNotification` and `CancelAllNotifications` functions of the `GameNotificationManager` class. For more information on canceling notifications, check out `https://docs.unity3d.com/Packages/com.unity.mobile.notifications@1.0/manual/index.html`.

This shows us how we can create notifications within our script, but right now the notifications are kind of plain. Thankfully, it's possible to customize notifications, which is what we'll be working on next.

Customizing notifications

Unity includes some default visuals to be used with notifications, but generally, replacing the content with our own will help our game stand out and be more visually appealing to players. In order to have custom icons for Android notifications, you are required to have a small icon with at least 48 x 48 pixels and have only white pixels with a transparent backdrop. The large icon must be at least 192 x 192 and can have whatever colors we'd like. You can create images of your own, or use the images named `Hi-ResIcon.png` and `Small-ResIcon.png` provided in the Example Code for this book in the `Chapter 08\Assets\` folder of the GitHub repository. Follow the steps given here for customization:

1. From the **Project** window, select the images you are planning to use for the small and large icons.
2. With the images selected, go to the **Inspector** window and open up the **Advanced** options.
3. Finally, check the **Read/Write Enabled** and **Alpha Is Transparency** properties. Click on the **Apply** button so the changes happen.

You can see the options in the **Inspector** window in the following screenshot:

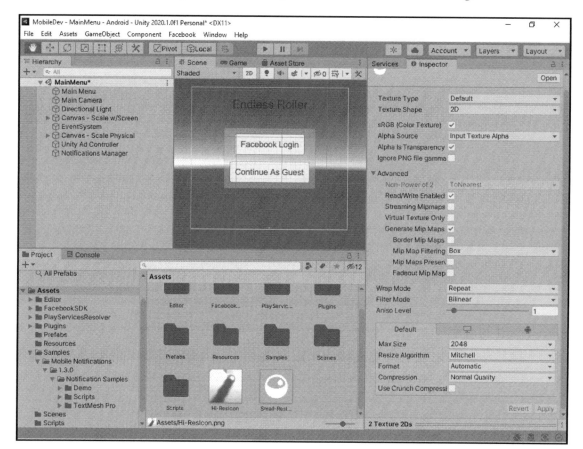

At this point, our images are ready and we can start to put them into our notifications. To do this, we will need to go to the **Project Settings** menu.

4. Open the **Project Settings** menu by going to **Edit | Project Settings**.

5. From there, go to the **Mobile Notifications** settings option.

6. From the menu, you'll see two options – **iOS** and **Android**. We will want to use the default properties for the iOS options so we will first select **Android**, if it isn't selected already.

7. Check the **Reschedule Notifications on Device Restart**. This will make it so that if someone plays the game again, they will no longer get the notification we created earlier. This will help the user not get annoyed at us spamming them too often.

8. Next, under **Notification Icons**, click on the plus (**+**) icon. Drag and drop the small icon image into the first **Texture 2D** option. Next, click on the plus (**+**) icon again and then change **Type** to **Large**. Afterward, assign your large icon to the **Texture 2D** spot:

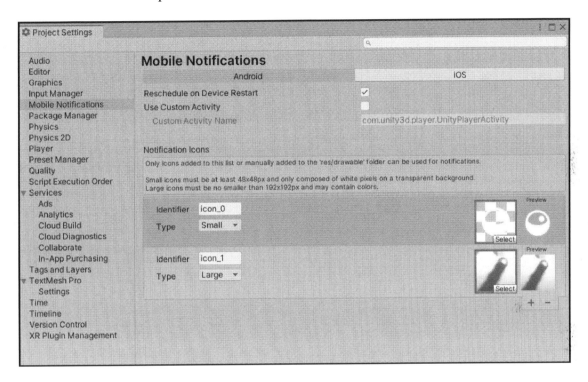

9. Then go back to the `NotificationsController` script and update the `ShowNotification` function to use our new icons:

```
public void ShowNotification(string title,
                             string body,
                             DateTime deliveryTime)
{
    IGameNotification notification =
notificationsManager.CreateNotification();

    if (notification != null)
    {
        notification.Title = title;
        notification.Body = body;
        notification.DeliveryTime = deliveryTime;
        notification.SmallIcon = "icon_0";
```

```
notification.LargeIcon = "icon_1";

    notificationsManager.ScheduleNotification(notification);
        }
    }
```

10. Save your script and return to the Unity Editor. Export your game to Android and you should see the icons update. Now the notification will show the small icon from the toolbar, as shown in the following screenshot:

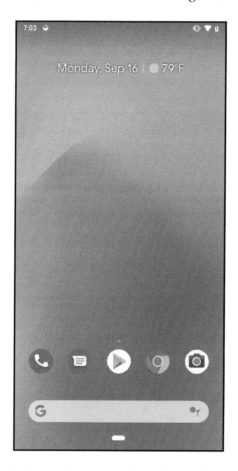

And it will use both icons when accessing the notification itself! This can be seen in the following screenshot:

It is also possible to modify other properties, such as the badge number used in iOS by using a line like the following:

```
notification.BadgeNumber = 5;
```

For more information on how you can customize your notifications, check out https://docs.unity3d.com/Packages/com.unity.mobile. notifications@1.0/manual/index.html.

This allows us to have our notifications look just the way we want them to with as much polish as we would like them to have.

Summary

At this point, we have seen how we can make use of Unity's Mobile Notifications package to create notifications for our players. We've learned how to schedule them to take place in the future as well as how to customize these notifications to have our own distinct visual style!

We now have everything in place for players to play and come back to our game, but we are only relying on what we created. In addition to that, we may want to see what our players are doing while playing our games. Then, we can use that information to improve and/or tweak our game.

In the next chapter, we will take a look at how we can do this using tools from Unity Analytics.

Using Unity Analytics

9

Making a game is a wonderful experience and a lot of hard work, but when designing projects, you have to rely on your experience and gut feelings in order to make it as awesome as possible. Often, in the game industry, we will use playtesting – a process where select people play the game and give feedback, and then we use the feedback we receive to improve the project.

This playtesting is most often done in person; however, by creating games for mobile, a lot of people will be playing your game after release and most of them will have an internet connection. With this combination of people playing the games while also being online, we can send data about how the game is being played to ourselves. This will still allow us to do playtesting with a large variety of people. Being able to look at our data will allow us to check whether the choices that are made to change the game are the right ones, and we will be able to make adjustments to our games on the fly.

This data could be about something as simple as where players tend to die in the game or things such as how often they come back to play, the daily average time they play, the number of users we have at a time, how long people play the game before stopping, and what choices they made. Over the course of this chapter, we will learn how to set up the ability to learn what our users are doing through the use of Unity's built-in Analytics system.

This chapter will be split into a number of topics. The chapter itself is a simple step-by-step process from beginning to end. Here is an outline of our tasks:

- Setting up Unity Analytics
- Tracking custom events
- Working with the funnel analyzer
- Tweaking properties with remote settings

Technical requirements

In this chapter, we will cover some of the different ways that we can integrate Unity's Analytics tools into our projects.

This chapter assumes that you have Unity Analytics activated already. If you haven't, refer to Chapter 5, *Advertising Using Unity Ads*, to learn how to create an account.

The code files for this chapter can be found at https://github.com/PacktPublishing/ Unity-2020-Mobile-Game-Development-Second-Edition/tree/master/Chapter%2009.

Setting up Analytics

Although we activated the Analytics option from Unity's Cloud Services in order to use Unity's Ads system in Chapter 5, *Advertising Using Unity Ads*, we didn't really dig into the system itself. Let's finish the setup for that now using the following steps:

1. From the Unity Editor, open the **Services** tab (shown in the top-right part of the next screenshot) by either selecting it or going to **Window** | **General** | **Services**.

2. From there, scroll down and click on the **Analytics** button as shown in the following screenshot:

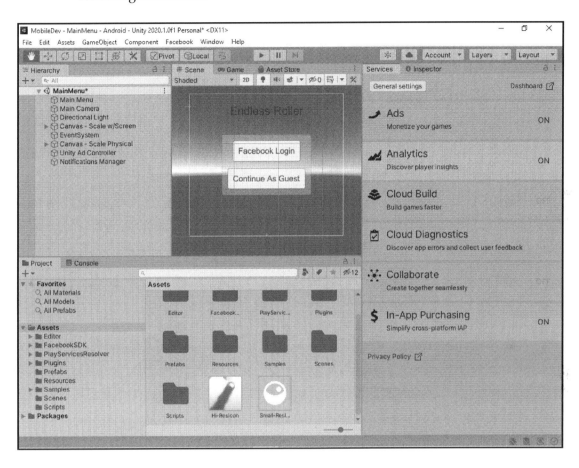

As long as **Analytics** is enabled, the editor sends an App Start event to the Analytics service when we press the **Play** button to start the game:

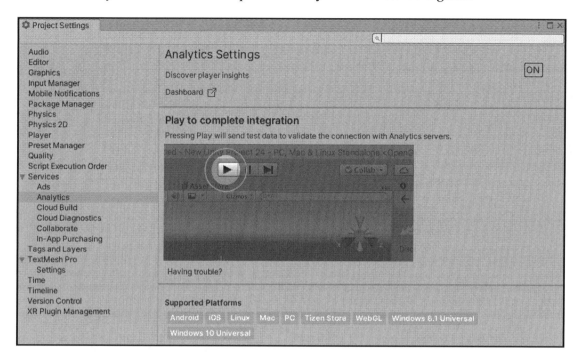

The nice thing about this is that we can ensure that this feature works correctly without having to export our game.

3. Press the **Play** button on the game. Once the game has been played, the app will send start sending Analytics events from the editor. However, they will not actually start processing data until you visit the dashboard at least once, so let's do that next.

4. From the **Services** tab at the top right, you'll see a button called **Dashboard**; click on it and it will open a web browser to the project's page:

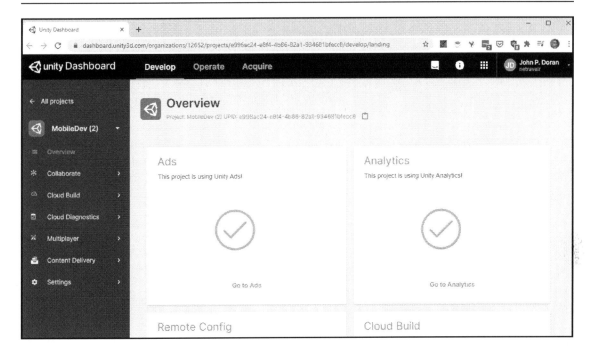

Unity used to have two built-in tools called the Validator and the Livestream, which would show you in real time the events that happened; however, they have since discontinued these tools (more information here: `https://forum.unity.com/threads/removal-of-validator-and-livestream-features-on-january-16th.810150/`). This means that we may have to wait up to 16 hours before we will actually see the events trigger within our projects.

You may still wish to verify that events are actually being sent. One way that we can do this is with a tool called Charles Proxy. It costs $50 but has a free 30-day trial. If you're interested in integrating it with Unity, check out `https://support.unity3d.com/hc/en-us/articles/115002917683-Using-Charles-Proxy-with-Unity`.

Now that we have Unity Analytics set up, let's start creating our own custom events to track!

Tracking Custom Events

Unity Analytics does a number of different things automatically to make it easy to work with. However, as a game designer, you may often want to check whether certain aspects of the game are being used or whether players are reaching certain pieces of content. To keep track of this, we can make use of the **Custom Events** system.

Custom Events are pieces of data that users send to the cloud as they play the game. Each Custom Event can have its own parameters, which will allow us to filter the data that we send when it is generated. We will discuss how you can send information over the cloud through the use of code.

Sending basic CustomEvents

The first kind of event we are going to send is just an event name. This can be used for something such as tracking the number of times people access a certain place or checking whether something invalid appears to be happening. To make it easy to trigger and track for testing purposes, we will cause an event to happen each time the game is paused. Let's look at the steps:

1. Open the `PauseScreenBehaviour` script and add the following `using` statement to the top of the script:

   ```
   using UnityEngine.Analytics;        // CustomEvent
   ```

   This namespace contains all of the functions used by Unity's Analytics system.

2. Update the `SetPauseMenu` function to include the following highlighted code:

   ```
   /// <summary>
   /// Will turn our pause menu on or off
   /// </summary>
   /// <param name="isPaused"></param>
   public void SetPauseMenu(bool isPaused)
   {
       paused = isPaused;

       // If the game is paused, timeScale is 0, otherwise 1
       Time.timeScale = (paused) ? 0 : 1;
       pauseMenu.SetActive(paused);

       if(paused)
       {
           var result = Analytics.CustomEvent("Paused");
   ```

```
        if (result == AnalyticsResult.Ok)
        {
            Debug.Log("Event Sent: Paused");
        }
    }
}
```

This code will call the `Analytics.CustomEvent` function when the `pauseMenu` has been turned on. The first parameter of `Analytics.CustomEvent` is a string, which is the name that you wish the event to have. This name will be used within Unity Analytics. The function returns an object of the type `AnalyticsResult`, which if set to `Ok` means that Unity sent the event without any problems and it should go to the cloud and be available after a period of time.

3. Save the script and then return to the Unity Editor. Once back, play the game and pause the game. As you can see, the event was sent over the cloud successfully!

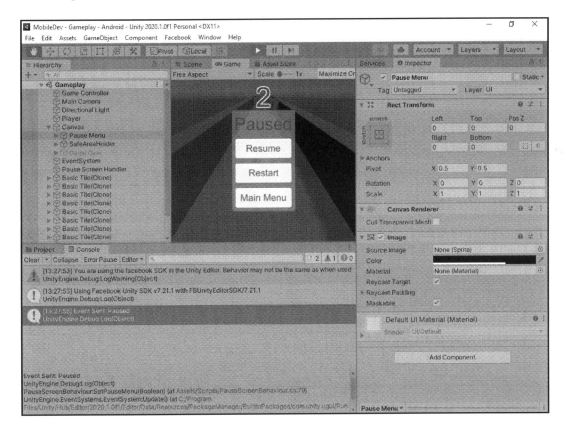

As mentioned before, it can take quite some time before information shows up on the Unity dashboard, but it's a good idea at this point to see where this information can be received later on.

4. Go ahead and scroll up in the **Services** window and select the **Dashboard** button in the top-right portion of the tab. From there, click on the **Go to Analytics** button:

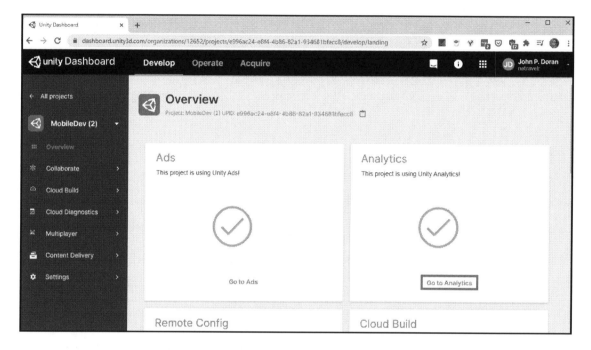

This will bring you to **Event Manager**, which is a place where you can see the Custom Events and parameters that have been received from the game. We will see this in more detail in the next section. As mentioned, currently there is nothing there to see; but given some time, you should see something there later:

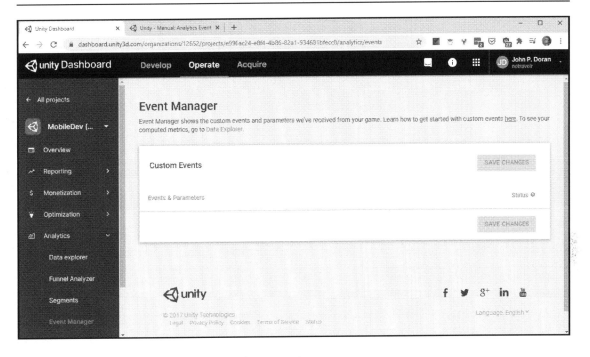

5. Next, click on the **Data explorer** option.

6. In the **Data explorer** tab, you'll see two buttons for **Metric** and **Custom Event**. You'll also see a chart that shows the **DAU (Daily Active Users)** that have been playing your project. We can also use this menu to observe whenever the **Paused** event is called.

> If you have just created the event, it may take up to 12 hours for the information to be received. Go ahead and check back later if that's the case. In the past, I've had to wait up to even 48 hours for the data, so do not be alarmed if it takes a while for it to show up.

7. Click on the **+** button to the left of **Custom Event** to add a Custom Event to this graph. Then, select the **Custom Event** dropdown and select **Paused**. Since we have just made the event, we won't see it in previous dates in Analytics, but we can see it a little easier if we click on the **Column Chart** button to change how the data is displayed:

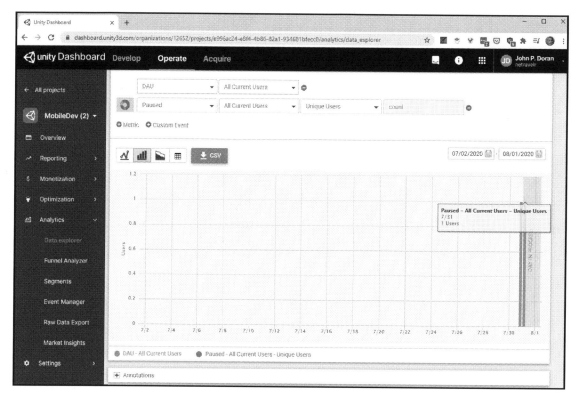

Notice that when we scroll down, we can see that **Data explorer** now shows that the **Paused** event has been called!

 In addition to the calling event, you can also add parameters to the events in a similar manner to how Unity's UI system works. For more information on that and the Analytics Tracker component, check out https://docs.unity3d.com/Manual/UnityAnalyticsAnalyticsTracker.html.

This can be a useful tool for designers on your team who prefer not to work within code and can easily be expanded for your own purposes.

Sending Custom Events with properties

One additional thing that we may want to track is how far players get before they lose. Let's take a look at how to do that now:

1. First, we will need to open up the `ObstacleBehaviour` script to modify what happens when the game ends.

2. To utilize Unity Analytics with parameters, at the top of the file, we will add the following `using` declarations:

```
using UnityEngine.Analytics; // Analytics
using System.Collections.Generic; // Dictionary
```

The top option is obvious, but we are also adding `System.Collections.Generic` in order to get access to the `Dictionary` class, which we will use in the next piece of code.

3. Next, we will update the `OnCollisionEnter` function to the following:

```
private void OnCollisionEnter(Collision collision)
{
    var go = collision.gameObject;
    var playerBehaviour = go.GetComponent<PlayerBehaviour>();

    // First check if we collided with the player
    if (playerBehaviour)
    {
        // Destroy (Hide) the player
        go.SetActive(false);
        player = go;

        var eventData = new Dictionary<string, object>
        {
            { "score", playerBehaviour.Score }
        };

        var result = Analytics.CustomEvent("Game Over", eventData);

        if(result == AnalyticsResult.Ok)
        {
            Debug.Log("Event Sent: Game Over - score: " +
                playerBehaviour.Score);
```

```
        }

        // Call the function ResetGame after waitTime has passed
        Invoke("ResetGame", waitTime);
    }
}
```

We've done a number of things within this script. To start off with, we have rewritten our check for the player to use the component as a variable now so that we don't have to call GetComponent again for the same thing. Aside from that, the main addition is the calling of the Analytics.SendEvent function with a second parameter. The second parameter (which is optional) is a dictionary, which we haven't discussed yet.

A **dictionary** is a class that represents a pair of keys and values. The key is an identifier of some sort, which allows us to have a reference to obtain the value. This is most often used with strings as the key so that you can refer to some other data type.

For more information on dictionaries, check out http://csharp.net-informations.com/collection/dictionary.htm.

4. Save the script and return to the Unity Editor.
5. Play the game and lose it. You will note in the **Console** window that now you are sending a **Game Over** event with your score value:

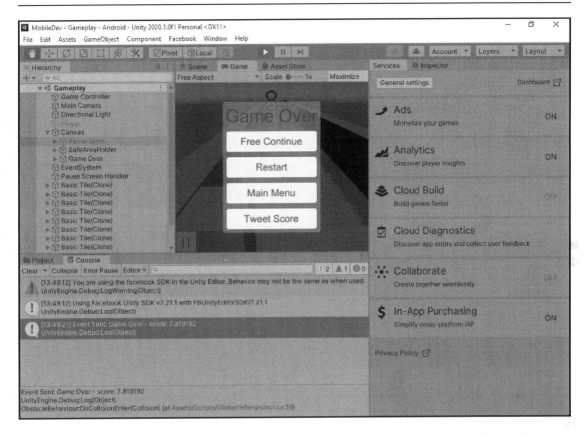

You may also dive into the dashboard to see the information as well, but Unity says it may take up to 6 hours before it will be visible. Events typically take a few hours to cycle. You will see them instantly on the **Console** window (from the `Debug.Log` call that we made to help you confirm that your code is working), but they don't populate in Analytics until the backend calculations have been processed at Unity's end, due to all of the events they receive.

6. After you've waited, go to the **Analytics** tab and click on the **Dashboard** button once again. From there, click on the **Go to Analytics** button.

We are brought again to **Event Manager**. **Event Manager** is the location where users can see the Custom Events that were received from users playing the game as well as the parameters that were passed to them. This typically takes the longest of all of the Unity Analytics tools to update, so if you do not see any events there, there is another way that you can check whether data has been received: using the **Raw Data Export** tool.

7. On the left-hand side of the Unity dashboard, under the **Analytics** section, click on the **Raw Data Export** button:

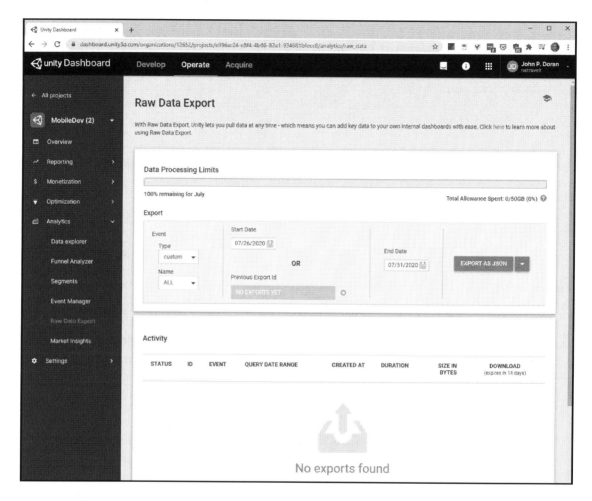

The **Raw Data Export** tool gives users access to the raw event data that Unity Analytics receives after being processed. This lets you use the data however you like outside of the Unity dashboard – for instance, you could use it to construct custom queries or data visualizations.

Note: The **Raw Data Export** tool requires you to have a Unity Pro subscription.

By default, the **Export** section is looking for Custom Events from a **Start Data** value to an **End Date** value. But you can customize this through setting the **Type**, **Start Date**, and **End Date** values. From here, you can get events regarding things such as when apps are started, what devices the game is being played on, and any transaction data that is generated.

By default, the files that are exported are JSON files. **JSON** stands for **JavaScript Object Notation** and is a format that is used to read/write text. The JSON file type is commonly used to transmit data and even save files. It's nice for programmers because it works with a key-pair system such as the **Dictionary** class that we used previously.

If we export the file as a JSON file, we would get something like the following for each piece of event data:

```
{"name":"Game
Over","ts":1596221196085,"userid":"8ae31bd296283084aac4984ad9eb6f75
","sessionid":"4916459330333886753","platform":"WindowsEditor","sdk
_ver":"u2020.1.0f1","debug_device":true,"user_agent":"UnityPlayer/2
020.1.0f1 (UnityWebRequest/1.0, libcurl/7.52.0-
DEV)","submit_time":1596221229000,"custom_params":{"score":"6.45771
5"},"country":"US","city":"Peoria","appid":"e996ac24-
e8f4-4b86-82a1-934681bfecc8","type":"custom"}
```

It may look like a bunch of text, but after some formatting, it looks a lot nicer to work with:

```
{
    "name":"Game Over",
    "ts":1596221196085,
    "userid":"8ae31bd296283084aac4984ad9eb6f75",
    "sessionid":"4916459330333886753",
    "platform":"WindowsEditor",
    "sdk_ver":"u2020.1.0f1",
    "debug_device":true,
    "user_agent":"UnityPlayer/2020.1.0f1 (UnityWebRequest/1.0,
        libcurl/7.52.0-DEV)",
    "submit_time":1596221229000,
    "custom_params":{"score":"6.457715"},
    "country":"US",
    "city":"Peoria",
    "appid":"e996ac24-e8f4-4b86-82a1-934681bfecc8",
    "type":"custom"
}
```

I made bold the two pieces of data we care about at the moment: the event that happened and the custom parameters we provided to it. This means that we are sending information correctly!

Another way that you can read the information that may be useful concerns the other that Unity Analytics supports for exporting: TSV. **TSV** stands for **tab-separated values** and is a file format that can easily be opened in programs such as Microsoft Excel and Google Sheets.

8. Click on the arrow next to the **EXPORT AS JSON** option and select **EXPORT AS TSV**.
9. Click on the **EXPORT AS TSV** button and wait for it to finish processing. You may need to reload your page later to receive the events:

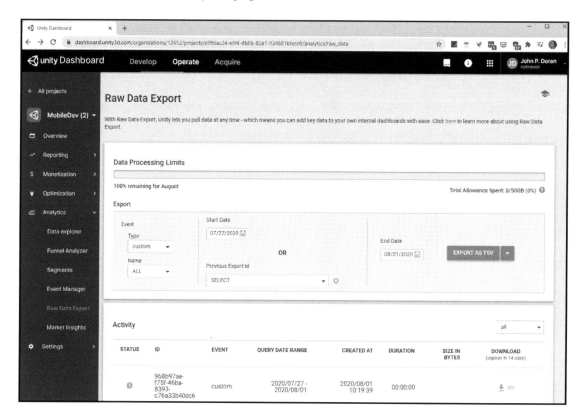

10. Once the data has finished processing, you can then click on **tsv** under the **DOWNLOAD** section. It'll then present some dates. Click on the current date and wait for the file to download.

11. Once downloaded, you'll see the file is of the GZ type, which is a standard GNU zip file. You should be able to unzip it utilizing unzipping software.

   I use the free 7zip on my Windows machine, which you can get from `https://www.7-zip.org/`. On macOS, you can utilize The Unarchiver, which is available on the App Store for free.

12. Once unzipped, you'll be given a file. At this point, you can just open it with a text editor such as Notepad, but to make it easier to parse, we can instead use some sort of sheets data. Rename the file, add the `.tsv` file extension to it, and then open it in Excel or Google Sheets. As you can see, the first section (**A**) has the names of the events that have happened over the day and the **N** section has the data that was passed to the function:

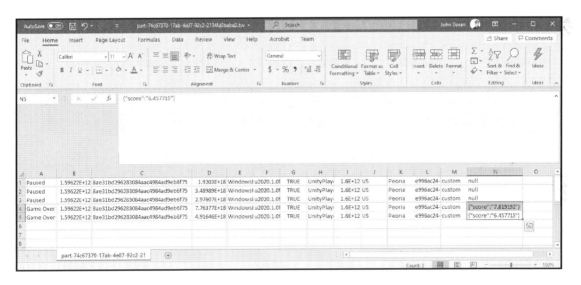

This means that Unity is receiving the information correctly!

Note that while in this example we used a single value, we can pass up to 10 parameters into the dictionary. However, the value must be one of the following types:

- `bool`
- `string`
- `int`
- `float`

Remember that you can always convert an object to a string in C# using the `ToString` function.

You can only send 100 custom events per hour per user, so you should not be doing too many custom events in the game.

For more information on `Analytics.CustomEvent` and other ways it can be called, check out `https://docs.unity3d.com/ScriptReference/Analytics.Analytics.CustomEvent.html`.

I suggest that you create custom events for whenever a user reaches an important milestone, for example, when they level up or when they make an **In-App Purchase (IAP)**.

Now that we know how to create different types of events, let's see how we can actually track events and learn more about what our players are doing utilizing the Funnel Analyzer tool.

Working with Funnel Analyzer

One of the many things we'd like to know about our players is how they are actually playing the game. Are users skipping our tutorial, for instance? To keep track of how players proceed through a series of events, we have funnels. Funnels help us to identify where player drop-off happens in our game.

If you happen to see a large number of people not getting to a certain step, you can assume that something that happened in the preceding step is causing people to stop playing our game.

For more information on how funnels can work as well as why you'd want to use them, check out `https://data36.com/funnel-analysis/`.

Funnels are based on the concept of Custom Events, which we used in the *Sending Custom Events with properties* section of this chapter. We can use Funnel Analyzer in order to look at the data sent via these funnels, which we can then use to make educated decisions on what changes should be made to the game. Follow the steps given here to add the tool:

1. From the dashboard, go to **Analytics** and select **Funnel Analyzer**:

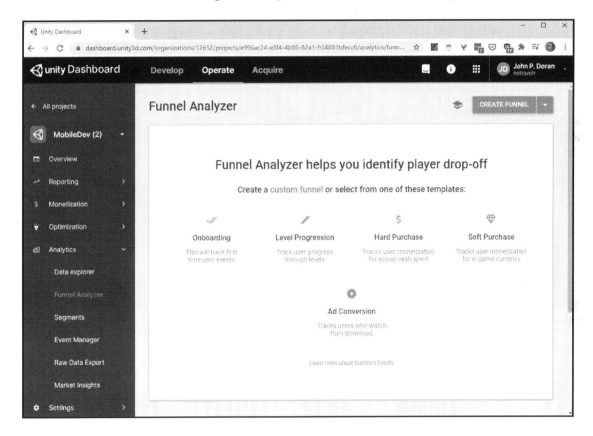

Right now, there are no funnels set up, so we should create one.

2. Click on the **custom funnel** option and fill the details as mentioned in the following screenshot. Then, scroll all the way down and then click on the **SAVE FUNNEL** button:

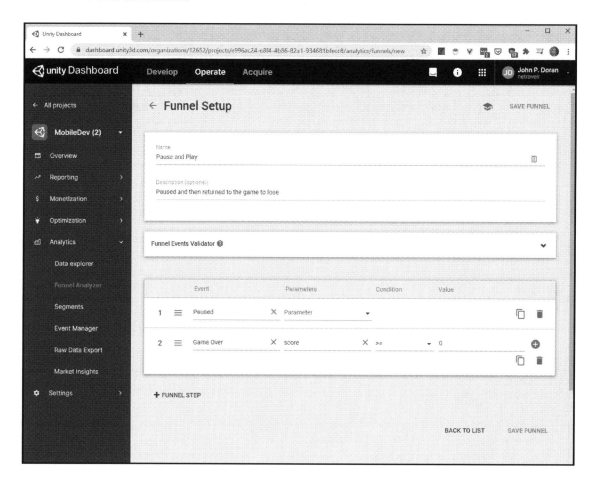

3. You'll get a notice saying that the funnel has been submitted, but it may take up to a day before we can see the results (at least 10-12 hours). Go ahead and click on **X** to exit out of the menu:

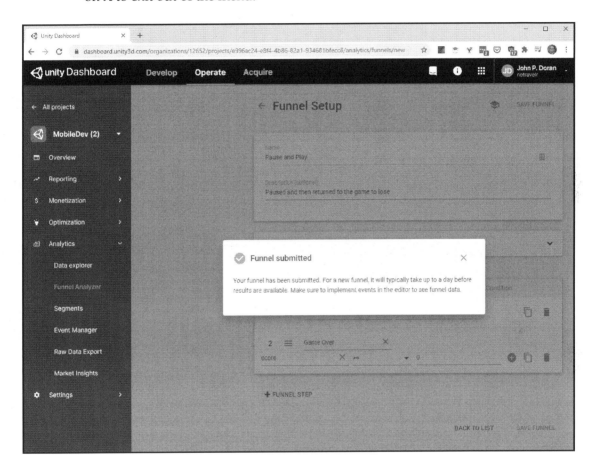

4. Now, go back into the Unity Editor and play the game a couple more times and ensure that you pause the game before causing a Game Over event to fill up some test data for us to check the next day:

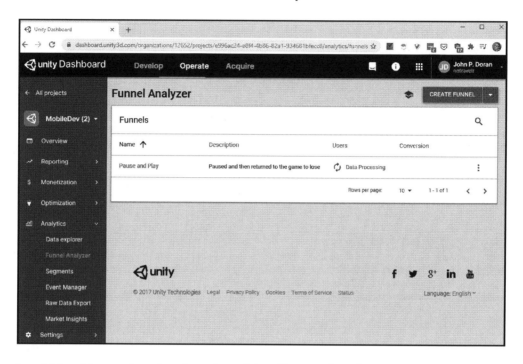

You should be able to select that funnel, and it will provide information on all the times it has been called.

The concepts used here can easily be expanded upon in other ways as well, like keeping track of how often users watch ads or make purchases in the game and what caused them to do so.

Now that we have seen how to create events, let's see one of the other main features of utilizing Unity Analytics: being able to change projects using the Remote Settings feature.

Tweaking properties with Remote Settings

Getting a new build of your game exported can take quite a bit of time. It takes time to actually make the changes in the editor, and then you have to export the game and upload a new version on each of the app stores you are targeting. Then, you have to spend time waiting on them to approve the app and for everyone to actually download it.

One of the things I talk to my students about is creating projects that can be easily changed without having to open the Unity Editor. This can be done using data-driven development practices – such as building levels or encounters using text files, Asset Bundles, or Unity's **Remote Settings** menu – to allow us to instantly modify variables in copies of the game that are already out.

One of the things we may want to be able to update is the difficulty of our game by changing the speed at which the player moves. So, let's take a look at how we can do that using the following steps:

1. The first thing we will need to do is create the variables that we would like to change. Open up the Unity dashboard and then click on **Go To Analytics** if needed. Once there, on the left-hand side, open up the **Optimization** section and then click on the **Remote Settings** tab located under it:

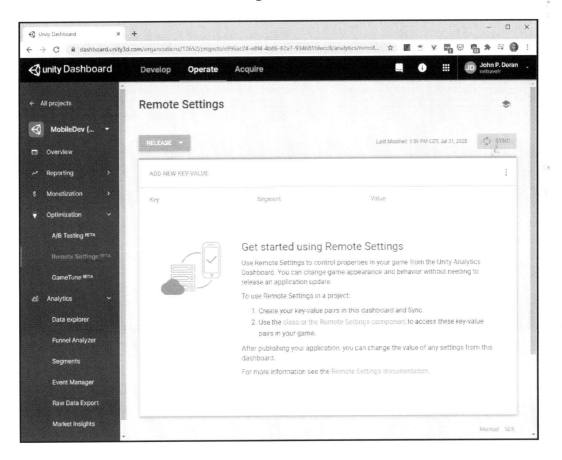

This section is the location where we can set and modify the values. Just like working with dictionaries, the settings are key-value pairs, and there are two configurations that can be used: **Release** or **Development**. The release is used by computers and devices running regular builds of your game. **Development** is the mode used by playing the game in the Unity Editor, as well as any builds created with the **Development Build** property set to **True** from the **Build Settings** window.

2. Click on the **ADD NEW KEY-VALUE** button at the top-left corner of the table. Under the **Enter Remote Setting Key** property, type RollSpeed. Under the **Type** dropdown, select **Float**. Lastly, put 5 in the **Enter Value** field. Finally, click on the **Save** button:

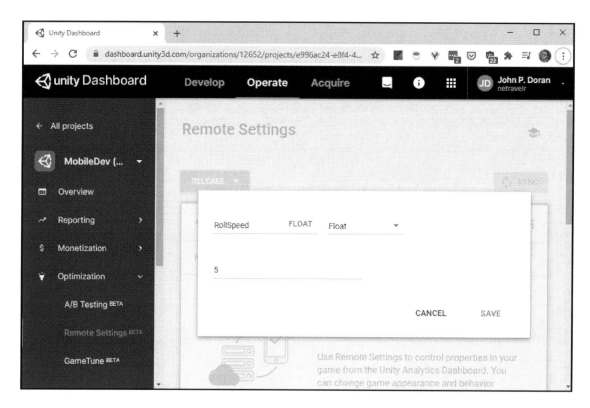

3. Then, let's do the same thing for the DodgeSpeed variable with a value of 5:

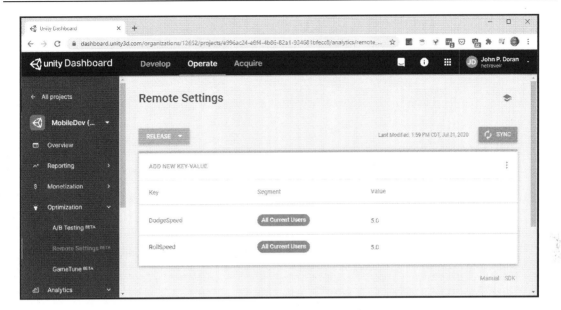

4. It's important to note that this doesn't actually make the change. Note how there is a big blue button that says **SYNC**. Click on that and then the changes will be deployed. It'll present a window asking whether you want to confirm the changes:

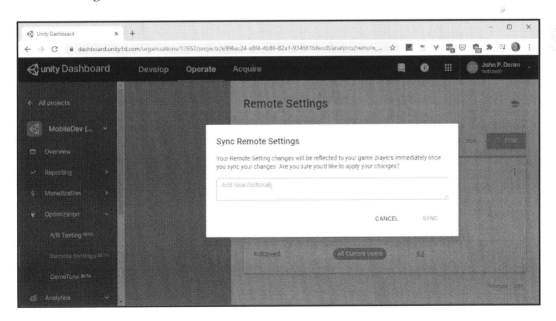

5. Go ahead and then click on **SYNC**.

6. Now that we have some values to grab, let's take a look at how we can actually do that. Head back into the Unity Editor.

7. In order to use **Remote Settings**, we will need to download and import the Remote Settings package. To do this, go to the Unity Asset Store at `https://assetstore.unity.com/`. As of Unity 2020, you no longer need to use the built-in asset store window. Go to **Window | Asset Store** (or press *Ctrl + 9*).

8. From the Asset Store, click on the search bar, type in `Remote Settings`, and press *Enter*:

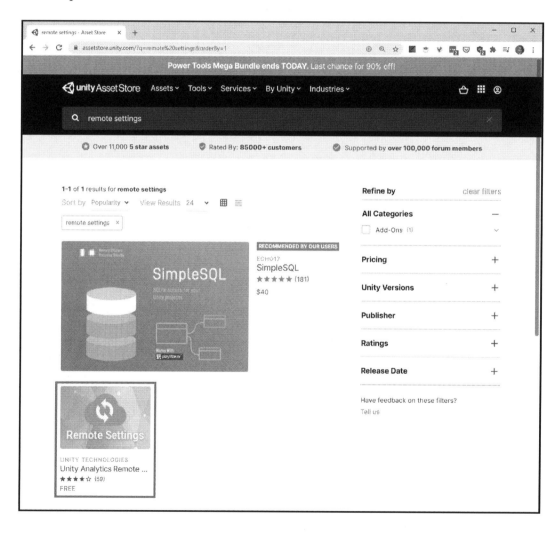

9. From there, click on the **Unity Analytics Remote Settings** option.
10. Next, click on the **Add to My Assets / Open In Unity** button to add it to our project:

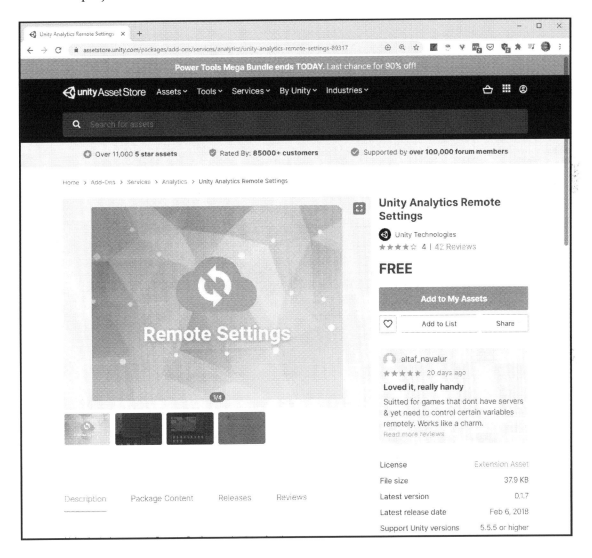

11. Then, the package manager should open with the asset selected. Click on the **Download** button and, once finished, click on **Import** with everything selected:

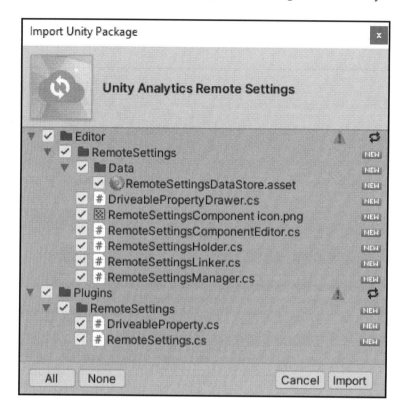

 I deleted the `MiniJSON.cs` file that was included with **Remote Settings** due to it already being defined within Unity's IAP scripts. This should be fixed by the time the book is published, but I am including it just in case it shows up.

12. One of the files has not been updated to the latest version of Unity, so we will need to fix that. Open the `RemoteSettingsLinker.cs` file and update the class definition to use the following highlighted code:

```
namespace UnityEngine.Analytics
{
    // During a build, collect classes referenced by RemoteSettings
    // components
    // in each scene and in prefabs, and write to a link.xml file
        // to prevent
    // those classes from being stripped.
```

```
public class RemoteSettingsLinker : IPreprocessBuildWithReport,
    IProcessSceneWithReport
{
    const string k_LinkPath =
        "Assets/Editor/RemoteSettings/link.xml";

    string lastActiveScene;
    Dictionary<string, HashSet<string>> types;
```

13. Save the file and upon returning to Unity, the fix should work.

14. Now that we have it imported, we need to enable it. To do that, we will need to go to **Window** | **Unity Analytics** | **Remote Settings**:

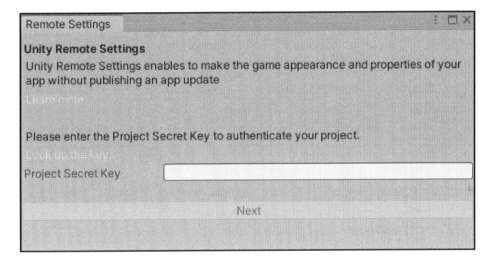

As you can see in the preceding screenshot, we need to plug in the project's secret key in order to make use of these features. To do this, we will need to once again go to the dashboard.

15. From the dashboard, go to the **Settings** section and select **Analytics Settings**.

16. Scroll down, and you should see the **Project Secret Key** property under **Feature Settings**:

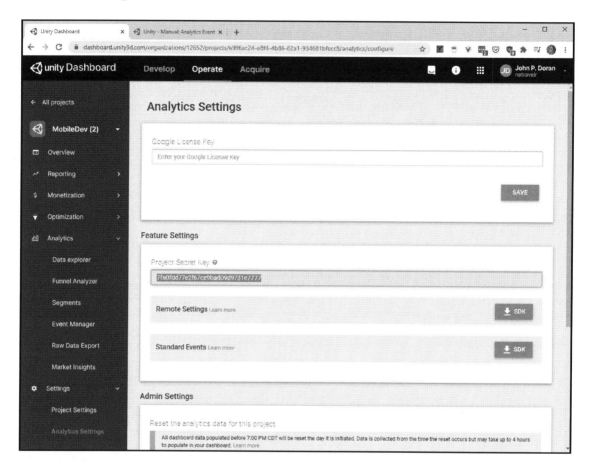

You should keep the value of **Project Secret Key** a secret, as it allows others to have access to your project.

17. Copy this value and then go back into Unity Editor, paste it into the slot, and click on the **Next** button. If all goes well, you should see the menu change:

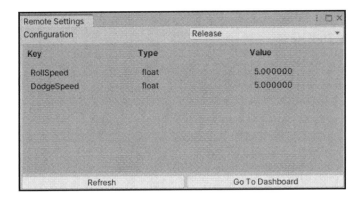

18. To make it easier to see, I'm going to drag the **Remote Settings** tab and drop it to the right of my **Scene** tab:

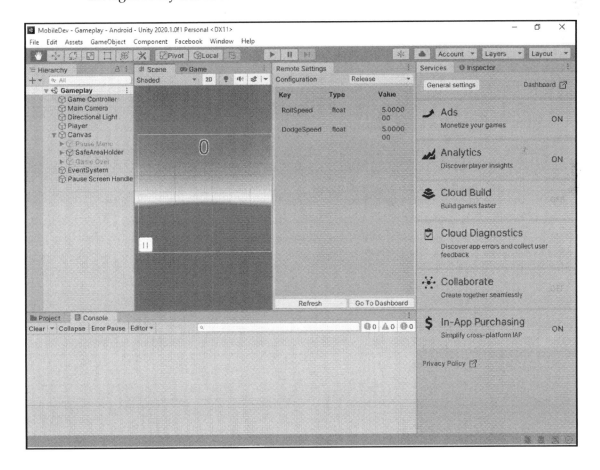

Now it's a lot easier to look at and work with. Again, this doesn't do anything yet, so let's fix that next.

19. Open up the Gameplay Scene if it isn't open already, select the **Player** object, and go to the **Inspector** window.

20. Next, go to **Add Component** | **Analytics** | **Remote Settings** to add the **Remote Settings** component to the object:

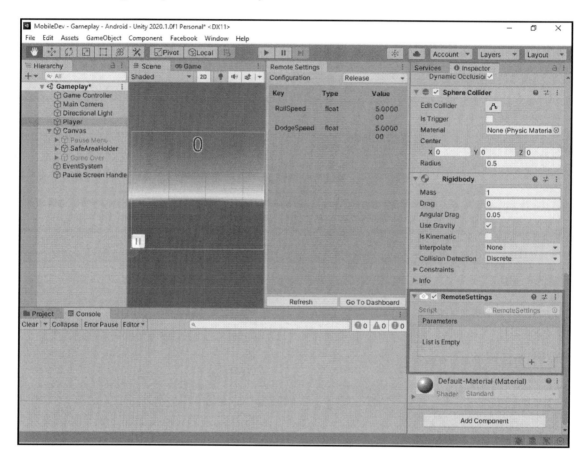

21. From there, click on the + button to add a new parameter for the component.

22. Drag and drop the **Player** GameObject from the **Hierarchy** tab into the **Object** section. Then, for the **No field** property, select **PlayerBehaviour | rollSpeed**. Then, for **Remote Setting Key**, select **Roll Speed** from the dropdown. This makes the `RollSpeed` variable in the `PlayerBehaviour` class set to the **Roll Speed** value in the **Remote Settings** menu.

23. Then, do the same thing for `DodgeSpeed`:

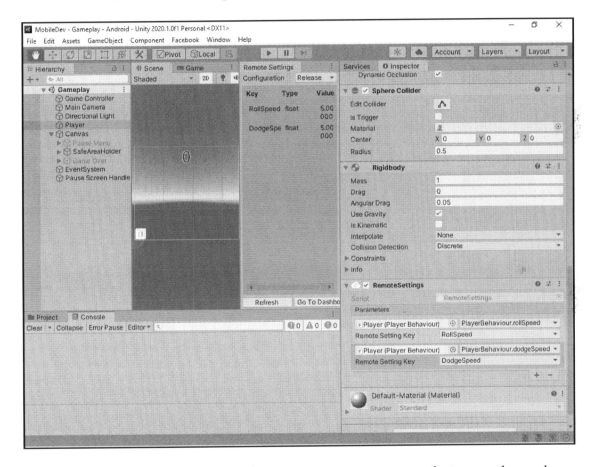

This would work correctly if we were to export our game, but currently, we do not have variables set up for the Development configuration. This means that when playing the game in the editor, nothing will change.

24. Dive back into the dashboard and go to the **Remote Settings** section again. Under the dropdown, change the **Release** value to **Development**:

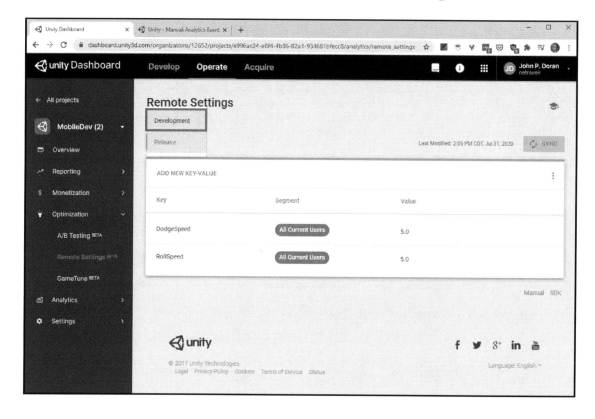

25. Once in **Development** mode, add in `DodgeSpeed` and `RollSpeed` again, but give them both a value of 0. Finally, click on the **SYNC** button to update the values:

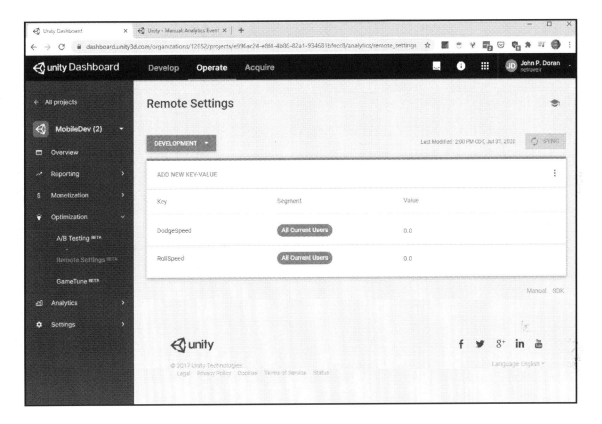

26. Next, dive back into the editor, and in the **Remote Settings** property, click on the **Refresh** button. You will note that the **Configuration** property now has a dropdown where you can select something. Go ahead and select **Development** and play the game:

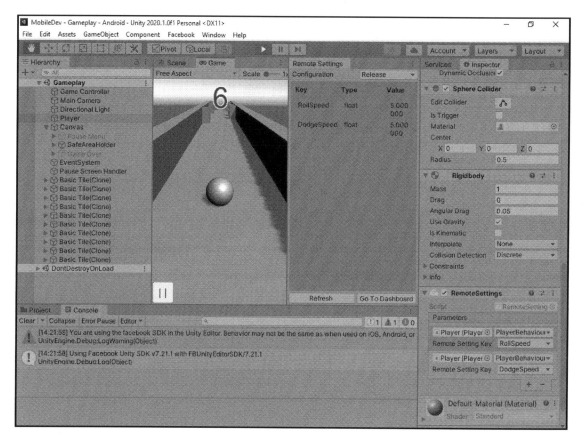

As you can tell, in this version of the game, the player cannot move at all due to how we set the properties. Now, you can test out the values and sync them in the editor and modify them for release when they're ready.

27. Since the `dodgeSpeed` and `rollSpeed` variables are now being set via the **Remote Settings** component, we can now hide them from the **Inspector** window. Replace their declarations in the `PlayerBehaviour` script, so that the class looks as follows:

```
/// <summary>
/// How fast the ball moves left/right
```

```
/// </summary>
[HideInInspector]
public float dodgeSpeed = 5;

/// <summary>
/// How fast the ball moves forwards automatically
/// </summary>
[HideInInspector]
public float rollSpeed = 5;
```

Here we've modified the two properties, adding the `[HideInInspector]` tag, which will hide the item in the **Inspector** window. We also changed the variables to use XML comments instead of tooltips, since they are no longer being displayed in the **Inspector** window.

28. Save the script and go to **Inspector**:

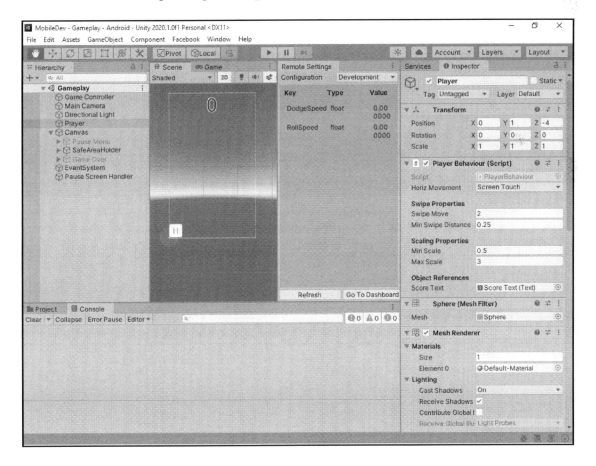

Now, the values will be set through the **Remote Settings** component, and users won't be confused about why their values are being replaced by what's in **Player Behaviour**.

29. Lastly, make sure you go back to the **Remote Settings** menu and change the **Development** variables back to a higher number and sync the changes before going on to the next chapter:

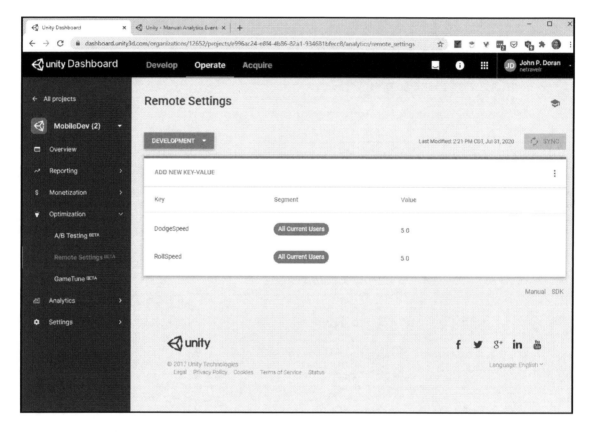

 There's a lot more that you can do with Remote Settings. You can learn more about Remote Settings and how to use it to work with non-default parameters at https://docs.unity3d.com/Manual/UnityAnalyticsRemoteSettingsComponent.html.

Being able to tweak these values while the game is live can be incredibly useful and allow you to share changes to the game without requiring your users to download a new version!

Summary

In this chapter, we explored a number of ways that we can make use of Unity's Analytics tool to make our games better, from how to tell what our players are doing to learning how we can adjust our game based on that feedback without users having to download an entirely new copy of our game.

Specifically, we learned how to set up the Unity Analytics section of the Unity Editor and then saw how we can make use of code to create events to be sent to the cloud for us to look at. With the data given, we learned how we could make use of funnels and Funnel Analyzer to learn more about our players. We then learned how we could use Remote Settings to make adjustments to our games on the fly.

With this, we have all of the implementation details of our game complete, but our game right now is pretty bare. In the next chapter, we will look into ways to make our game more polished using features such as particle systems and screen shake.

Making Your Title Juicy **10**

We now have a basic game, but it's just that... basic. In this chapter, you will learn some of the secrets that game developers use to take the basic prototype of their game and turn it into something with a lot of polish that feels satisfying to play, which is known as making our games juicy.

Also known as *game feel*, juiciness is a kind of catch-all term for all the things that we do in a game to make it pleasing for its users to interact with. This is something that is done with most mobile games that are out there today, and lacking this kind of interactivity will make others believe our project is lacking in polish.

In this chapter, you will learn some of the different ways that you can integrate features of juiciness into our projects. We will start off by learning how to make use of animations. We will then see how we can use Unity's material system in order to add visual appeal to our objects. We will then improve the overall visual quality of our game through the use of post-processing effects. Lastly, we will use one of the most powerful tools in a game developer's toybox, the particle system, to improve feedback when the player moves in the environment.

This chapter is split into a number of topics. It contains a simple step-by-step process from beginning to end. Here is the outline of our tasks:

- Animation using LeanTween
- Adding tweens to the pause menu
- Working with materials
- Using post-processing effects
- Adding particle effects

Technical requirements

This book utilizes Unity 2020.1.0f1 and Unity Hub 2.3.1, but the steps should work with minimal changes in future versions of the editor. If you would like to download the exact version used in this book, and there is a new version out, you can visit Unity's download archive at `https://unity3d.com/get-unity/download/archive`. You can also find the system requirements for Unity at `https://docs.unity3d.com/2020.1/Documentation/Manual/system-requirements.html` in the **Unity Editor system requirements** section. To deploy your project, you will need an Android or iOS device.

You can find the code files present in this chapter on GitHub at `https://github.com/PacktPublishing/Unity-2020-Mobile-Game-Development-Second-Edition/tree/master/Chapter%2010`.

Animation using LeanTween

Currently, our game's menus are completely static. This is functional but does not make players excited about playing our game. To make the game seem more alive, we should animate our menus. Being able to use Unity's built-in animation system is great, and it can be quite useful if you want to modify many different properties at once. If you don't need precise control, if you're only modifying a single property, or if you want to animate something purely via code, you can also make use of a tweening library. If it is given a start and an end, the library will take care of all the work in the middle to get that property to that end within the time and speed you specify.

One of my favorite tweening libraries is Dented Pixel's *LeanTween*, which is open source and usable for free in commercial and non-commercial projects and is optimized for mobile devices and used in many games, including Pokémon Go. In the following sections, we will first install and set up LeanTween and then see how we can use it to animate our title screen UI menus.

LeanTween setup

LeanTween allows us to spin, shake, punch, move, fade, and tweak objects in many different ways with only one line of code per task. It also gives us the ability to fire custom events during the start, middle, and end of the animations, allowing us to effectively do whatever we want to create an animation in a way that is incredibly powerful once you get familiar with it.

Now that we know we want to add tweens to our project, let's start off by actually adding the LeanTween engine to our project. Implement the following steps:

1. Open up the **Asset Store** tab by going to `https://assetstore.unity.com/` in your web browser of choice. Once there, at the top of the search bar, type in `LeanTween` and then press **Enter**.

2. From there, you'll be brought to a list of items with the first one being **LeanTween**; select it, and you will be brought to LeanTween's product page:

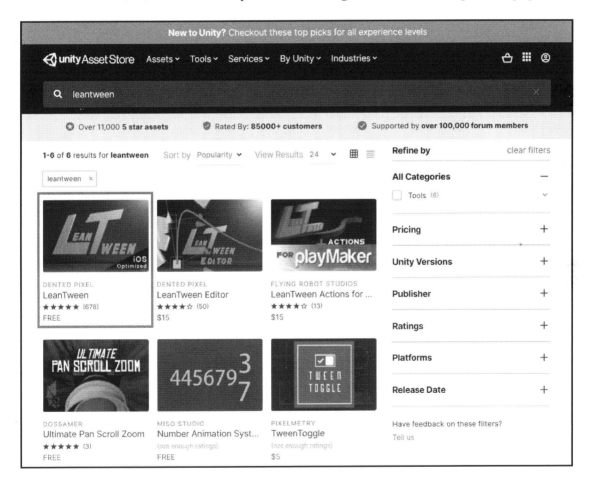

3. Once at the project page, click on the **Add to My Assets / Open In Unity** button.

4. Once logged in, click on **Download** once again, and if it doesn't happen automatically, click on the **Import** button.

5. You should see an **Import Unity Package** window pop up. From there, you can check or uncheck whatever files you want to keep. We will just use the contents of the Framework folder here; however, the others may be useful to you should you wish to use them on your own.

6. Once you're finished selecting what you want, click on the **Import** button:

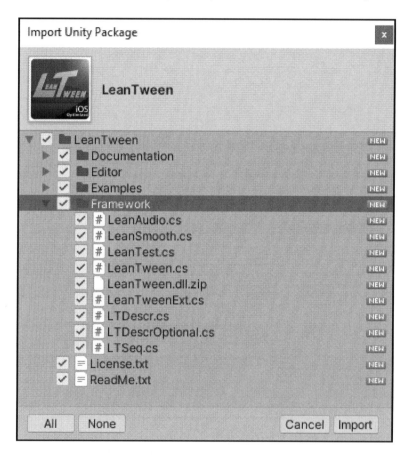

7. We don't need the **Asset Store** tab anymore, so go ahead and close it. You'll notice that now we have the files we have selected inside our **Project** tab in the Assets/LeanTween/Framework folder:

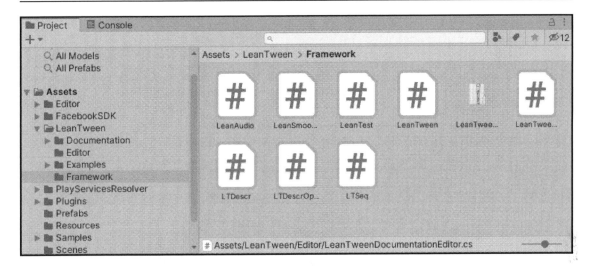

With that, we have LeanTween set up.

 There are other tweening libraries that you may want to consider, such as iTween and DoTween. For some more information and a comparison of them, check out `http://dotween.demigiant.com/#enginesComparison`.

Now that we have a tweening system in place, let's see how we can actually use it!

Creating a simple tween

Made popular in animation before transitioning to game development, the process of tweening (or *inbetweening*) is where, given a starting and ending value, the computer will generate the intermediate frames between the two states, giving the appearance of the beginning value evolving smoothly into the second value. A tween is the information that we have to provide in order to start the tweening process.

Now that we have LeanTween included in our project, we can use it inside our code. To do that, perform the following steps:

1. From the Unity Editor, open the **MainMenu** level by going to the **Project** window and double-clicking on the **MainMenu** scene.
2. Now, move to the `Scripts` folder and open the `MainMenuBehaviour` by double-clicking on it.

3. We will add the following new function, which we will use to have the object move from the left side of the screen to the center:

```
/// <summary>
/// Will move an object from the left side of the screen
/// to the center
/// </summary>
/// <param name="obj">The UI element we would like to
/// move</param>
public void SlideMenuIn(GameObject obj)
{
    obj.SetActive(true);

    var rt = obj.GetComponent<RectTransform>();

    if (rt)
    {
        // Set the object's position offscreen
        var pos = rt.position;
        pos.x = -Screen.width / 2;
        rt.position = pos;

        // Move the object to the center of the screen (x of 0
          // is centered)
        LeanTween.moveX(rt, 0, 1.5f);
    }
}
```

Before we move anything using LeanTween, we will first set the position of our object (the `obj` parameter) off-screen by setting the x position. It's important to note that when dealing with UI elements in Unity, by default, we are dealing with screen space, which, as you can recall from Chapter 3, *Mobile Input/Touch Controls*, means that we are moving in terms of pixels.

From here, we'll see that we are calling the `moveX` function from LeanTween. The version we are using takes in three parameters, the first being the `RectTransform` object we wish to move and the second being the x position to move it to. Based on how we set up the Anchors and Pivots, a position of 0 on the x axis is actually centered, so we pass in 0. Lastly, we have the amount of time (in seconds) in which we want the transition to happen.

4. Now that we have this function, let's actually call it. In the `Start` function of the `MainMenuBehaviour` script, change it so that it now looks as follows:

```
virtual protected void Start()
{
    // Initialize the showAds variable
    UnityAdController.showAds = (PlayerPrefs.GetInt("Show Ads", 1)
        == 1);

    if (facebookLogin != null)
    {
        SlideMenuIn(facebookLogin);
    }

    // Unpause the game if needed
    Time.timeScale = 1;
}
```

The first thing we do is bring in the Facebook login menu to the screen by calling the `SlideMenuIn` function, which in turn will tween the menu to the center of the screen. LeanTween, by default, makes use of the game's `Time.timeScale` property to scale movement. When we leave the game from the pause menu and go back to the main menu, the game will still be paused. This ensures that the game will be unpaused by the time we want to slide this menu in. When we start building the pause menu, we'll see how we can make our tweens work even when the game is paused.

If you play the game now, you'll notice that the Facebook login screen will now move from off-screen back into the center of the screen.

Right now, the object moves in a fairly static manner. One of the ways we can add life to this tween is by giving it some additional features, such as an `easeType`.

5. Add the following highlighted code to the `SlideMenuIn` function:

```
public void SlideMenuIn(GameObject obj)
{
    obj.SetActive(true);

    var rt = obj.GetComponent<RectTransform>();

    if (rt)
    {
        // Set the object's position offscreen
        var pos = rt.position;
        pos.x = -Screen.width / 2;
```

```
            rt.position = pos;

            // Move the object to the center of the screen (x of 0 is
            // centered)
            LeanTween.moveX(rt, 0,
                1.5f).setEase(LeanTweenType.easeInOutExpo);

        }
    }
```

What is happening here is that the `LeanTween.moveX` function actually returns an object of type `LTDescr`, which is actually a reference to the tween that was created. To that tween, we can add additional parameters by calling additional functions onto the tween. In fact, an alternate way to write this is the following:

```
// Move the object to the center of the screen (x of 0 is centered)
var tween = LeanTween.moveX(rt, 0, 1.5f);
tween.setEase(LeanTweenType.easeInOutExpo);
```

However, most of the examples in LeanTween's documentation use the former method, chaining a number of different events to happen at once.

 To see what some of the other commonly used methods are besides `easeType` in LeanTween, check out `https://tedliou.com/archives/leantween-ui-animation/`.

6. Finally, we will next add the ability so that when we select a button to go to another menu, we will have the current menu slide out:

```
/// <summary>
/// Will move an object to the right offscreen
/// </summary>
/// <param name="obj">The UI element we would like to
/// move </param>
public void SlideMenuOut(GameObject obj)
{
    var rt = obj.GetComponent<RectTransform>();
    if(rt)
    {
        var tween = LeanTween.moveX(rt, Screen.width / 2, 0.5f);

        tween.setEase(LeanTweenType.easeOutQuad);

        tween.setOnComplete(() =>
        {
            obj.SetActive(false);
```

```
            });
        }
    }
```

Note that this is similar to the previously written function, except now we are using also another function called setOnComplete, which can either take in a function or an expression lambda, which works basically as a function without a name and is often used in **Language-Integrated Queries (LINQ)**. In this case, because I wanted to have access to obj, I used a lambda. What this will do is, after the object is off-screen, we will automatically turn it off; but we have the potential to do anything. This can be incredibly powerful, as we can do anything that we'd normally be able to do via code.

For more information on lamba expressions, check out https://docs. microsoft.com/en-us/dotnet/csharp/programming-guide/statements- expressions-operators/lambda-expressions.

7. Then, we will need to update the ShowMainMenu function to actually display the menus:

```
public void ShowMainMenu()
{
    if (facebookLogin != null && mainMenu != null)
    {
        SlideMenuIn(mainMenu);
        SlideMenuOut(facebookLogin);

        // No longer needed as menus will be animating
        //facebookLogin.SetActive(false);
        //mainMenu.SetActive(true);

        if (FB.IsLoggedIn)
        {
            // Get information from Facebook profile
            FB.API("/me?fields=name", HttpMethod.GET, SetName);
            FB.API("/me/picture?width=256&height=256",
            HttpMethod.GET, SetProfilePic);
        }
    }
}
```

8. Save the script and dive back into the game:

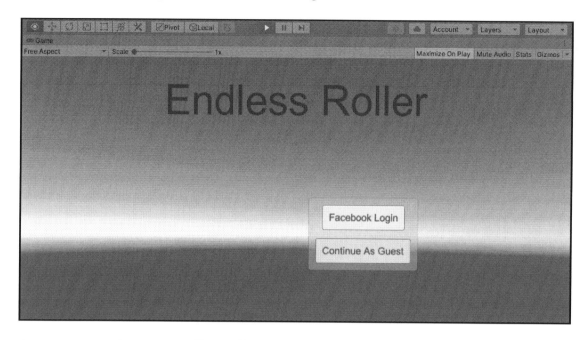

As you can see, the menus will now fly in and out when on the main menu.

 You can find a list of all of the possible parameters you can pass into these functions at `http://www.pixelplacement.com/itween/documentation.php`.

With the preceding example, you should be able to see just how easy it is to add motion to our projects and how it can improve the overall quality of the product, making it more enjoyable to interact with.

Adding tweens to the pause menu

Now that we have the main menu finished, let's continue doing this with the pause menu:

1. Go ahead and open up our **Gameplay** scene. Update the
   PauseScreenBehaviour script to have the following implementation of
   SetPauseMenu:

```
/// <summary>
/// Will turn our pause menu on or off
/// </summary>
/// <param name="isPaused"></param>
public void SetPauseMenu(bool isPaused)
{
    paused = isPaused;

    // If the game is paused, timeScale is 0, otherwise 1
    Time.timeScale = (paused) ? 0 : 1;

    // No longer needed
    //pauseMenu.SetActive(paused);

    if (paused)
    {
        SlideMenuIn(pauseMenu);
    }
    else
    {
        SlideMenuOut(pauseMenu);
    }

    if (paused)
    {
        var result = Analytics.CustomEvent("Paused");

        if (result == AnalyticsResult.Ok)
        {
            Debug.Log("Event Sent: Paused");
        }
    }
}
```

Note that because `PauseMenuBehaviour` inherits from `MainMenuBehaviour`, it also can call the `SlideMenuIn` and `SlideMenuOut` functions, respectively, as long as they are marked as `protected` or `public`.

Now if we run the game, nothing will appear to happen when we hit the pause menu. This is because—as I mentioned previously—tweens are scaled by `Time.timeScale`, which we just changed. To fix this, we can make use of another LeanTween function called `setIgnoreTimeScale`, which we will set to `true` in both functions we wrote previously in the `MainMenuBehaviour` script. For one last additional polish, we will add the `LeanTween.alpha` function to have the menus fade in and out as well.

2. Add the following highlighted code to the `SlideMenuIn` method:

```
/// <summary>
/// Will move an object from the left side of the screen
/// to the center
/// </summary>
/// <param name="obj">The UI element we would like to
/// move</param>
public void SlideMenuIn(GameObject obj)
{
 obj.SetActive(true);

 var rt = obj.GetComponent<RectTransform>();

 if (rt)
 {
 // Set the object's position offscreen
 var pos = rt.position;
 pos.x = -Screen.width / 2;
 rt.position = pos;

 // Move the object to the center of the screen (x of 0 is
centered)
 var tween = LeanTween.moveX(rt, 0, 1.5f);
 tween.setEase(LeanTweenType.easeInOutExpo);
 tween.setIgnoreTimeScale(true);

 LeanTween.alpha(rt, 1, 0.5f);
 }
}
```

3. Add the highlighted code to the `SlideMenuOut` method:

```
/// <summary>
/// Will move an object to the right offscreen
/// </summary>
/// <param name="obj">The UI element we would like to
/// move </param>
public void SlideMenuOut (GameObject obj)
{
    var rt = obj.GetComponent<RectTransform>();
    if(rt)
    {
        var tween = LeanTween.moveX(rt, Screen.width / 2, 0.5f);

        tween.setEase(LeanTweenType.easeOutQuad);

        tween.setIgnoreTimeScale(true);

        tween.setOnComplete(() =>
        {
            obj.SetActive(false);
        });

        LeanTween.alpha(rt, 0, 0.5f);
    }
}
```

4. Save both scripts and dive into the editor to try it out:

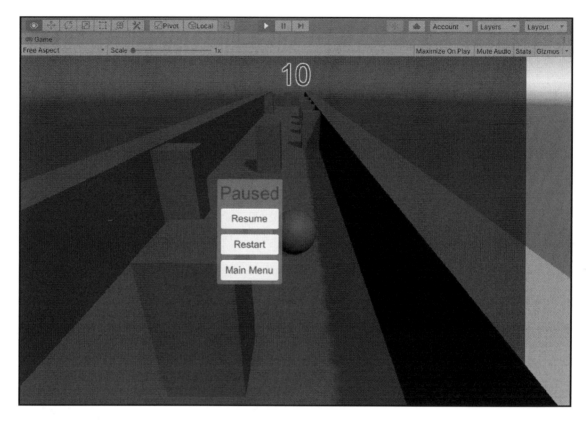

Perfect! We now have the screen flying in just like we wanted it to.

In the previous two sections, we learned how to create tweening events and how to apply them to different scenarios. In this next section, we will see another way that we can improve the visuals of our project through the use of materials.

Working with materials

Earlier, we always used the default material for everything in our project. This has worked out well for us, but it may be a good idea for us to talk a little bit about creating custom ones to improve the visuals of our player. Materials are instructions on how to draw 3D objects within Unity. They consist of a shader and properties that the shader uses. A **shader** is a script that instructs the material on how to draw things on the object.

Shaders are a huge subject that entire books have been written on, so we can't dive too much into them here, but we can talk about working with one that is included in Unity, the **Standard Shader**. Implement the following steps:

1. First, open the **Gameplay** scene. Then, let's create a new folder in the **Project** window called `Materials`:

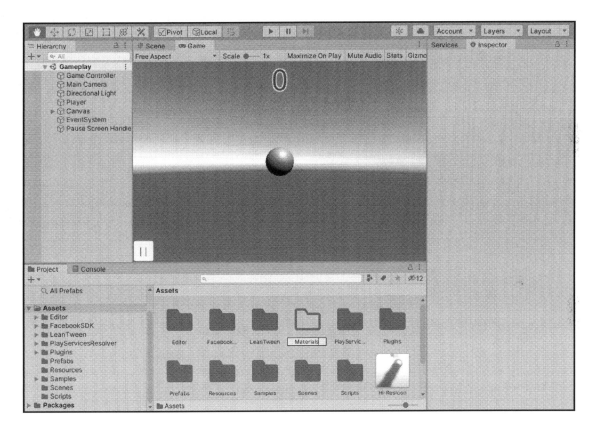

2. Open up the `Materials` folder we just created, and then once inside, create a new material by right-clicking within the folder and then selecting **Create** | **Material**:

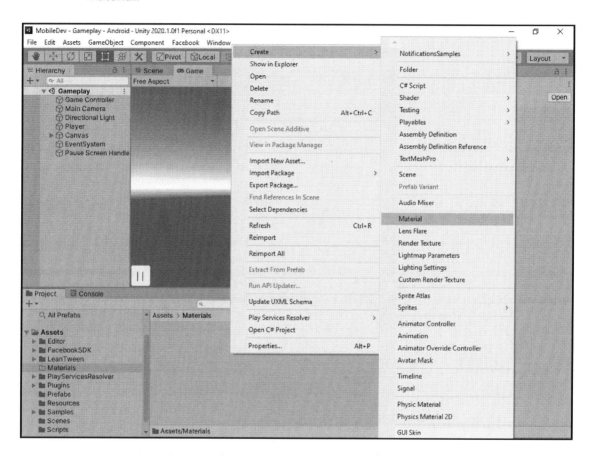

3. Name this new material `Ball`.

4. In the **Inspector** window, you'll be brought to the **Shader** menu with the properties for the **Standard** shader. Set the **Metallic** property to `0.8` and the **Smoothness** property to `0.6`.

5. Now, go to the **Scene** view and drag and drop the **Ball** material onto our player object:

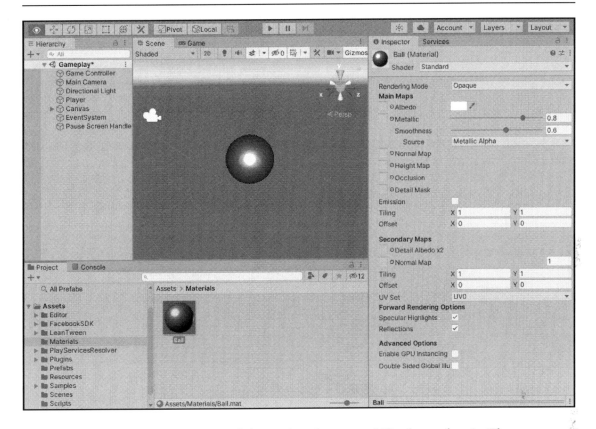

The metallic parameter of a material determines how *metal-like* the surface is. The more metallic a surface is, the more it reflects its environment. The smoothness property determines how smooth the surface is; a higher smoothness will have light bounce off it uniformly, making the reflections clearer.

 For more information on the standard shader and its parameters, check out `https://docs.unity3d.com/Manual/StandardShaderMaterialParameters.html`.

Materials are only one of the ways that we can improve the visual quality of our project. In fact, one of the most drastic ways that we can modify our project's visuals is through the use of post-processing effects, which we will be looking at next.

Using post-processing effects

One of the ways that we can improve the visual quality of our game with little effort is by using post-processing effects (previously called **Image Effects**). Post-processing is the process of applying filters and other effects to what the camera will draw (the image buffer) before it is displayed on screen.

Unity includes a number of effects in its freely available post-processing stack, so let's go ahead and add it using the following steps:

1. Open up the **Package Manager** again by going to **Window | Package Manager**. From there, go to the **Packages** dropdown from the top left and set it to **Unity Registry**. Afterward, scroll down until you see the **Post Processing** option and select it:

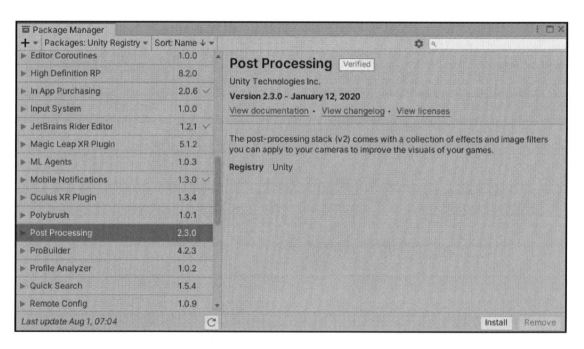

2. Once selected, click on the **Install** button and wait for it to complete.

3. Switch to the **Scene** window, and then, from the **Hierarchy** window, select our **Main Camera** object and select **Add Component** in the **Inspector** window and type in Post Process. Then move your mouse over the **Post-process Layer** selection and click to add the script to your project. The **Post-process Layer** component handles the blending of post-processing volumes and what the post-processing should be based on.

4. Under the **Post-process Layer** component, change the **Layer** to **Everything**. This will make it so everything in our scene will be used in terms of blending between volumes.

5. We will next need to add the **Post-process Volume** component to our **Main Camera** game object. Do this by clicking on the **Add Component** button and then selecting the **Post-process Volume** option:

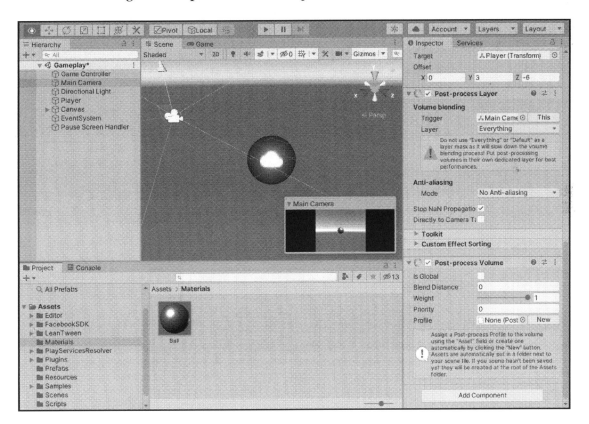

Note that this component requires a profile. We can go ahead and add that next.

6. We can create a new **Post-processing Profile** by right-clicking on the **Project** window, opening the `Assets` folder, and selecting **Create | Post-processing Profile**, and then naming it `MobilePostProcessing`:

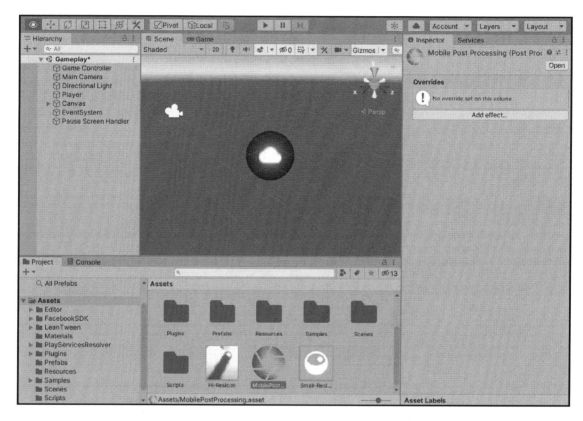

7. Go back to the **Main Camera** object and attach this object to the **Profile** property of the **Post-process Volume** component. Afterward, go to the **Post-process Volume** component and then click on the check for the **Is Global** property. This will make it so the volume we have created will always be visible on our player's screen no matter where their camera is positioned in the world.

8. Because `Post-processing Profile` is a separate file, we can make changes to it while playing the game without worrying about losing our changes. With that in mind, start the game and pause it once gameplay has started.
Now, there's a large number of possible effects that can be added to modify how the game looks.

Note that for each one you add, the frame rate of the devices we are trying to run our game on will be decreased. Keep testing your device with these options and note how it works.

9. Next, under the section of the **Post-process Volume** component, you'll see a section called **Overrides**. Click on the **Add effect...** button and then select **Unity | Vignette**. Click on the arrow to the left of the name to open up the potential options. From there, check the **Intensity** property and increase it to 0.45:

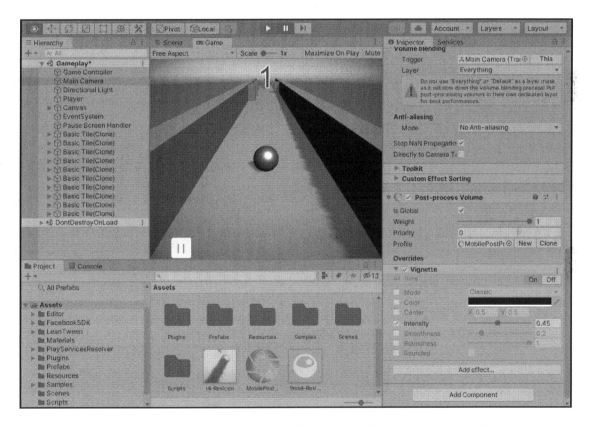

If the UI menu disappears, switching from the **Scene** view and back to the **Game** view seems to fix this issue.

Note how there now seems to be a blackened edge around the game.

10. Next, enable the **Smoothness** and set it to 0.35 to make it even darker by clicking on the top right of the section to expand it:

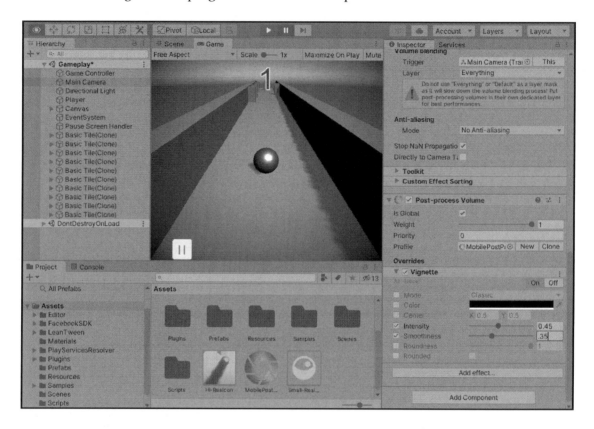

Vignetting is the term used for the darkening and/or desaturating toward the edges of an image compared to the center. I like to use this when I want to have players focus on the center of the screen.

11. Click on the **Add effect...** button again and this time, select **Unity | Grain**.

12. Check and set the **Intensity** to 0.15 and you'll note that the screen has become fuzzier. While not a great idea if it is set too large, note that decreasing the **Size** to 0.3 and unchecking **Colored** will help with the appearance of things:

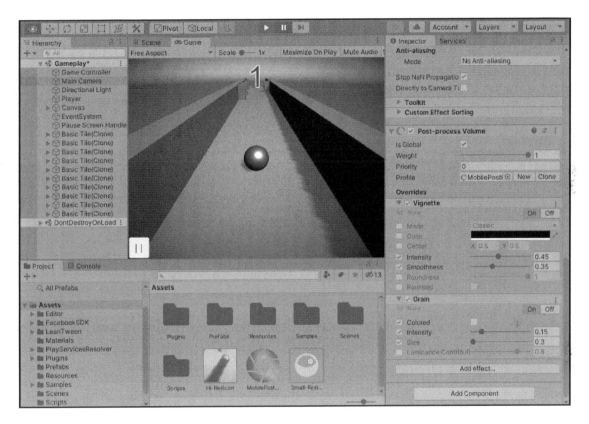

If you've been to a movie theater that still uses film, you may have noticed how there were little specks of things in the filmstock while playing over time. The **Grain** effect in Unity simulates this film grain, causing the effect to become more pronounced the more the movie is played. This is often used in horror games to obscure the player's vision.

13. Another property to add is **Unity | Bloom**, which makes bright things even brighter. Enable the property and then set the **Intensity** to 10. From there, set **Soft Knee** to 0.6 to help brighten things up:

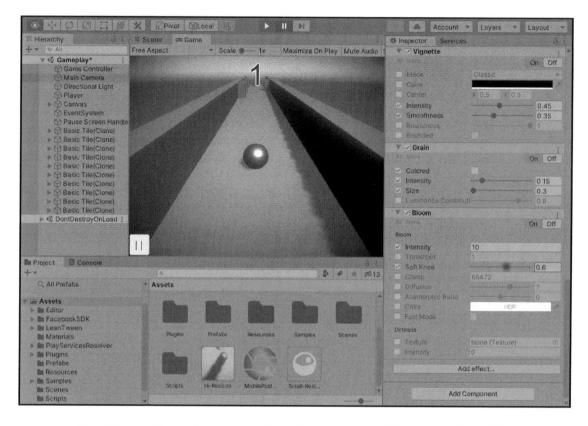

The **Bloom** effect attempts to mimic the imaging artifacts of real-world cameras, where things in areas with light will glow along the edges, thus overwhelming the camera.

14. Lastly, stop the game and then go back to the **Post-process Layer** component and, under **Anti-aliasing**, change the **Mode** to **Fast Approximate Anti-aliasing (FXAA)** and then check **Fast Mode**:

Aliasing is an effect where lines appear jagged on the screen. This happens if the display we are trying to play our game on doesn't have a high enough resolution to display properly. Anti-aliasing attempts to reduce that appearance by attempting to combine colors nearby these lines to remove the prominence at the cost of it appearing blurrier.

For more information on post-processing in Unity, check out `https:// docs.unity3d.com/Packages/com.unity.postprocessing@2.1/manual/ index.html`.

There are a number of other properties to look into and adapt to get your project looking just the way you want it. Explore them and find what works well for the vision you are looking to achieve!

Adding particle effects

The game itself currently works, but it could use some more polish. One of the things we do to increase the polish of the game is to make use of particle systems. Typically used for effects that are natural or organic such as fire, smoke, and sparks, particle systems create objects that are designed to be as low-cost as possible, called particles. Due to this, we can spawn many of the particles at once with a minimal performance cost. One of the easiest types of particle systems to create is a trail to follow our player, so let's add one of those now using the following steps:

1. Select **Player** in the **Hierarchy** window, and then right-click and select **Effects | Particle System**.
    This will make this system a child of the player, which will be good for what we are going to do.
2. From the **Particle System** component, change the **Start Speed** to 0 and the **Simulation Space** to **World**. Then, change the **Start Color** to something to make it easy to see, such as purple.
3. Open up the **Shape** section by clicking on it. Change **Shape** to **Sphere** and set the **Radius** to 0 (it will automatically change to 0.0001).
    This is a step in the right direction. The purple particles are now following the player, as shown in the screenshot:

However, there's still a number of things we can do to improve this. Instead of just a single color, we can change it so that it randomly alternates between two colors.

4. To do that, go to the right side of **Start Color**, and you'll see a little downward-facing arrow. Click on that and then select **Random Between Two Colors**. Then, change the color to one of two purple colors for some randomness.

5. Then, next to **Start Size**, click on the right arrow, select **Random Between Two Constants**, and then set the values between 0.5 and 1.2.

6. With that, set the **Start Speed** property to be a random value from 0 to 0.2.

7. Then, open up the **Emission** section and set the **Rate Over Time** property to 100:

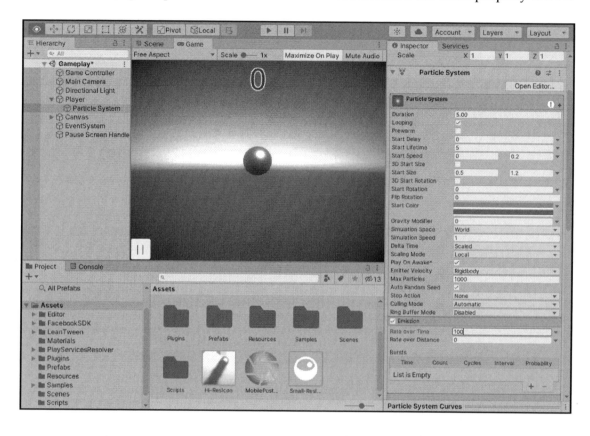

8. Save the game and play:

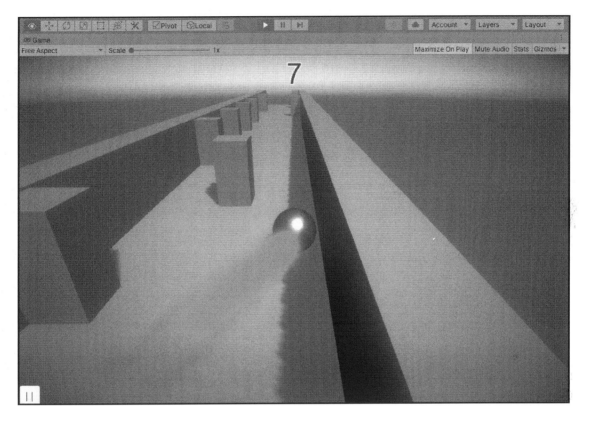

As you can see, the particle system looks great on both our PC and mobile devices.

 If you're interested in exploring more details on things that can be done to polish projects, you can check out my other Unity book, *Unity 5.x Game Development Blueprints*, also available from Packt.

Of course, there are many other areas that can be improved through the use of adding particle systems. Perhaps whenever the player hits a wall, we can display some sparks; when we swipe, we could play another effect; when the player pauses the game, we could have something falling on the screen. The possibilities are endless!

Summary

We now have improved our game by a huge amount by only doing a few simple things to improve the quality of the title. We first animated our menus with a few lines of code using tweens from LeanTween and saw how a few lines of code can improve the visual quality of our UI in a number of ways. We next saw how to create materials to improve the visual quality of our ball and then used some post-processing effects to polish the contents of our screen. Finally, we discussed how to use particle effects to create a nice trail following our player.

With these concepts, you now have the skills to dramatically improve the juiciness of your game projects and can improve the game feel so that players actually enjoy interacting with your game.

By this point, our game is finally ready for the big leagues. In the next chapter, we will explore how to get our game onto the App Store.

11
Game Build and Submission

Over the course of this book, we have gone over many aspects of building games for mobile devices. The last step in our game development journey is actually releasing the game out into the wild and having people actually play it. All of those long hours of hard work have now come together into something that the masses will be able to enjoy.

When doing this, there are a number of things to keep in mind and this is exactly what we will be discussing next.

In this chapter, we will go over the process of submitting your game to the Google Play Store or iOS App Store with tips and tricks to help the process go smoother. By the end of this chapter, you will know exactly how to create developer accounts for both stores as well as how to put your game on the respective stores.

This chapter will be split into a number of topics. It will contain a simple step-by-step process from beginning to end. Here is the outline of our tasks:

- Building a release copy of our game
- Putting your game on the Google Play Store
- Putting your game on the Apple iOS App Store

Technical requirements

This book utilizes Unity 2020.1.0f1 and Unity Hub 2.3.1, but the steps should work with minimal changes in future versions of the Editor. If you would like to download the exact version used in this book, and there is a new version out, you can visit Unity's download archive at `https://unity3d.com/get-unity/download/archive`. You can also find the system requirements for Unity at `https://docs.unity3d.com/2020.1/Documentation/Manual/system-requirements.html` in the **Unity Editor system requirements** section. To deploy your project, you will need an Android or iOS device.

You can find the code files present in this chapter on GitHub at `https://github.com/`
`PacktPublishing/Unity-2020-Mobile-Game-Development-Second-Edition/tree/master/`
`Chapter%2011.`

Building a release copy of our game

We exported copies of our game previously in `Chapter 2`, *Project Setup for Android and iOS Development*, but there are some additional steps that we should do before actually releasing the game on an app store:

1. The first step will be to confirm you are currently set to deploy your project to our mobile platform of choice. You can check this by going into the **Build Settings** menu by navigating to **File | Build Settings**.

2. From there, you should see the Unity logo to the right of the **Android** or **iOS** selection. If you do not, select it and then click on the **Switch Platform** button and wait for it to finish reimporting the assets for the project:

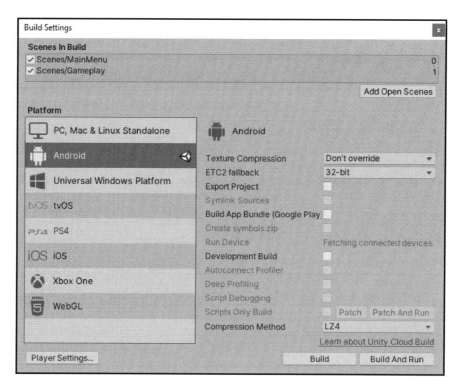

3. After confirming whether we are building for **Android** or **iOS**, open up the **Player** settings menu by clicking on the **Player Settings...** button from the menu or by going to **Edit | Project Settings | Player**.

4. If you haven't done so already, set the **Company Name** and **Product Name** values to your own values. In my case, I used `John P. Doran` and `Endless Roller`, respectively.

5. You'll then see a **Default Icon** item. Drag and drop the `Hi-ResIcon` image into the `Assets` folder and then drag and drop it into the **Default Icon** slot. This will cause the **Icon** section of the Android settings to automatically scale the image to fit whatever device you are targeting:

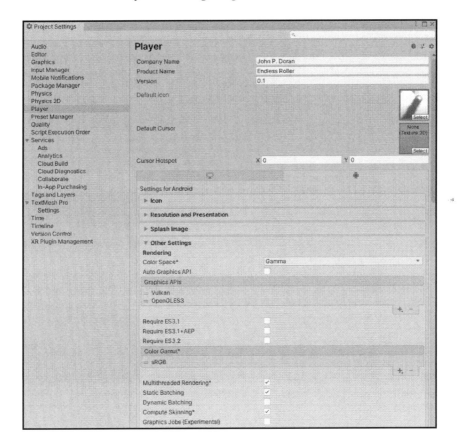

Of course, you can also use your own image, and you can use transparency if you would like to.

6. Under the **Resolution and Presentation** section, you can enable or disable different rotations and aspect ratios as desired. We adjusted the game to fit these, but this may be useful to know about as you work on your own projects or you wish to restrict users to one experience or another.

7. The **Splash Screen** option can be used to display your own logo in addition to Unity's if you have the Personal Edition of Unity. If you have Pro, you may disable it here.

8. Confirm under **Other Settings** that the **Package Name** property is not set to the default values. The general method of naming is com.CompanyName.GameName.

9. Next, open up **Publishing Settings**. This is where we are going to be putting in information about who our game's publisher is (in this case, I'm assuming it's you). Whenever you build a game for Android, you need a **Keystore**, which allows you to sign off on the game, approving it for the build process. Click on the **Keystore Manager** button. From there, you'll be brought to a menu.

10. From the menu, click on the **Keystore...** dropdown and then select **Create New | Anywhere...** and choose a location for this file:

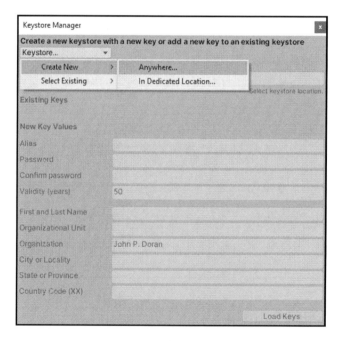

Keep in mind where this is going to be located, as you will be using it in the future to create new versions of your game

11. Then, you'll need to set a **Password** that you will need to know as you'll be using it over and over. Afterward, in the **Confirm password** textbox, you should enter the same thing as you did before.

12. From there, under the **New Key Values** section, you'll need to add in the same information as before—the password with confirmation and then your name and other information. You can see what I put down in the following screenshot. Once finished, click on the **Add Key** button:

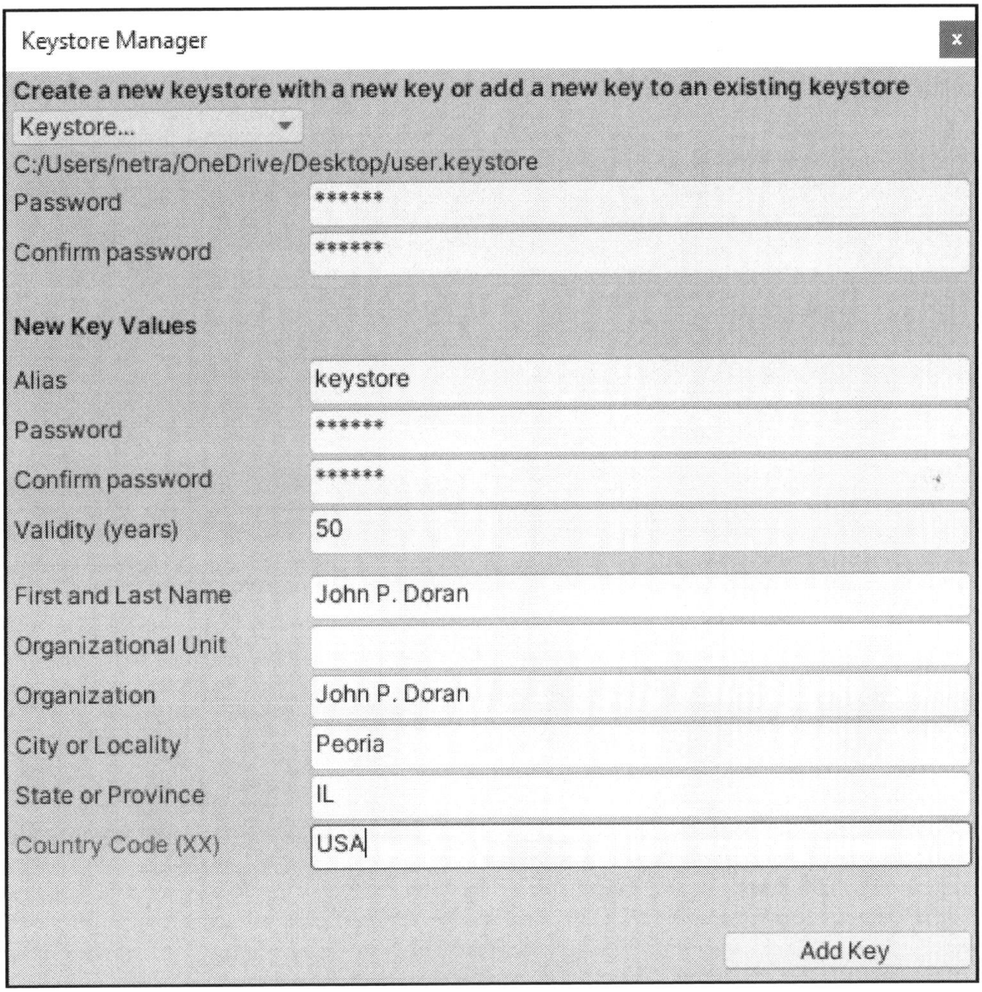

Keystore Manager	x

Create a new keystore with a new key or add a new key to an existing keystore

Keystore... ▼

C:/Users/netra/OneDrive/Desktop/user.keystore

Password	******
Confirm password	******

New Key Values

Alias	keystore
Password	******
Confirm password	******
Validity (years)	50
First and Last Name	John P. Doran
Organizational Unit	
Organization	John P. Doran
City or Locality	Peoria
State or Province	IL
Country Code (XX)	USA

Add Key

13. You'll have a popup asking whether you'd like to set the new keystore as your **Project Keystore** and **Project Key**. Click on **Yes**. You should then see this screen:

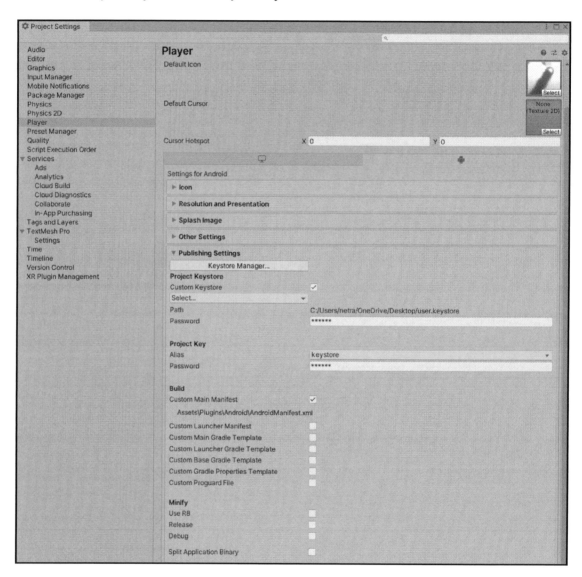

With that, we have everything set up that we need to put the game up on the store. To start, we will discuss how to put the game on the Google Play Store before moving on to the Apple App Store.

Putting your game on the Google Play Store

Now that your game is built, you will need to actually put it up on Google's Play Store. To put games up on the Google Play store, you are required to pay a one-time $25 dollar fee. This may or may not seem like a large amount of money, but it is much cheaper than the iOS App Store and is a one-time fee, so for those who are a bit more budget-conscious, you may wish to dive into Google first and make some profit before moving on to Apple's store. We will first look at the Google Play Console before filling out all of the details needed in order to submit our game to the store. We will also discuss how to mark our game as a beta to get feedback from others before making the final submission.

Setting up the Google Play Console

The first step is to gain access to the Google Play Console. This allows you to publish an Android app on Google Play as well as Google Play Game Services if you'd like. Implement the following steps:

1. Open up your web browser and go to `https://play.google.com/apps/publish`. This page is the **Google Play Console**, which allows you to add apps to the Google Play store.
2. If you aren't signed in to your Google account, you'll need to sign in, otherwise, you'll be brought to a page that needs you to agree to the developer agreement:

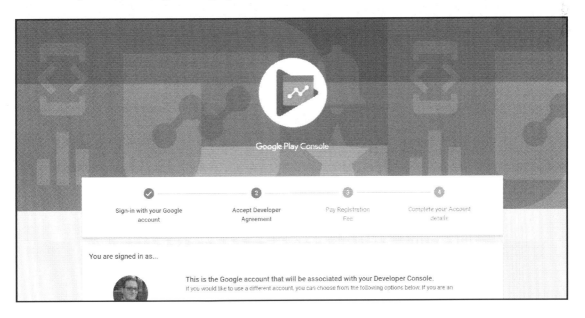

3. Scroll down and you'll see a checkbox saying, **I agree and I am willing to associate my account registration with the Google Play Developer distribution agreement**. Read the agreement, and if you agree, click the checkbox.

4. Afterward, click on the **Continue to Payment** button. You will need to enter your credit card information and continue until the payment is complete. From there, you'll see a window saying that you'll receive a receipt by mail and then click on the **Continue Registration** button.

5. You'll then need to enter in the details under the **Developer Profile**. This will include the developer name, the email you'd like to be contacted by, your website if you have one, and a contact number in case Google needs to contact you about your apps. You'll also be given the option to receive emails from Google Play, but it's not required for this course.

6. Once you have finished, click on the **Complete Registration** button. If all goes well, you'll be brought to the **Google Play Console**:

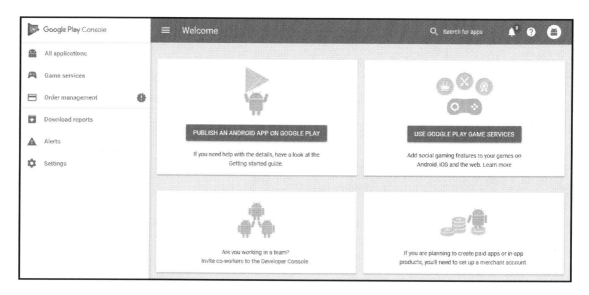

Once you have an account, you can now start the process of actually publishing a game to the Google Play store. To start that process, we will need to add a project to our account, which is what we will be doing next.

Publishing an app on Google Play

The process of publishing an app to Google Play involves filling out a number of different fields with information about your game as well as art assets for screenshots. To do this, implement the following steps:

1. Click on the **PUBLISH AN ANDROID APP ON GOOGLE PLAY** button. You'll be brought to a page where you need to select a **Default language** and then the **Title** of your game. Then, click on the **Create** button:

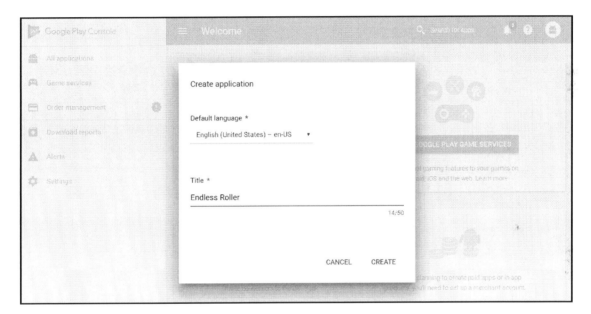

2. You'll then be brought to a page where you'll need to fill in information about your game, starting with a **Short description** and then a more detailed **Full description**:

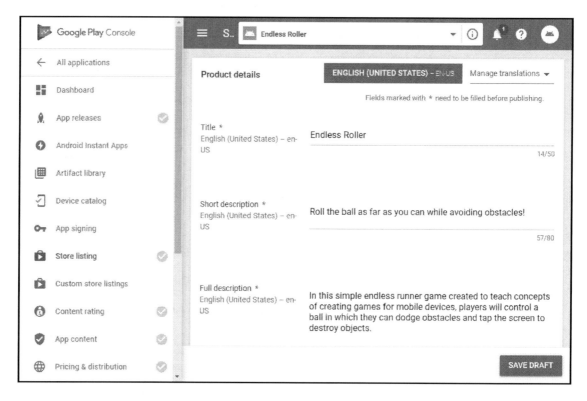

3. You'll then need to provide graphical assets to be used to display your game. You are required to have at least two screenshots and then some additional icons and graphics:

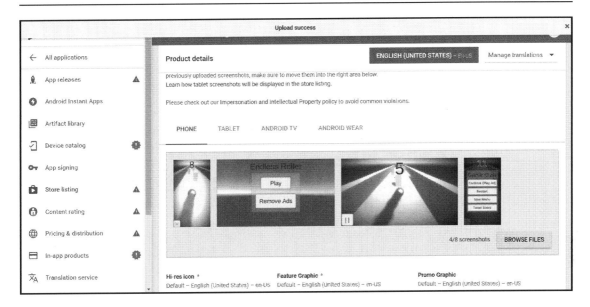

4. You'll then need to include some more images for icons and other featured graphics. The ones with an asterisk (*) are required. You can find some already made ones in the example code with this book, but I suggest that you create your own once you've customized this game to your liking:

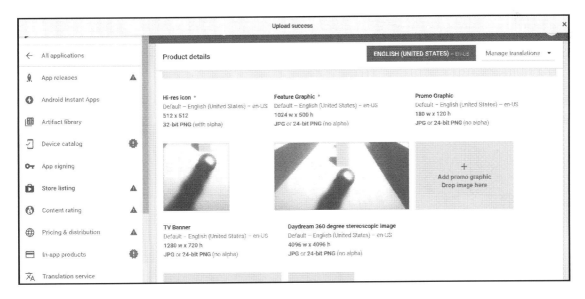

5. Now, scroll down and you'll need to select an **Application type** (I picked **Games**) and a **Category** (I chose **Arcade**).

6. Finally, confirm your contact info and check whether you have a privacy policy or not.

7. Afterward, scroll all the way to the top and then click on the **SAVE DRAFT** button:

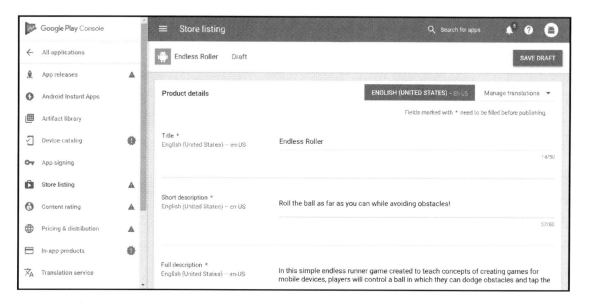

8. Next, click on the **Pricing & distribution** option on the left-hand side. By default, you need to decide whether you want your app to be paid or free. I'm going to go with free, but if you click on the **Set up a merchant account** button, you can take payment as well.

9. You'll need to scroll down and select the countries you'd like to have people be able to download your game in. Generally, unless we are doing some kind of testing or beta program, we will generally hit the **Available** button to allow the entire world to play:

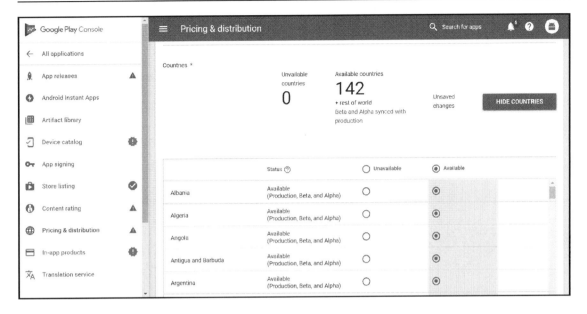

10. Scroll down and you'll need to answer whether your game is directed toward children under 13 and also state whether your game has ads or not. In my case, the app is not directed toward children and the game contains ads:

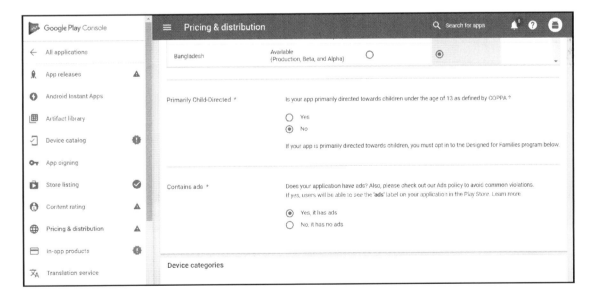

11. Now, scroll down till you get to the **Consent** section and check the final two options after reading and agreeing to their stipulations:

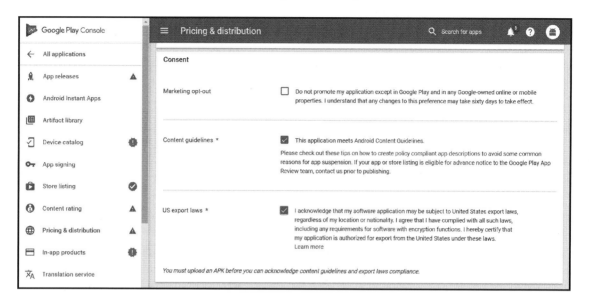

12. When you reach the end, scroll all the way up and click on the **SAVE DRAFT** button again.

13. Next, we will need to bring in our APK file to the store. Click on the **App releases** section. From there, we need to select what version of the game we want to release. Production means that the game is completely done, but assuming we are looking for feedback and/or want to make the project better, we will want to select **Beta** or **Alpha**. I'll go ahead and select **Beta** and click on the **Manage Beta** option:

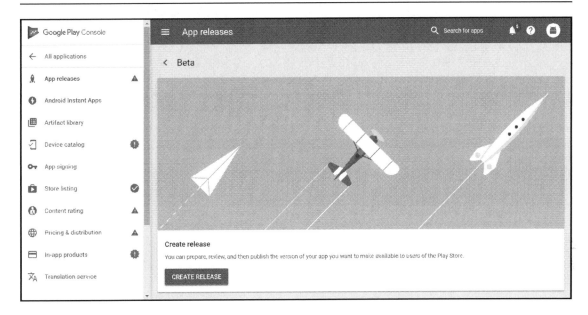

14. From there, click on the **Create Release** button. You'll then be given the opportunity to enroll the app into **Google Play App Signing**. Go ahead and click on **Continue** and accept the terms if you would like. Afterward, you will be brought to a screen to allow you to add an APK:

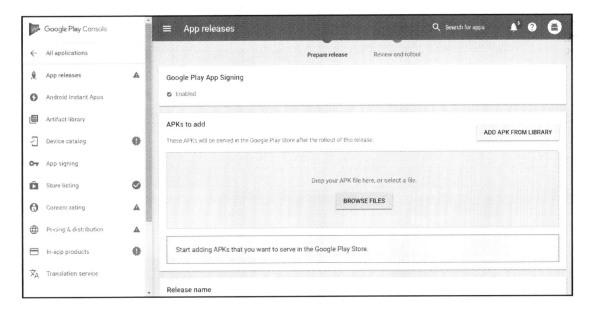

15. Click on the **Browse Files** button and go to the folder you've exported your game to. If you exported your game as we did in `Chapter 2`, *Project Setup for Android and iOS Development*, you may notice an error like the following:

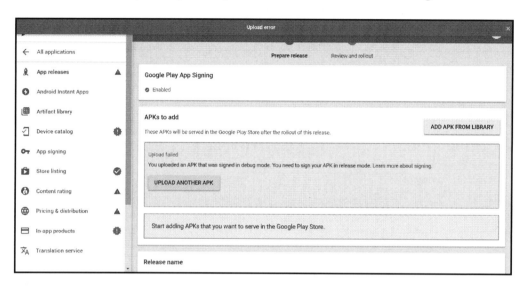

Ensure that you follow the instructions in the *Building a release copy of our game* section.

If all goes well, you'll be brought to a screen that looks as follows:

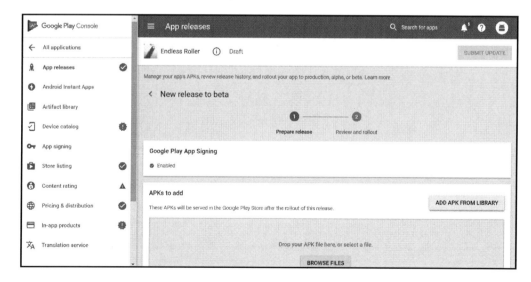

16. If you scroll down, you should see a version of the game on the screen. You'll be asked what is new in this release. I wrote `Initial release` and then clicked on the **Save** button.

17. Next, click on the **Content rating** button. You may be required to put in a physical address. If so, click on the **Account details** page and fill it out, and then click on the **Continue** button on this page:

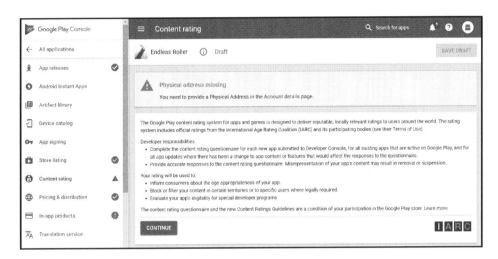

18. From here, you'll need to enter your email address again and then select your app category. In our case, it's likely **Game**:

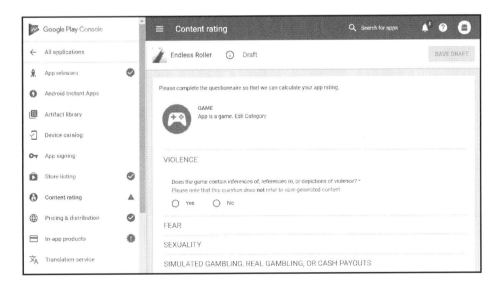

19. Then, answer each of the questions offered until you arrive at the **Save Questionnaire** button that you will click and then click on the **Calculated Rating** button.

20. Afterward, you should see a calculated rating for you to note:

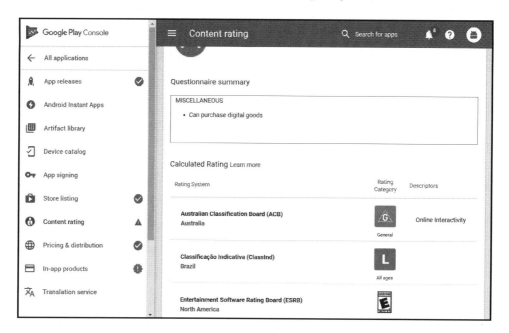

21. Scroll down all the way to the bottom and then click on the **Apply Rating** button. If all goes well, you should notice that the top of the screen says **Ready to publish**. Click on that button:

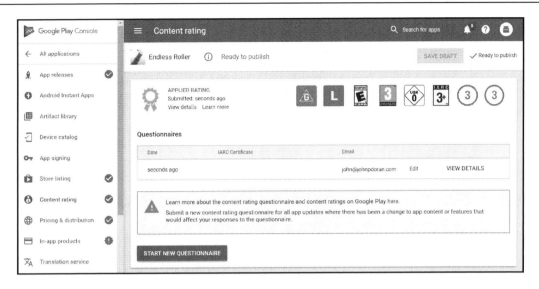

22. Click on the button that says **Manage Releases**. From there, scroll down to the **Beta** section again and then click on the **Manage Beta** button. Here, you're able to select your method of **Open Beta testing**.

23. Under **Choose a testing method**, select **Open Beta Testing**. Afterward, you can select a **Feedback Channel** to specify how you want people to provide feedback. Afterward, click on the **SAVE** button:

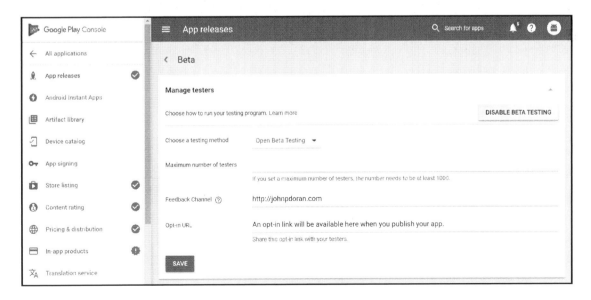

24. Next, return to the **App releases** page and click on the **Edit Release** button under **Beta**. From there, click on the **REVIEW** button at the bottom of the screen:

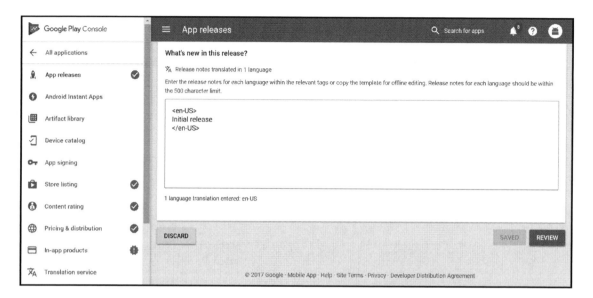

25. Finally, scroll all the way down, and you'll see the **START ROLLOUT TO BETA** option; click on it:

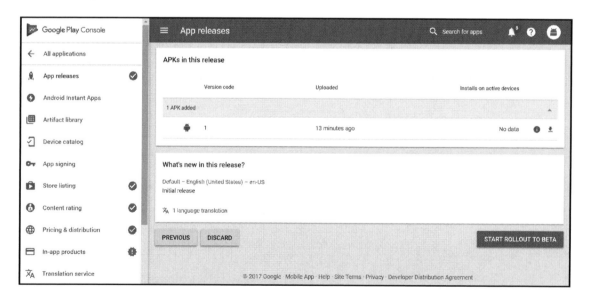

With that, our game is currently **Pending publication**:

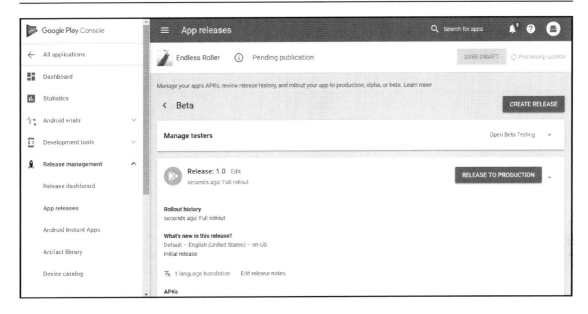

After waiting a moment, your game should be published and you can share it with the world. If you go to the **Manage testers** section, you should notice an **Opt-in URL** that you can share and have others play:

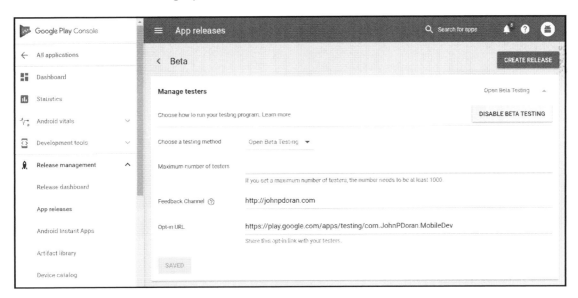

And with that, we've gone over all of the steps needed to get our game on to the Google Play store. With that experience finished, we can now approach the process of getting on to Apple's iOS App Store, which we will be doing next.

Putting your game on the Apple iOS App Store

Just like the Google Play store, there is an additional fee to put your game on the App Store. Unlike the Google Play store, the fee is $99 plus tax every year. However, a lot of people believe that having their titles on iOS devices is worth the extra cost. In this section, we will go through the process of getting our game on the App Store. We will start by setting up your Apple Developer account and creating a provisioning profile. Afterward, we'll utilize the iTunes Connect tool to actually add the app to the store, and utilize Xcode to make an archive with which we can upload the project to the app store, so it can finally be reviewed for submission.

Apple Developer setup and the creation of a provisioning profile

In order to deploy an app onto an iOS device, you are required to use a Mac computer, but before we move on to the iTunes store, we first need to have all of the certificates and permissions figured out ahead of time.

Implement the following steps:

1. On a Mac computer, go to `developer.apple.com`:

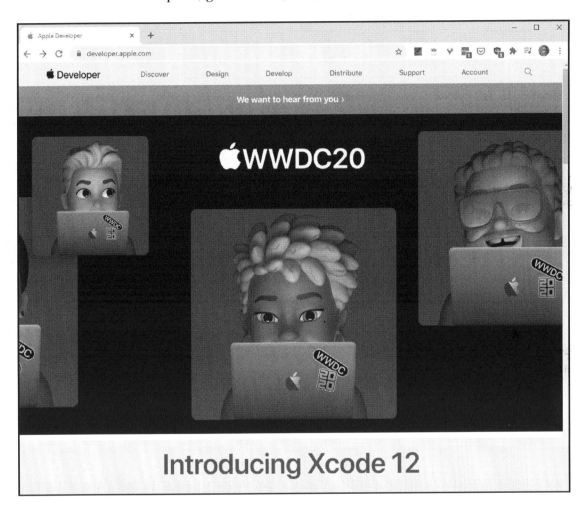

2. From there, click on the **Account** button on the top right of the screen, fill in your **Apple ID** and **Password**, and press *Enter* to sign in:

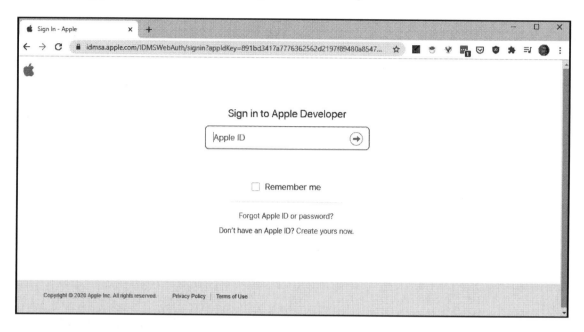

If you have a two-factor identification method set up, you may need to verify that you are indeed yourself.

3. From there, click on **Accounts**. Now, at this point, you will need to make the payment for the $99 annual fee. This process should be fairly straightforward, and once you have finished that aspect of things, you will come to a page similar to the following:

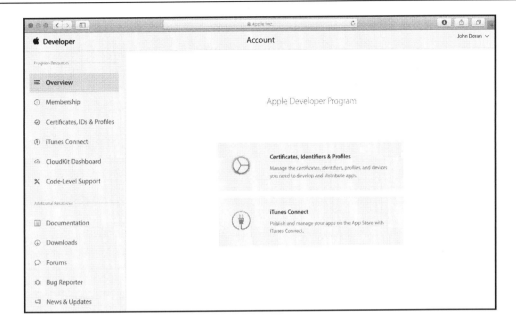

4. Select the **Certificates, Identifiers & Profiles** screen to start the process of creating apps. If you just paid the $99 fee, you may see an error stating that **The selected team does not have a program membership that is eligible for this feature. If you need assistance, please contact Apple Developer Program Support. https://developer.apple.com/support**, as you can note in the following screenshot:

Don't worry, that just means that the payment hasn't processed on Apple's end yet. Try again in about 30 minutes to an hour, and the screen should work okay.

5. We will need to set up some certificates to allow us to export to the iOS App Store. From the **All** certificates page, click on the + sign in the top-right corner of the screen:

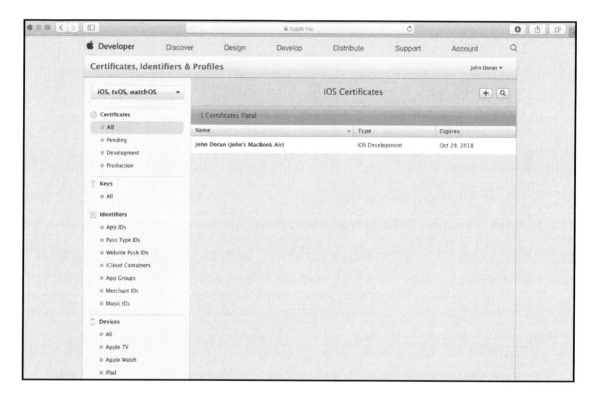

6. When the page asks what kind of certificate we need, select the **App Store and Ad Hoc** option under the **Production** section, and then click on **Continue**:

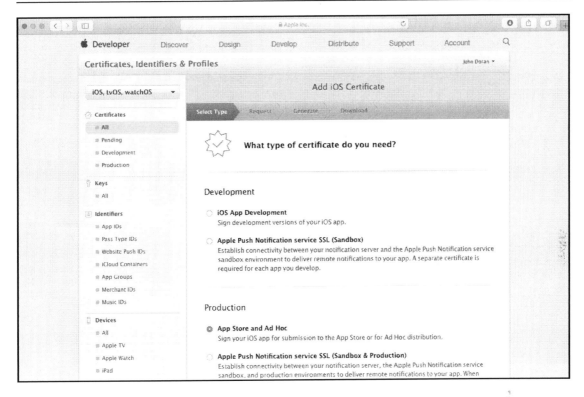

7. Next, we need to create a **Certificate Signing Request** (CSR). You'll be brought to a page that goes through the process of creating one, but, in our case, we will start off by opening the `Applications\Utilities` folder on our Mac and opening the **Keychain Access** program.

8. From there, go to **Keychain Access | Certificate Assistant | Request a Certificate From a Certificate Authority...**:

9. Once there, fill in the information with your email address in the **User Email Address** property, then, for the **Common Name**, put in a name, and leave the **CA Email Address** blank. Then, under the **Request is** property, select **Saved to disk**:

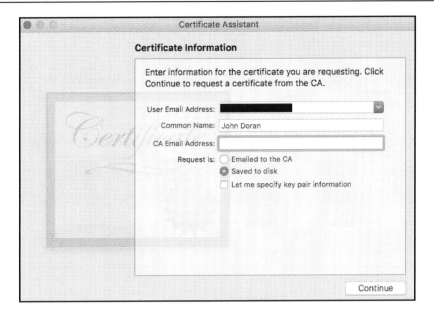

10. Then, click on the **Continue** button and select a spot to save it. I personally used my Desktop, but you can use any location you please, so long as you remember where it is later on:

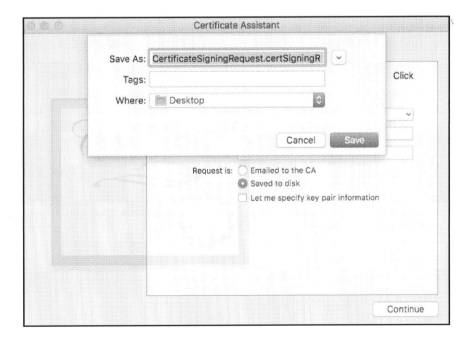

11. Afterward, it will state that the request has been created on the disk. Go ahead and click on **Done** and then return to your web browser.

12. Scroll down and then click on the **Continue** button. From there, you'll be brought to the **Generate your certificate** page. Click on the **Choose File** button and then select the file we just created. Then, click on the **Continue** button:

13. You'll then be brought to a screen saying that your certificate is ready. Go ahead and click on the **Download** button and save it to your disk:

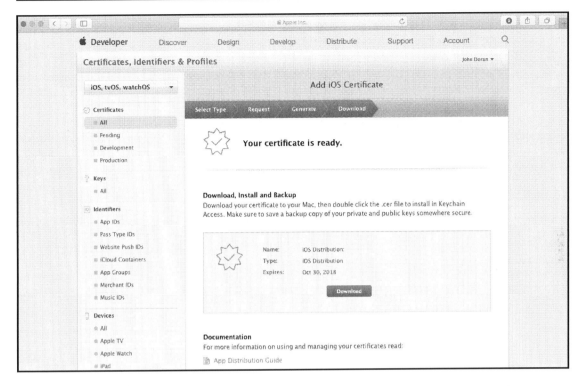

14. Afterward, double-click on the `.cer` file to give the data access to **Keychain**.
You'll be asked whether you want to add the certificates; go ahead and click on
Add:

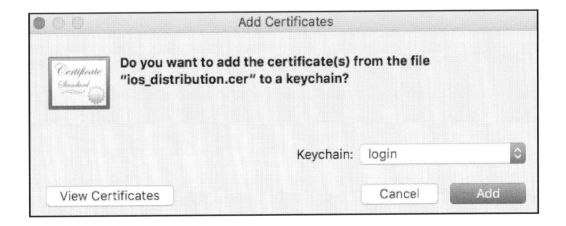

15. The next step is to create an App ID. To do this, go to the left sidebar and click on the **iOS App IDs** section. I currently have one App ID already due to Xcode opening our `Endless Roller` project, which we can customize by clicking on the **Edit** button. However, if you didn't do so earlier and have a different **Bundle ID** than the ones listed, let's go through the details next:

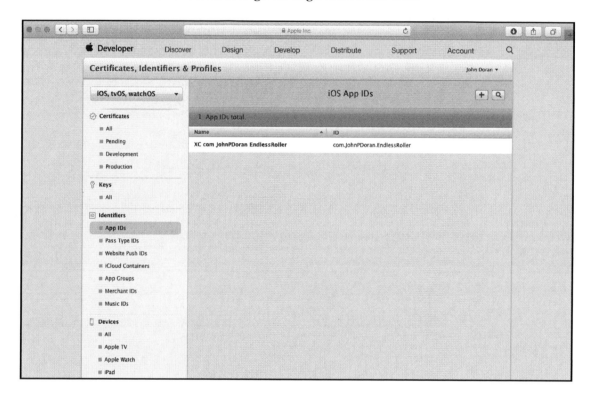

16. We can create a new ID by clicking on the **+** button in the top-right corner of the screen.

17. From there, under **App ID Description**, put in the name of your game—in my case, I used `Endless Roller`. Then, under the **App ID Suffix**, put in the **Bundle ID** in the same manner as it was in Unity. In my case, it was `com.JohnPDoran.EndlessRoller`. Under **App Services**, select the options that you are using, but, in this case, we're not, so we can just scroll all the way down and then click on the **Continue** button:

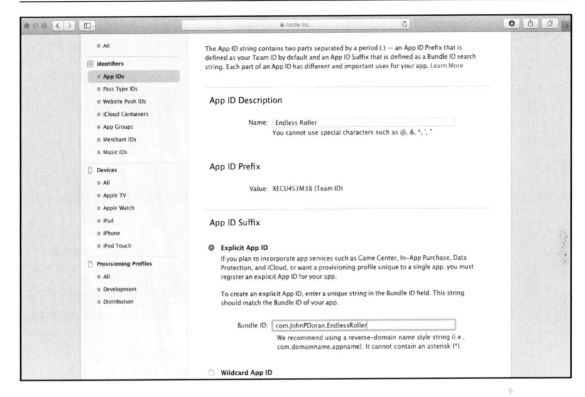

In this case, this would not work due to there already being an ID with this specific **Bundle ID**. This is because you need to have unique ones. With that in mind, I just went in and edited the original App ID to `Endless Roller` and then completed it.

The last aspect we will need to set up here is a **Provisioning Profile**. Apple defines that a *"provisioning profile is a collection of digital entities that uniquely ties developers and devices to an authorized iPhone Development Team and enables a device to be used for testing."* This means that it's a link between a device and the developer account that is making the project.

For more information on provisioning profiles, check out `https://medium.com/@abhimuralidharan/what-is-a-provisioning-profile-in-ios-77987a7c54c2`.

18. To do this, click on the **All** button under the **Add iOS Provisioning Profiles** section. From there, click on the + icon in the top right. Under **Distribution**, you are going to select the **App Store** and then click on **Continue**:

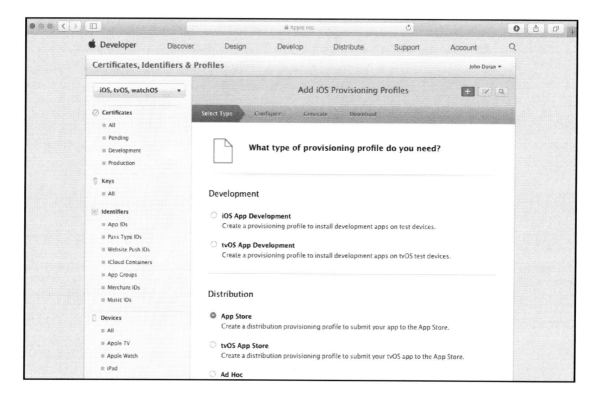

19. From there, you'll need to select your **App ID**. `Endless Roller` may be selected, otherwise, search for it in the drop-down list and select it, and then click on **Continue**:

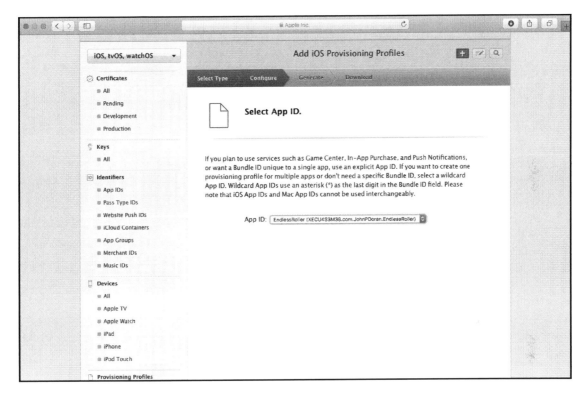

20. Then, select your certificate and click on **Continue**.

21. Finally, we will need to put in a **Profile Name**—I'll put in `Endless Roller`—and then click on **Continue**:

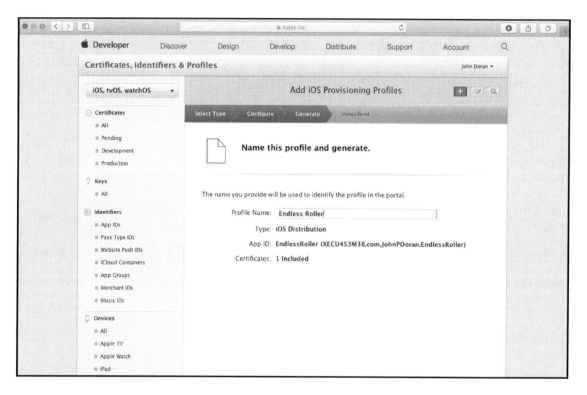

22. You'll be brought to a page with the profile. Go ahead and download it and keep it safe as we'll need to use it later:

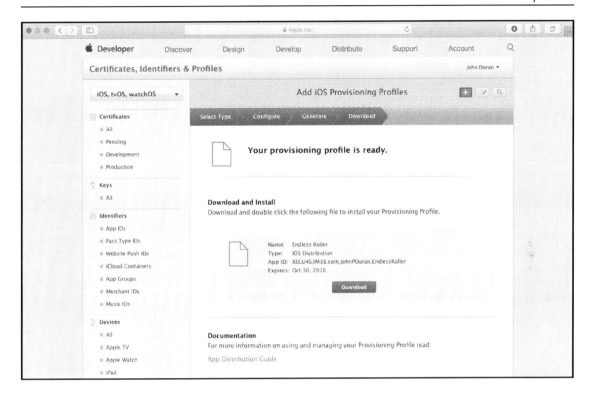

With that, our provisioning profile is ready.

Adding an app to iTunes Connect

Now that we have the provisioning profile, we can actually put our app on the store. To do that, perform the following steps:

1. In your web browser, go to `http://itunesconnect.apple.com` and click on the **My Apps** button:

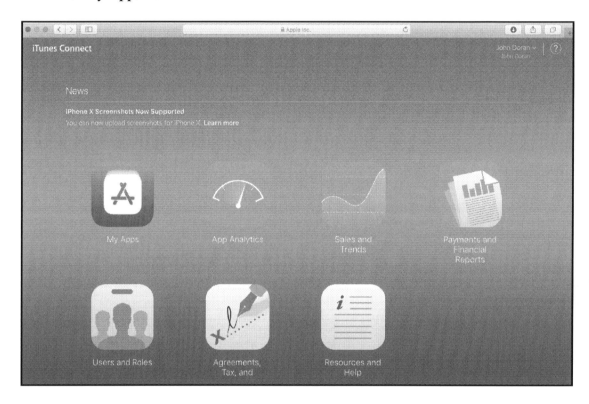

If you intend to sell your apps, you will also be required to go to the **Agreements, Tax, and Banking** section and put in your banking information.

2. From there, go to the top-left corner and click on the **+** icon to add a new app to our profile by selecting **New App**:

3. On this menu, select **iOS** as your **Platforms** and insert the name of your game under **Name**. Apple requires each name to be unique, so keep in mind you will not be able to use `Endless Roller` again. Under **Primary Language**, select **English (U.S.)** and then select your **Bundle ID**. Then, under **SKU**, put in an identifier (I used `EndlessRoller`). Then, click on the **Create** button:

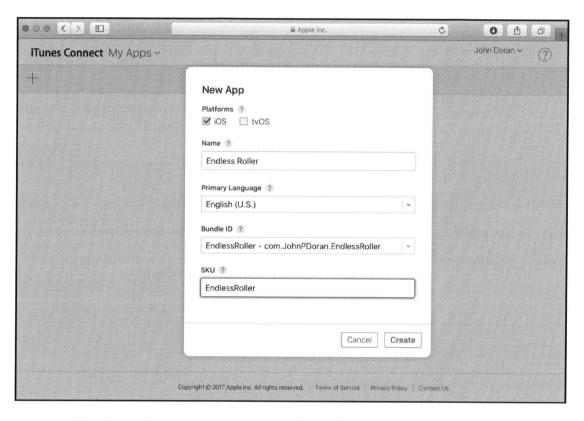

4. You'll then be brought to the **App Information** screen. From there, change the **Category** to **Games** and then, under **Subcategory**, select **Arcade**, and then click on **Save**:

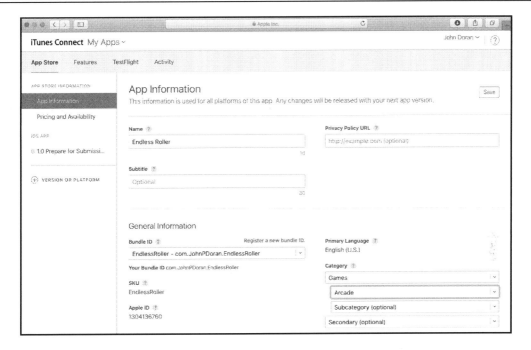

5. Next, go to the **1.0 Prepare for Submission** section and click on it to start filling in the information for the title. Start off by filling in the **Description** textbox with the information that you used earlier on Google Play. Then, under **Keywords**, put in possible things that people could search for in order to find your game:

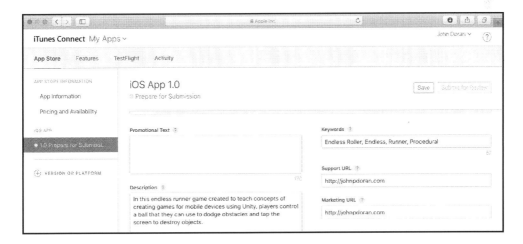

6. We'll then need to provide an app icon to be used. The image must be 1024 x 1024 in PNG format. Under **Copyright**, go ahead and put your name.

7. Lastly, you'll need to provide some screenshots of your game to use. If you click on the **iOS Screenshot Properties** page, you'll see details on how your screenshots should be created (specifically, the size of the images). The one used in this chapter is for the iPhone 5.5" display, but you can also submit for the optional 5.8" one to support the iPhone X:

8. Note that in the **Build** section, it states that you need to submit your build using Xcode. Let's go ahead and do that after we finish up the last step.

9. Go into the **Pricing and Availability** section and select a price. In my case, I'll be using **USD 0 (Free)**, but, as always, you can pick what you'd like. Since there's no cost under the **Volume Purchase Program**, go ahead and select **Available with no discount** since there's no reason for there to be one, and then click on the **Save** option:

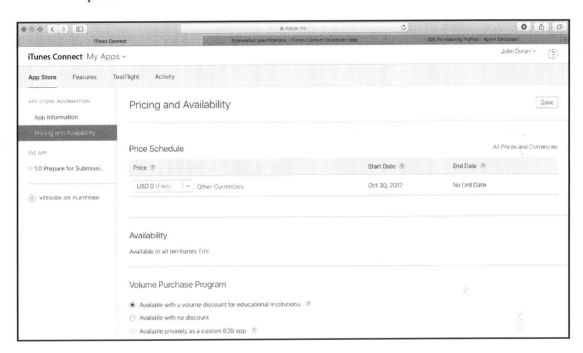

10. Once all of the information is filled in, go ahead and open up Xcode again and your exported project (follow the same steps as in `Chapter 2`, *Project Setup for Android and iOS Development*). From there, go to **Product | Archive** and wait for it to finish:

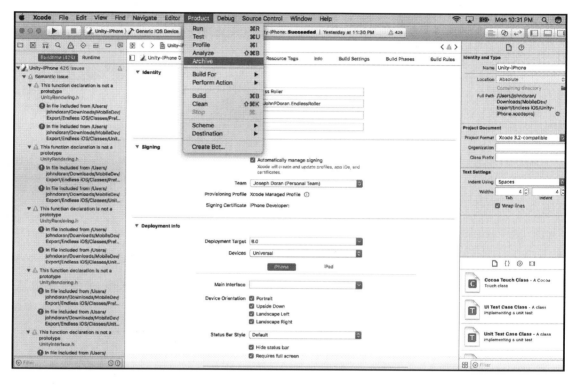

11. This generally takes a while, so wait for it to complete. You may be asked to use an access key. Go ahead and click on the **Allow** button.

12. Upon finishing, you should be brought to the following menu. Go ahead and select the **Upload to App Store...** button:

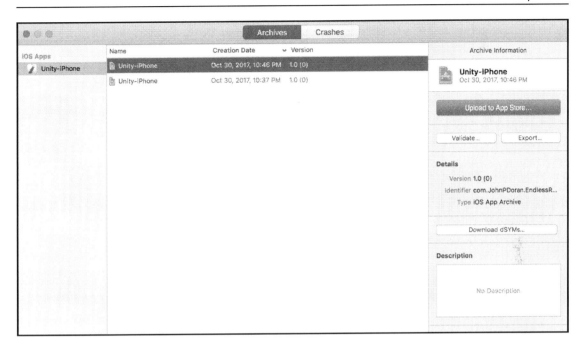

13. You'll be asked to select some options. In general, use the default options, and afterward, it will give you an `.ipa` file uploaded to the store. Before uploading, it will give you one last look with information about each aspect of the project. Go ahead and click on the **Upload** button and wait for it to finish:

This will not show up immediately on **iTunes Connect**; you may have to wait for a moment (or a couple of hours) before it's updated. However, once it is ready, you'll see it under the build section we mentioned earlier.

14. Once it's loaded up, you should be able to click on the **Select a build** button before you submit your app.

15. From there, select the build we created and then click on the **Done** button:

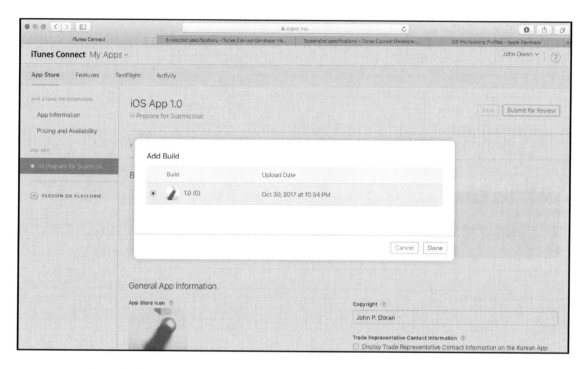

16. Then, click on the **Save** button. Once you're finished with everything and have double-checked all of your information, you can go ahead and click on the **Submit for Review** button to wait for feedback from Apple.

Generally, it takes up to 3-4 weeks for first-time developers to receive feedback, although it can be longer or shorter depending on seasonal demand. As you release more and more titles, it takes less time each time around. If approved, you'll receive an email that lets you know that the app is up, or they may list details on things that need to be modified before approval for placement on the store can be given.

Summary

With that, you learned how to publish your games on both Google Play and the Apple iOS App Store. You first learned how to build a release copy of your game, then learned how to put the game on Google Play by setting up the Google Play Console, and then finally, how to publish your app on the store. You then learned how to put a copy of the iOS version of your game on the App Store and all of the setup involved there.

I hope that you've enjoyed this exploration of features and that you continue to explore the possibilities of this space. In the next chapter, we will discover one of the newest additions to mobile game development: augmented reality.

12
Augmented Reality

Made popular with Niantic's *Pokemon GO* and *Harry Potter: Wizards Unite*, **Augmented Reality (AR)** is a way of blending digital elements with the real world. Specifically, it is a technology that superimposes a computer-generated image on a user's view of the real world, hence providing a composite view, meaning that both the real world and then digital elements put on top of it are displayed to the player.

In this chapter, we will explore how to set up our project to utilize AR for both Android and iOS devices and how we can customize them. This project will be a simple AR project in which the player can look at various surfaces in the game environment and spawn objects on top of them. The goal of this chapter will be to explore the basic concepts of AR and see how they can be used in a project.

This chapter will be split into several topics. It will contain a simple, step-by-step process from beginning to end. Here is the outline of our tasks:

- Setting up a project for AR
- Detecting surfaces
- Interacting with the AR environment
- Spawning objects in AR

Technical requirements

This book utilizes Unity 2020.1.0f1 and Unity Hub 2.3.1 but the steps should work with minimal changes in future versions of the editor. If you would like to download the exact version used in this book, and there is a new version out, you can visit Unity's download archive at `https://unity3d.com/get-unity/download/archive`. You can also find the system requirements for Unity at `https://docs.unity3d.com/2020.1/Documentation/Manual/system-requirements.html` in the **Unity Editor system requirements** section. To deploy your project, you will need an Android or iOS device.

You can find the code files present in this chapter on GitHub at `https://github.com/`
`PacktPublishing/Unity-2020-Mobile-Game-Development-Second-Edition/tree/master/`
`Chapter%2012`.

Setting up a project for AR

Before we can start adding notifications to our project, we will need to add three packages
that Unity makes available to enable AR for both iOS and Android devices. In our case, we
are going to be utilizing both ARCore and ARKit to create our project and the AR
Foundation package to act as an intermediary so we can use both ARCore and ARKit while
using a similar connection. Since this is a brand new way to create projects, we will actually
create a new Unity project to demonstrate how to use it. Follow the steps given here:

1. To get started, open Unity Hub on your computer.
2. From startup, we'll opt to create a new project by clicking on the **New** button.
3. Next, under **Project Name** put in a name (I have chosen `Mobile AR`) and
   under **Templates** make sure that **3D** is selected:

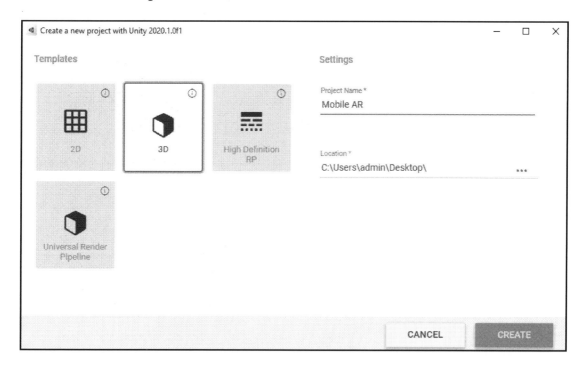

4. Afterward, click on **CREATE** and wait for Unity to load up.

5. From the Unity Editor, go to **Window | Package Manager**.

6. If it hasn't been set already, click on the **In Project** drop-down menu from the toolbar of the **Packages** menu and select **Unity Registry**.

7. From here, you will need to select at least one of the following: **ARKit XR Plugin** if you want to support iOS devices and **ARCore XR Plugin** for Android, and click **Install** for both of them. Afterward, scroll down the available options until you reach **AR Foundation** and select it. Once there, click the **Install** button:

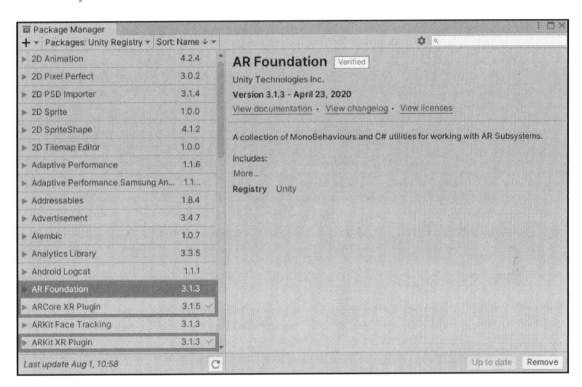

While AR Foundation does most things that you'd want to do with AR, there are a few things that are for iOS or Android only. For more information on what AR Foundation can do and what ARCore and ARKit provide individually, check out `https://blogs.unity3d.com/2018/12/18/unitys-handheld-ar-ecosystem-ar-foundation-arcore-and-arkit/`.

We now have all of the packages we need so we can exit the **Package Manager**.

8. Next, open up the **Build Settings** menu by going to **File | Build Settings**. From there, change your platform to either **iOS** or **Android** and click on the **Switch Platform** button. Afterward, click on the **Player Settings...** option.

9. Under the **Other Settings** section, modify **Package Name** for Android or **Bundle Identifier** for iOS. I used `com.JohnPDoran.MobileAR` but you can use whatever you'd like in the same kind of reverse URL format. Copy/paste the values into the other option if you are planning on targeting both platforms. Next, complete *step 10* if you are planning on using iOS and *step 11* if you are planning on using Android or complete both the steps if you plan on using both, iOS and Android.

10. If you are using iOS, make sure that, in the iOS **Platform Settings** section, the **Requires ARKit support** option is checked as well. This means that you also need to make sure that your **Target minimum iOS Version** is `11.0` or higher. You'll also need to set your **Architecture** property to **ARM64** instead of the **Universal** default.

11. For those using Android, go to the Android's **Player Settings...** and select **Player** option and then under the **Graphics APIs** section, select the **Vulkan** option and press the – button to remove it from the list. Also, uncheck the **Multithreaded Rendering** option. The reason we have to disable this functionality is that, as of the time of writing, it is not compatible with ARCore. You'll also want to set **Minimum API level** to **Android 7.0 'Nougat' (API level 24)** or higher. Now, from the **Player Settings...** menu, select the **XR Plugin Management** option, and then select **Install XR Plugin Management** and check the **ARCore** field.

With that, we've taken care of all of the settings needed to support our project and have it export correctly!

Now that we have AR Foundation included, we can now create a basic scene for a VR project.

Basic setup

Since the player can be anywhere when the game starts, we can't use a camera in the traditional sense so we will start by removing the original one. Follow the steps given here:

1. From the **Hierarchy** panel, select the **Main Camera** object and delete it by right-clicking and selecting **Delete** or pressing the *Delete* key.

   There are two key objects that we will need to create before we can start implementing our own features, an **AR Session** and an **AR Session Origin**.

2. Right-click in the **Hierarchy** panel and select **XR | AR Session**:

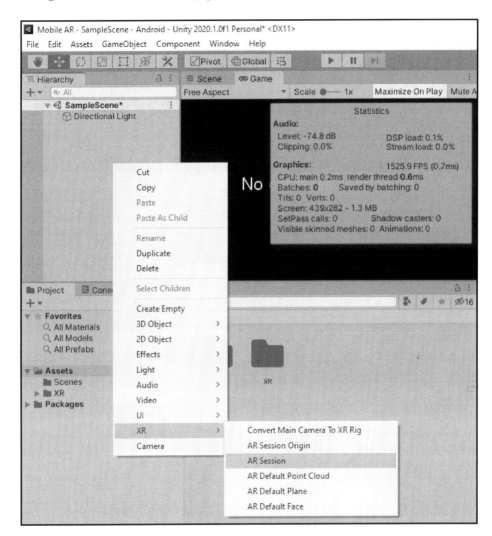

The **AR Session** is what controls the life cycle of any AR experience, which allows us to enable or disable AR features depending on the platform we are working on.

 The **AR Session** is also responsible for telling you where your particular device supports AR. For information on handling this, check out `https://docs.unity3d.com/Packages/com.unity.xr.arfoundation@2.0/manual/index.html#checking-for-device-support`.

3. Create an **AR Session Origin** by right-clicking and selecting **XR | AR Session Origin**.

   The **AR Session Origin** is used to scale and offset virtual content while the game itself is playing. You may notice that the object has a child, **AR Camera**, which is the camera that will follow the game as it is running.

   Before we deploy to the device to ensure everything is working correctly, let's add a cube to our scene so we can see that it is working correctly.

4. Switch to the **Scene** view if you haven't done so already. Then, from the top menu, click on **GameObject | 3D Object | Cube**:

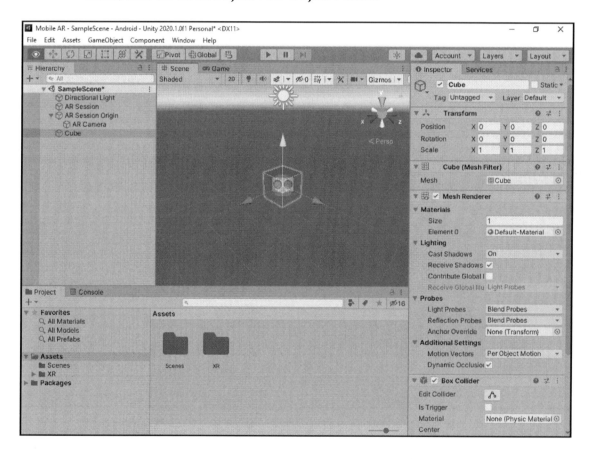

5. Now build your project and put the game on the device in the same manner as discussed in `Chapter 2`, *Project Setup for Android and iOS Development*.

 For iOS users, you may notice when you build the project, it will tell you that the project is lacking a `.xml` file. If this appears, click on the **Yes, fix and build** option when prompted.

6. Upon running your project, give access to the camera if needed and open the game. Once the project shows your environment, step back as the game starts:

The reason why we have to step back to see the cube is that the position of all objects is based on the area the phone was physically at when the game started. The cube is also quite large because at a default scale of 1,1,1 that means that it is 1 meter or around 3.3 feet wide on each side in relation to real-sized objects. We obviously don't want to require the user to step back upon starting the game so we will need to keep track of where usable surfaces are in our environment, which is what we will be doing next.

Detecting surfaces

To detect surfaces within our real-world environment, we will need to make use of a new component, the **AR Plane Manager**. The **AR Plane Manager** allows us to create, remove, or update game objects in our scene based on the surfaces within the real-world environment. The following steps will automatically create invisible planes with colliders that we could possibly use for gameplay reasons:

1. We no longer need the original cube we created, so we can delete it from the scene by right-clicking it and selecting **Delete** or by selecting it and pressing the *Delete* key.

2. From the **Hierarchy** panel, select the **AR Session Origin** object. From there, add the **AR Plane Manager** component to it by clicking on the **Add Component** button at the bottom of the **Inspector** window and then typing in the name of the component and pressing *Enter*.

At this point, we will have surfaces being generated to our scene while being run but for things such as debugging, it would be a good idea to visually see the planes that are being generated. So, that's what we will do next using the following steps:

1. From the top menu, go to **GameObject | XR | AR Default Plane**.

   This object has several different components that are used in creating a visual plane, of note are the **AR Plane** and **AR Plane Mesh Visualizer** components. **AR Plane** represents a plane detected by the AR device, and **AR Plane Mesh Visualizer** is in charge of using the data from **AR Plane** to modify the **MeshFilter** and **MeshCollider** components to overlay the detected wall and the **Line Renderer** component to display the boundaries. The **Mesh Renderer** will draw the information displayed from these modifications.

2. From the **Project** window, create a new folder called `Prefabs`.

3. Drag and drop the **AR Default Plane** object into the **Prefabs** folder to turn it into a prefab. If it is done correctly, you should notice the game object's text in the **Hierarchy** window is now blue:

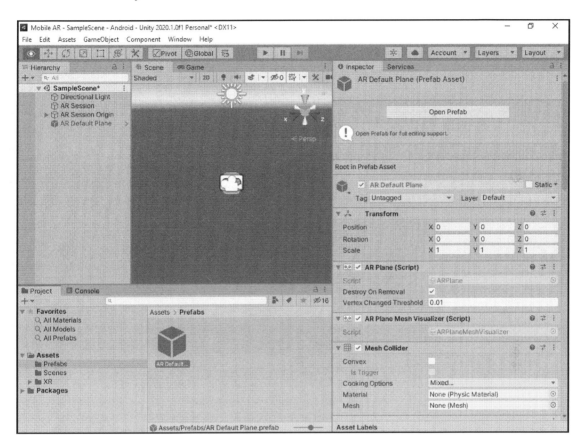

4. Once created, you can delete the **AR Default Plane** object in the **Hierarchy** window.

5. Select the **AR Session Origin** object and drag and drop the **AR Default Plane** prefab into the **Plane Prefab** property of the **AR Plane Manager** component:

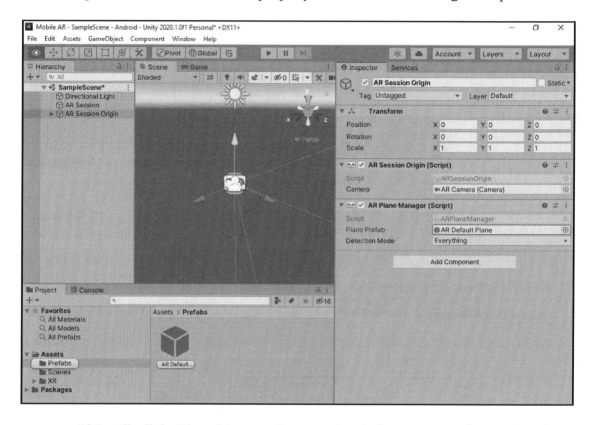

This will tell the **Plane Manager** that, any time it detects a new plane within the scene, to spawn a plane prefab and have it draw the details for it.

6. Save your project and build your game again. Once it is running on your device, walk around your room, moving the camera as you do so:

The longer you stay within an area with movement, the longer the phone will have to build a more realistic depiction of the surfaces in your environment.

Feel free to open the prefab we created and modify how your planes will be visualized!

It's great that we can now see things happening in the game environment but we currently have no way to actually interact with the world—that is what we will be looking into in the next section.

Interacting with the AR environment

One of the ways that we can have the player interact with the world is by allowing them to spawn objects within the scene to help players see where items will spawn. We can create an indicator to show where they will actually spawn to. Let's look at the steps to do just that:

1. Create a quad using **GameObject** | **3D Object** | **Quad**.

   Quads represent a plane, the simplest type of geometry. In our case, we will use the quad as an indicator to the player where they will be spawning an object if they tap on the screen.

2. With the quad selected, go to the **Inspector** window and go to the **Transform** component and set **Position** to (0,0,0), **X Rotation** to 90, and **Scale** to (0.2, 0.2, 1).

We made the quad smaller to be 20 centimeters long and rotated it so it could represent a floor better. We do not want these values to change but we will eventually want to move and rotate this object to follow our player when they move the camera. To protect this data, we can instead create a parent object for it. That way, whenever the parent moves or rotates, the child will move and rotate in the same manner.

3. Create an empty game object by selecting **GameObject | Create Empty**. Select the object and rename it `Placement Indicator`. Then, go to the **Transform** component and set **Position** to (0,0,0).

4. From the **Hierarchy** window, drag and drop the **Quad** game object on top of the **Placement Indicator** to make it a child:

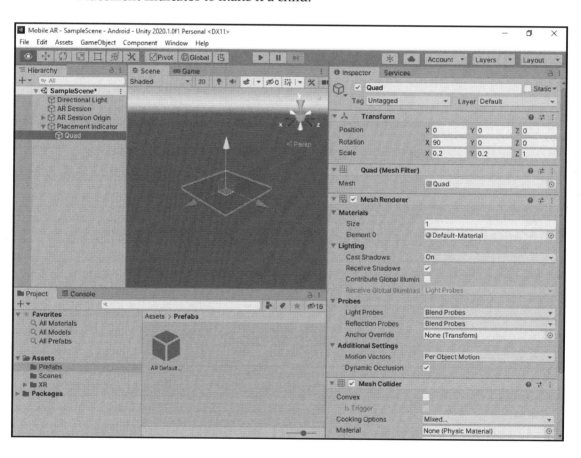

Now that we have an object to work with, we need some way to figure out where the player's camera is facing so we can move the object. We can do this through the use of a new component, the **AR Raycast Manager**.

5. From the **Hierarchy** window, select the **AR Session Origin** object. From there, add the **AR Raycast Manager** component to it.

   The **AR Raycast Manager** exposes the ability to raycast to AR Foundation. This will allow us to perform a raycast within the physical environment that we are in. A raycast, also known as hit testing, allows us to create a ray, which is an invisible line that allows us to check whether there is something that collides from its point of origin and direction. This is used oftentimes in games for things such as checking whether a bullet would hit the player.

Now that we have this setup done, let's see how we can work with these components in code and see how we can use the information to place AR objects within real-world spaces using the following steps:

1. Go to the **Project** window and go back to the **Assets** folder. From there, create a new folder called `Scripts`.
2. Go inside of the **Scripts** folder and create a new C# script called `PlaceARObject`.
3. At the top of the file, add the following `using` statements:

   ```
   using UnityEngine.XR.ARFoundation; // ARRaycastManager
   using UnityEngine.XR.ARSubsystems; // TrackableType
   ```

4. Add the following properties to the class:

   ```
   /// <summary>
   /// A reference to the Raycast Manager for being able to perform
   ///   raycasts
   /// </summary>
   ARRaycastManager raycastManager;

   /// <summary>
   /// A reference to the AR camera to know where to draw
   ///   raycasts from
   /// </summary>
   Camera arCamera;
   ```

5. Then, we need to initialize the properties in the `Start` function:

   ```
   /// <summary>
   /// Start is called before the first frame update. Initalize our
   /// private variables
   ```

```
/// </summary>
private void Start()
{
   raycastManager = GameObject.FindObjectOfType<ARRaycastManager>();
   arCamera = GameObject.FindObjectOfType<Camera>();
}
```

6. Finally, we need to replace our `Update` function and use `LateUpdate` instead:

```
/// <summary>
/// LateUpdate is called once per frame after all Update functions
 ///  have been called
/// </summary>
private void LateUpdate()
{
    // Figure out where the center of the screen is
    var viewportCenter = new Vector2(0.5f, 0.5f);
    var screenCenter =
      arCamera.ViewportToScreenPoint(viewportCenter);

    // Check if there is something in front of the center of the
     // screen
    // and update the placement indicator if needed
    UpdateIndicator(screenCenter);
}
```

7. In the preceding snippet, we are using an `UpdateIndicator` function that currently doesn't exist, so let's add that in next:

```
/// <summary>
/// Will update the placement indicator's position and rotation
/// to be on the floor of any plane surface
/// </summary>
/// <param name="screenPosition">A position in screen space</param>
private void UpdateIndicator(Vector2 screenPosition)
{
    var hits = new List<ARRaycastHit>();

    raycastManager.Raycast(screenPosition,
                           hits, TrackableType.Planes);

    // If there is at least one hit position
    if (hits.Count > 0)
    {
        // Get the pose data
        var placementPose = hits[0].pose;

        var camForward = arCamera.transform.forward;
```

```
        // We want the object to be flat
        camForward.y = 0;

        // Scale the vector be have a size of 1
        camForward = camForward.normalized;

        // Rotate to face in front of the camera
        placementPose.rotation =
            Quaternion.LookRotation(camForward);

        transform.SetPositionAndRotation(placementPose.position,
                                          placementPose.rotation);
    }
}
```

8. Save the script and return to the Unity Editor. Attach the `PlaceARObject` script to the **Placement Indicator** game object.

9. Export your game to your device of choice and verify that it is working:

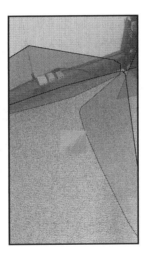

As you can see, the plane will now move and rotate so that it is always facing us! You may notice the plane has a flickery texture. This is due to the z-fighting concept we discussed previously in `Chapter 4`, *Resolution-Independent UI*. Basically, both objects have the same position so it's up to Unity to decide what order to draw them in. We can fix this by placing the quad slightly above the plane's position, which we will do now.

10. Update the `UpdateIndicator` function to use the following code at the end:

```
// Rest of UpdateIndicator...

// Rotate to face in front of the camera
placementPose.rotation = Quaternion.LookRotation(camForward);

// Move the quad slightly above the floor to avoid z-fighting
var newPosition = placementPose.position;
newPosition.y += 0.001f;

transform.SetPositionAndRotation(newPosition,
                                 placementPose.rotation);
}
```

11. Save the script and export the game again. As you can see, now the quad is placed cleanly above the given surface:

Now that we have an indicator of sorts, let's make it so we can actually spawn an object in AR.

Spawning objects in AR

The simplest way to spawn an object in AR would be to make it so when the player taps on the screen it will spawn an object where our **Placement Indicator** object is. But before we do that, we first need to make an object that we'd want to create within the scene.

Follow the steps given here:

1. Create a sphere by going to **GameObject** | **3D Object** | **Sphere**.

2. From the **Inspector** window, set **Position** to (0,0,0) and set **Scale** to (0.2, 0.2, 0.2).

3. Add a **Rigidbody** component to the sphere by going to **Component** | **Physics** | **Rigidbody**.

   By adding the **Rigidbody** component, we are letting Unity know that we want this object to be affected by things such as gravity and react to collision events and forces being applied to it. At this point, you could customize the object as much as you'd like, change the mesh and collider, and so on.

4. Go to the **Project** window, and open the **Prefabs** folder. Create a prefab of our sphere by dragging and dropping it from the **Hierarchy** window to the **Project** window:

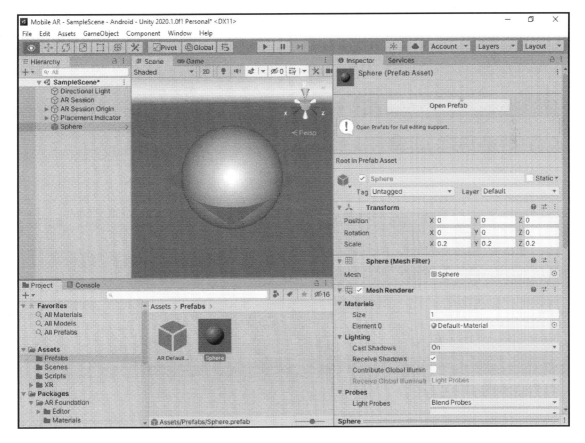

5. Now that the object is a prefab, we can delete it from the **Hierarchy** window.

6. Open the `PlaceARObject` script and add the following property to it:

```
[Tooltip("The object to spawn when the screen is tapped")]
public GameObject objectToSpawn;
```

7. Then, update the `LateUpdate` function to the following:

```
/// <summary>
/// LateUpdate is called once per frame after all Update functions
  /// have been called
/// </summary>
private void LateUpdate()
{
    // Figure out where the center of the screen is
    var viewportCenter = new Vector2(0.5f, 0.5f);
    var screenCenter =
      arCamera.ViewportToScreenPoint(viewportCenter);

    // Check if there is something in front of the center of the
      // screen
    // and update the placement indicator if needed
    UpdateIndicator(screenCenter);

    // If we tap on the screen, spawn an object
    if (Input.GetMouseButtonDown(0))
    {
        // Spawn the object above the floor to see it fall
        Vector3 objPos = transform.position + Vector3.up;

        if(objectToSpawn)
        {
            Instantiate(objectToSpawn, objPos, transform.rotation);
        }
    }
}
```

8. Save the script and return to the Unity Editor.
9. From the **Hierarchy** window, select the **Placement Indicator** object. From the **Inspector** window, set the **Object To Spawn** property to our **Sphere** prefab:

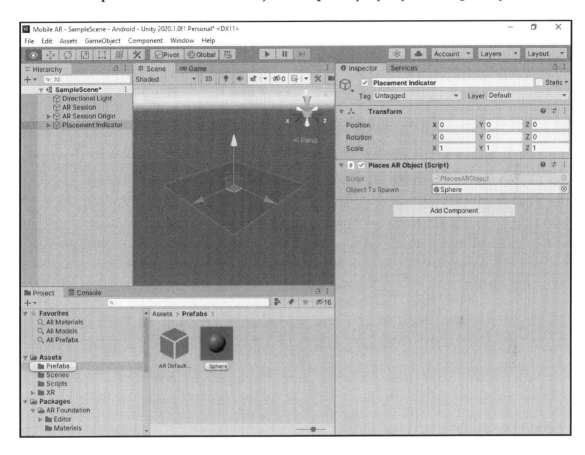

10. Save your project and build it to your device and tap the screen to have spheres spawn onto the screen:

As you can see, we can now spawn objects into our scene and we can see them interact with each other correctly! Taking this further, you can create whatever type of gameplay experience you'd like!

Summary

Throughout this chapter, you have learned how to utilize Unity's AR toolsets to augment reality by adding artificial computer-generated objects into the real world. This new and growing technology is still being developed and the skills gained from working in it will likely grow in importance in the future as things such as **Virtual Reality (VR)**, **Mixed Reality (MR)**, and other forms of **Extended Reality (XR)** become more and more commonplace.

In this chapter, you learned how to install ARKit for iOS, ARCore for Android, and AR Foundation for a multiplatform AR solution. Once installed, you learned how to set the platform settings for both iOS and Android AR development. Afterward, we did the basic setup to have Unity use its AR tools to allow users to add a simple mesh to the environment. We then built upon that to detect surfaces within the real world using the AR Plane Manager and learned how to visualize it by using the AR Default Plane object. We then learned how to interact with the AR environment using the AR Raycast Manager to detect when we hit the meshes within the real world and have objects in the computer-generated world react to it. Finally, we saw how to spawn objects in AR using this information.

This should give you all of the information you need to start experimenting on your own and see whether you can create your own games for both mobile devices and games within an AR environment. So, go forth and use the knowledge from this book to make your games the best they can be and I look forward to playing them!

Other Books You May Enjoy

If you enjoyed this book, you may be interested in these other books by Packt:

Unity 2020 Virtual Reality Projects - Third Edition
Jonathan Linowes

ISBN: 978-1-83921-733-3

- Understand the current state of virtual reality and VR consumer products
- Get started with Unity by building a simple diorama scene using Unity Editor and imported assets
- Configure your Unity VR projects to run on VR platforms such as Oculus, SteamVR, and Windows immersive MR
- Design and build a VR storytelling animation with a soundtrack and timelines
- Implement an audio fireball game using game physics and particle systems
- Use various software patterns to design Unity events and interactable components
- Discover best practices for lighting, rendering, and post-processing

Unity Certified Programmer: Exam Guide

Philip Walker

ISBN: 978-1-83882-842-4

- Discover techniques for writing modular, readable, and reusable scripts in Unity
- Implement and configure objects, physics, controls, and movements for your game projects
- Understand 2D and 3D animation and write scripts that interact with Unity's Rendering API
- Explore Unity APIs for adding lighting, materials, and texture to your apps
- Write Unity scripts for building interfaces for menu systems, UI navigation, application settings, and much more
- Delve into SOLID principles for writing clean and maintainable Unity applications

Leave a review - let other readers know what you think

Please share your thoughts on this book with others by leaving a review on the site that you bought it from. If you purchased the book from Amazon, please leave us an honest review on this book's Amazon page. This is vital so that other potential readers can see and use your unbiased opinion to make purchasing decisions, we can understand what our customers think about our products, and our authors can see your feedback on the title that they have worked with Packt to create. It will only take a few minutes of your time, but is valuable to other potential customers, our authors, and Packt. Thank you!

Index